Shakespeare's

Shakespeare's
Midwives

Shakespeare's Midwives

Some Neglected Shakespeareans

Arthur Sherbo

DELAWARE

Newark: University of Delaware Press
London and Toronto: Associated University Presses

Associated University Presses
440 Forsgate Drive
Cranbury, NJ 08512

Associated University Presses
25 Sicilian Avenue
London WC1A 2QH, England

Associated University Presses
P.O. Box 39, Clarkson Pstl. Stn.
Mississauga, Ontario,
L5J 3X9 Canada

The paper used in this publication meets the requirements
of the American National Standard for Permanence of Paper
for Printed Library Materials Z39.48-1984.

Library of Congress Cataloging-in-Publication Data

Sherbo, Arthur, 1918–
    Shakespeare's midwives : some neglected Shakespeareans / Arthur Sherbo.
        p.   cm.
    Companion volume to: The birth of Shakespeare studies.
    Includes bibliographical references (p.   ) and index.
    ISBN 0-87413-449-8 (alk. paper)
    1. Shakespeare, William, 1564–1616—Criticism and interpretation—History—18th century.   2. Shakespeare, William, 1564–1616—Criticism and interpretation—History—19th century.
    3. Shakespeare, William, 1564–1616—Criticism, Textual.
    4. Criticism—Great Britain—History—18th century.   5. Criticism—Great Britain—History—19th century.   I. Title.
    PR2968.S55   1992
    822.3'3—dc20   91-50932
                                                                                 CIP

PRINTED IN THE UNITED STATES OF AMERICA

Contents

List of Abbreviations

In citing works in the notes, short titles have generally been used. Works frequently cited have been identified by the following abbreviations:

Diaries   Claude E. Jones, ed. *Isaac Reed Diaries, 1762–1804,* Berkeley and Los Angeles, University of California Press, 1946.

Folger   Folger C.b.10 Letters to and from George Steevens.

GM   *Gentleman's Magazine.*

Letters   *The Percy Letters,* by various editors. 6 vols. Baton Rouge: Louisiana State University Press; New Haven, Conn.: Yale University Press, 1944–61.

Life   James Boswell, *Life of Johnson.* Edited by G. B. Hill; revised and enlarged by L. F. Powell, 6 vols. Oxford, at the Clarendon Press, 1934–50.

Lit. Anecd. John Nichols, *Literary Anecdotes of the Eighteenth Century,* 9 vols. London: Nichols, Son and Bentley, 1812–15.

Lit. Illustr. John Nichols, *Illustrations of the Literary History of the Eighteenth Century,* 8 vols. London: Nichols, son, and Bentley, 1817–58.

Acknowledgments

I have been chary over the years in acknowledging the debt I owe Miss Lorraine Hart who has typed incredibly convoluted manuscripts, written in a virtually illegible hand, while also acting as a corrector of the press, as it were. I hope with this and other publications to make amends. To a lesser extent this holds true for the staffs of the Special Collections department of the Michigan State University Library and to the staff of the Rare Books Room of the Cambridge University Library. My greatest debt is to my friend and one-time colleague, Professor Gwynne Blakemore Evans, who read this work in an earlier and bloated version and practiced kindly surgery upon it. I hope the scars are not too evident. If I have overlooked others who helped in some way or other, I can only plead forgetfulness. Manuscript material is by courtesy of the Trustees of the Boston Public Library and by the Folger Shakespeare Library in Washington, D.C.

Introduction

Shakespeare's Midwives: Some Neglected Shakespeareans is, quite obviously, a companion volume to my *Birth of Shakespeare Studies: Commentators from Rowe (1709) to Boswell-Malone (1821)*, published in 1986. I quote the first two sentences of my introduction to that work as a means of expanding on its theme, the necessity for cooperation in editions of Shakespeare. "The compleat explanation of an author not systematick and consequential, but desultory and vagrant, abounding in casual allusions and light hints, is not to be expected from any single scholiast, [for] a commentary must arise from the fortuitous discoveries of many men, in devious walks of literature," What I have done is to conflate a sentence from Dr. Johnson's Preface to Shakespeare (up to "scholiast") and one from a letter from him to Thomas Warton of April 14, 1758, seven years before the Preface was published. George Steevens enunciated the same theme in 1766 in an advertisement anticipatory of his collaboration with Johnson in the 1773 *Shakespeare*. A number of men contributed notes to that edition and to the 1778 Johnson-Steevens *Shakespeare*.[1]

Edmond Malone emphasized the same basic principle in the brief Advertisement he appended to his two-volume *Supplement to the Edition of Shakespeare's Plays Published in 1778*, which appeared in 1780. In partial justification of the number of recent editions of Shakespeare published close upon one another in the last decade and a half before his *Supplement*, Malone wrote that "those who complain of the repeated impressions of this great poet, would do well to consider, whether the hopes which were many years since entertained, of seeing a perfect edition of his works produced by the effort of a single person, were not rather sanguine than reasonable." While acknowledging, prematurely, that the text of Shakespeare seemed "indeed now finally settled" and, thanks to "the last editor" [Steevens], that there was little left "obscure or unexplained," he still insisted that "the field of illustration is so extensive, that some time may yet elapse before the dramas of Shakespeare shall appear in such a manner as to be

11

incapable of improvement." He quoted Johnson's Preface in support of his statement that the "illustration" of Shakespeare from Elizabethan books, "now difficult to be procured," must "necessarily be the slow and gradual work of time; the result of various inquiries, instituted for different purposes." Johnson had written that many of Shakespeare's allusions "yet remain undiscovered, which may be gradually retrieved by future commentators." And while "various additional observations by several of the former commentators" were "inserted" in the *Supplement*, "to these the editor has been enabled to add the annotations of some gentlemen who now first appear as scholiasts on our author." A scant three years later Malone published *A Second Appendix to Mr. Malone's Supplement to the Last Edition of the Plays of Shakespeare: Containing Additional Observations by the Editor of the Supplement*, a publication he justified by quoting from the Advertisement to the *Supplement:* "till our author's whole library shall have been discovered, till the plots of all his dramas shall have been traced to their sources, till every allusion shall be pointed out, and every obscurity elucidated, somewhat will still remain to be done by the commentators on his work." Incidentally, Malone took occasion in his *Second Appendix* to thank one or two friends for their help, for he, too, had let it be known that he was open to suggestions in his projected *Second Appendix.*

Isaac Reed, editor of the next edition of the Johnson-Steevens *Shakespeare* to appear, still felt it necessary, in 1785, to justify yet another republication. Indeed, this is the subject of the first paragraph of his brief, seven-paragraph Advertisement.

> The WORKS OF SHAKESPEARE, during the last twenty years, have been the objects of publick attention more than at any other period. In that time the various editions of his performances have been examined, his obscurities illuminated, his defects pointed out, and his beauties displayed, so fully, so accurately, and in so satisfactory a manner, that it might reasonably be presumed little would remain to be done by either new Editors or new Commentators: yet though the diligence and sagacity of those gentlemen who contributed towards the last Edition of this Author may seem to have almost exhausted the subject, the same train of enquiry has brought to light new discoveries, and accident will probably continue to produce further illustrations, which may render some alterations necessary in every succeeding republication.

Possibly these repeated statements about the necessity to keep at the business of editing Shakespeare's works in the light of new discoveries may strike the modern Shakespearean scholar as more than a little naive. Perhaps, however, there is still need for a community of scholars.

While some of these scholars and men of letters sometimes jealously guarded certain nuggets of information which were eventually to be used in work under way, they were for the most part uncommonly generous in sharing their knowledge. Those resident in the three focal points in the English scholarly world—London, Cambridge, and Oxford—were called upon time and again to examine books and manuscripts, to collate texts, and even to arrange for the loan of books from one of the university libraries. With the opening of the Reading Room of the British Museum on 1 January 1759, scholars living in London were in a position to reciprocate the kindnesses of some of their outlying friends, although neither Cambridge nor Oxford is at any great distance from London. The scholarly career of Thomas Percy (1729–1811) is instructive as regards the interchange of information among scholars, since much of his correspondence is extant and in print. Percy did most of his scholarly work while vicar of Easton-Mauduit, Northamptonshire, where he lived for twenty-nine years. In 1778 he became Dean of Carlisle and in 1782 Bishop of Dromore in Ireland. While Percy corresponded with many scholars, the greatest number of his letters were to Edmond Malone, Richard Farmer, and Thomas Warton. His correspondence with these three English men of letters spanned the years from 1761 to 14 May 1811, with Malone writing to Percy on this date, only three and a half months before Percy's death and some thirteen months before his own. Percy also corresponded with Sir David Dalrymple, Lord Hailes (1726–92) from 1762, while he was working on the *Reliques of Ancient English Poetry,* to 1789. In the Preface to the *Reliques,* Percy wrote "To Sir David Dalrymple, Bart., of Hailes, near Edinburgh, the Editor is indebted for most of the beautiful Scottish poems, with which this little miscellany is enriched, and for many curious and elegant remarks with which they are illustrated." His interest in Scottish literature further stimulated by the work on the publication of the *Reliques* (1765), Percy entered into correspondence with another Scottish scholar, George Paton (1721–1807). And when Percy sought to be informed about Welsh literature, he had recourse to Evan Evans (1731–88), with whom he exchanged letters from 1761 to 1776. The best way to recapture the excitement these men felt in their scholarly exchanges is, of course, to read the letters themselves. The results of most of their scholarship naturally resides in those works which they wrote and published themselves, but an appreciable and valuable part of their scholarly labors lies in their contributions to the work of other scholars, especially in the notes to the successive editions of Shakespeare.

A further idea of the composition of the class that responded to Johnson and Steevens in their requests for aid in editing Shakespeare can be had from James Sutherland's analysis of Johnson's biographies of those forty-three poets "whose lives fell either wholly or partially within the eighteenth century." He writes that

> sixteen were educated at Oxford, eleven at Cambridge, three at Trinity College, Dublin, and three at Edinburgh University. Of the remaining ten, three (Rowe, Dyer, Hammond) were Westminster boys. Two (John Hughes and Isaac Watts) were Dissenters, and one (Pope) a Roman Catholic. These were debarred by statute from matriculation at Oxford and Cambridge. Two (Dorset and Sheffield) were noblemen, and, as often happened with the sons of noblemen, were privately educated. This leaves us with only John Gay and Richard Savage, and Gay certainly got a good grounding in classics at his school in Barnstaple. If any of those forty-three poets can be spoken of as uneducated, it is Savage, and even he attended for some years "a small grammar-school near St. Albans." No fewer than ten of our poets were Westminster boys, five were at Winchester, four at Eton. Of their parents a considerable number were either noblemen or landed gentlemen, but rather more of them were professional men—lawyers, doctors, or clergymen. Eight of the poets (or about one in five) were the sons of parsons, and no less than thirteen of them (almost one in three) became parsons themselves.[2]

All of which is to say, in somewhat different form, that men of culture constituted a small select group, almost a closed society, in England at this time.

Nor must it be thought that Sutherland's analysis of these eighteenth-century poets is without relevance in the history of Shakespeare scholarship. Nicholas Rowe was the first editor of Shakespeare's plays and he was followed by Alexander Pope. John Hughes revised the text of Rowe's *Shakespeare* and compiled the index, while Pope was assisted in one way or another by John Gay amd Elijah Fenton in his *Shakespeare*. Hughes, by the way, also edited *Hamlet*, but on his own, not for Rowe. Dr. Mark Akenside, M.D., was the first (or possibly the second) critic to suggest that Hamlet's madness was not all feigned. William Collins suggested a source for *The Tempest* to Thomas Warton and his suggestion found its way into the commentary on Shakespeare. Many of these poets were translators—Pope, Fenton, Broome, and Tickell of Homer; Pope, Addison, Garth, Duke, and Yalden of Ovid; Rowe and Hughes of Lucan; Pitt, and a number of others, of Virgil; Ambrose Philips and Gilbert West of Pindar; Pitt of Vida's *Art of Poetry*; Granville of Demosthenes. Some had edited various works other than Shakespeare's—Sprat edited Cowley's Latin poems and Fenton prepared an edition of Waller's poetry. Others were historians—Gilbert West wrote an *Institution of the Garter*; Lyttleton, a *History of Henry II*; William King, an *Account of Denmark* as well as a *History of the Heathen Gods*; Sprat, a *History of the Royal Society* as well as one on the Ryehouse plot. Mallet wrote lives of Sir Francis Bacon and of the Duke of Marlborough; Addison wrote on coins, among other things; Prior was an art collector and connoisseur of painting; Blackmore wrote on history and theology; and Collins and Gray both projected histories of English poetry, a project finally realized by Thomas Warton who, while not of the confraternity of Johnson's poets by reason of chronology (he outlived Johnson), was not only a poet, critic, and antiquarian, but also a major contributor to Shakespeare studies. Add the name of Jonathan Swift and his nonfictive works to all the foregoing and one has further evidence of the closed society which I predicated above and which responded with notes and observations to the appeals of successive editors of Shakespeare.

Thomas Warton's name and his *History of English Poetry* (as well as his earlier *Observations on the Faerie Queene of Spenser*) bring to mind other major contributors to Shakespeare studies in the eighteenth century, that is, exclusive of the great editors, Johnson, Steevens, Malone, Reed, and others. Richard Farmer is deservedly well known for his *Essay on the Learning of Shakespeare* but hardly at all known for his further contributions to the number of over three hundred notes. Bishop Percy, busy with his *Reliques*, the Northumberland Household Accounts, and a number of other interests, literary and antiquarian, found time to contribute a growing number of notes to the editions of Shakespeare, starting with five notes in the Appendix to Johnson's edition of 1765. The rival historians of music, Sir John Hawkins and Dr. Charles Burney, did their bit, the former to a much greater degree than the latter. Others sent in their notes or made their suggestions in letters or in conversation, some to the extent of a single note, others in the hundreds. A partial roll of names that are or should be familiar to students of the eighteenth century would include those of Sir William Blackstone, Richard Porson, the Reverend Mr. Samuel Henley, the Reverend Mr. John Bowle, Francis Douce, John Henderson, John Philip Kemble, John Monck Mason, John Nichols, Sir Joshua Reynolds, Henry Todd, Peter Whalley, and Horace Walpole. But then there are the lesser known contributors, and they are many. George Tollet, the recluse country bachelor, contributed a great number of notes— over four hundred. Another major contributor was the retired ironmonger, Thomas Holt White, brother of the celebrated Gilbert White of Selborne. Scores and scores of others contributed in one way or another, sometimes pseudonymously (Eboracencis, T. Row, T.C.), more often anonymously. In addition to being lawyers, doctors, clergymen, and retired ironmongers, they were academics, noblemen, artists, typesetters, musicians, actors, architects, printers, officials of the British Museum, engravers, schoolmasters, amateur antiquaries, statesmen, government officials, "learned ladies," Grub Street writers, historians, "ingenious gentlemen," botanists, naval officers, sportsmen, classicists, and scientists—to name those professions, avocations, and trades that come most immediately to mind.

The contributions of the seven men whom I have selected for discussion and analysis are of such a magnitude as to have swelled the preceding volume, *The Birth of Shakespeare Studies: Commentators from Rowe (1709) to Boswell-Malone (1821)*, to possible but rather unwieldy dimensions. Indeed, I had originally included, in the yet unnamed work that became *The Birth of Shakespeare Studies . . .*, the contributions of Isaac Reed and Richard Farmer. But both Reed, editorial factotum as I dubbed him in the book I wrote on him (1989), and Farmer, author of the *Essay on the Learning of Shakespeare* (1767), were sufficiently interesting to warrant separate full-length treatment. The book on Richard Farmer will have been published when the present work is still being prepared for publication.

Most modern editions of Shakespeare's works are solo performances, although one thinks of collaborations such as W. Aldis Wright's with W. George Clark or of John Dover Wilson's with Sir Arthur Quiller-Couch. More often, individual plays are farmed out to different editors, and we have the Yale edition or the Arden edition. Acknowledgments of assistance, where there are any, are to the general editor of the series, wives, typists, and the occasional colleague. Sometimes a suggestion or an identification is acknowledged in a footnote, but these too are rare. It seems that we may be in the Age of the Single Scholiast, when entire editions, not only of Shakespeare but of other major literary figures, are entrusted to or undertaken by one person who does not advertise for help, except *in extremis*, as witness the occasional brief letter in *TLS* asking for information on the whereabouts of letters, documents, MSS, etc. Possibly the conditions for such appeals for help as Steevens's no longer exist, although contemporary London and the *TLS* would seem to afford the best opportunities for the success of such an appeal, if it were forthcoming. But then again, perhaps our presumptive coming of age as single scholiasts implies a degree of scholarly sophistication that stands in the way of public admission of the need for assistance. A request for information about privately held letters and MSS is one thing, for these are the materials basic to one kind of scholarly effort or another (biography on the one hand and canonical or textual studies on the other), but a plea for general and wide-ranging assistance in any and all aspects of an edition of Shakespeare is something else entirely. It is less than anticlimactic, therefore, to suggest that the Age of the Single Scholiast, if indeed we are in it, is upon us because a number of gentlemen, possessed of old books or of fortuitous discoveries, responded to these general appeals for help in the eighteenth century.

Times, of course, have changed. The Age of the Single Scholiast, its existence still in doubt, has been or may be made possible by the emergence of the huge research libraries in capitol cities and large universities, as well as in their smaller counterparts. Printed bibliographies, editions of older literature, source studies—all the necessary paraphernalia—are at hand or can be reached, either by a polite letter, interlibrary loan, or even, when necessary, by actual visit. No place is very distant in these days of supersonic speeds. But not only the times have changed; editions, too, are vastly different, in some aspects, from their eighteenth-century predecessors. With the exception of the New Variorum *Shakespeare*, modern editions are economical of commentary. To be sure, the multi-editor edition, issued one volume per play, allows the individual editor much scope in his introduction, so that in his prefatory matter he can tend to a number of things that would otherwise be consigned to the space below the text. This is all very well and economical, and one does not as a result read a line of Shakespeare's text, virtually lost at the top of a page, only to be asked to read comments on the line (or on one word in the line) that take up the rest of the page and spill over on to the next—and maybe even on to the next after that. The New Variorum often does; many eighteenth-century editions also do, and are all the more interesting for it. I am thinking now, of course, of the research or reference edition, not of the school edition. The former is for the scholar and the would-be scholar; the latter, for students for whom Shakesepare's text, the plays and poems themselves, are and should be the be–all and end–all of their efforts and pleasure. Dr. Johnson, as usual, said it magnificently in his Preface.

> Notes are often necessary, but they are necessary evils. Let him, that is yet unacquainted with the powers of Shakespeare, and who desires to feel the highest pleasure that the drama can give, read every play, from the first scene to the last, with utter negligence of all his commentators. When his fancy is once on the wing, let it not stoop at correction or explanation. When his attention is strongly engaged, let it disdain alike to turn aside to the name of Theobald and of Pope. Let him read on through brightness and obscurity, through integrity and corruption; let him preserve his comprehension of the dialogue and his interest in the fable. And when the pleasures of novelty have ceased, let him attempt exactness, and read the commentators.

Fine advice and such as should be given to all beginning readers of Shakespeare.

My invitation in *The Birth of Shakespeare Studies* to those who wished to browse through sample notes from the editions discussed is here repeated. The abbreviations for Shakespeare's plays are from the *Shakespeare Quarterly Bibliography*, Volume 36, Number 6 (1985), pp. 690–91. S is Shakespeare.

P. 25	Tyrwhitt on S's flattery of King James in *MM*.
Pp. 30–31	Tyrwhitt on the locale of I. v in *Lr*.
Pp. 31–32	Tyrwhitt on the source of *MV*.
Pp. 33–34	Tyrwhitt on s.d. to IV. ii in *Ado*.
P. 55	Tollet on Maid Marian
Pp. 59–60	Tollet on S's coinages
P. 61	Tollet on "broome groves" in *Tmp*.
Pp. 77–78	Blackstone on "Safe toward your love and honour" in *Mac*.
Pp. 81–82	Blackstone on "These Knights will hack" in *Wiv*.
P. 82	Blackstone on sleeping tops in *TN*.
P. 85	Blackstone on expedition and genuscission in *MW*.
P. 93	Steevens on the wager in *Ham*.

Shakespeare's Midwives

1
Thomas Tyrwhitt, Editor of Chaucer

At some time prior to 1780 Thomas Tyrwhitt (1730–1786) examined for Edmond Malone "a fragment of a MS poem" on the subject of Pericles, Prince of Tyre in Richard Farmer's possession,[1] probably having met Farmer through George Steevens. Tyrwhitt, like Farmer, had published an essay on Shakespeare and had contributed a substantial number of notes to various editions of Shakespeare. D. Nichol Smith, in a lecture on Malone, wrote that

> Of all the scholars at the end of the eighteenth century [he had mentioned Johnson, Tyrwhitt, Farmer, Percy, Steevens, the Wartons, Reed, and Ritson], I should be disposed to say that Tyrwhitt was the ablest, and I wonder if he is unique in being held in high honor by both classical and English students. Bentley's divagation into English studies did not bring him repute. But Tyrwhitt, who gained fame on the Continent by his classical emendations and whose edition of Aristotle's *Poetics* won the not-easily-won commendation of Ingram Bywater, is honored by English scholars for his edition of *The Canterbury Tales*. It set Chaucerian studies on their proper way and still remains not merely one of the great editions of Chaucer but also, alike in its wealth of information and its influence, one of the most important editions of any of the greater English authors.[2]

Tyrwhitt also won high praise from Walter Skeat for his part in the controversy over the "Rowley" poems, but relatively little has been written about his contributions to Shakespeare studies. John Nichols, it is true, wrote that "as his knowledge [of the old English writers] was directed by a manly judgment, his critical efforts have eminently contributed to restore the genuine text of Shakespeare," adding that he had given "many other judicious remarks" on Shakespeare to Steevens for the 1778 *Shakespeare* and to Isaac Reed for the 1785 edition (*Lit. Anecd.*, III. 147–48n). The new *CBEL*, vol. II, following Nichols, notes that "Tyrwhitt also contributed to Steevens' *Shakespeare* 1778 and to Reed's

Shakespeare 1785." And while the *DNB* properly notes that Tyrwhitt also contributed to Malone's *Supplement* (1780), no authority mentions that Tyrwhitt made his first contributions to the Johnson-Steevens edition of 1773, contributions to the number of ninety-three notes. More importantly, no one has analyzed these and the other one hundred forty-five notes, one hundred forty in 1778 and five in 1785, with which he enriched the commentary on Shakespeare's plays. Nor has much account been taken of the eighteen notes or suggestions he is credited with in Malone's *Supplement*, notes on the poems and on the Shakespeare apocrypha.

As an undergraduate at Oxford, Tyrwhitt, as did so many other young men, tried his hand at poetry, almost inevitably opting for heroic couplets in a long "Epistle to Florio at Oxford" which, if one is sufficiently hardy, can be read in the *GM* (1835. ii. 595–60). And he tried his hand at translation, some Pope into Latin and some Pindar into English. But his first scholarly publication was the anonymous *Observations and Conjectures Upon Some Passages of Shakespeare*, 1766, which, he explained, came into being because the publication of Samuel Johnson's edition late in 1765 tempted him into "looking over once more the enchanting scenes of that admirable Poet." He concluded his introductory paragraph by stating, "My intention is merely to set down my own observations and conjectures upon some passages of *Shakespeare*, which have either been passed over in silence, or attempted, in my opinion, without success, by former Commentators." The work is a modest one, running to fifty-four pages and containing some fifty conjectural emendations and only about ten or twelve "observations," unless one wishes to detach the remarks on other editors, notably those on Johnson, from the conjectures, and count them as separate observations. The most remarkable of Tyrwhitt's observations is on the canonicity of *Titus Andronicus*, for he was the first to call attention to Francis Meres's *Palladis Tamia, or, the Second Part of Wit's Commonwealth* with its list of plays by Shakespeare, among them *Titus Andronicus* (pp. 15–16). He was unlucky enough to think that the work was by somebody named Maister, his copy probably having a defective title-page, for Farmer, in the second edition of his *Essay Upon the Learning of Shakespeare*, pointed out that the work bears the author's name, i.e., "Francis Meeres Maister of Artes of both Universities" (*Letters*, II. 170n.). Also notable are Tyrwhitt's remarks on the language of *Troilus and Cressida* (p. 48) and on Shakespeare's flattery of King James in *Measure for*

Measure (pp. 36–37). Both are worth quoting. The former reads,

There are more hard, bombastical phrases in the serious part of this Play, than, I believe, can be picked out of any other six Plays of Shakespeare. Take the following specimens, in this Scene:——*Tortive,*——*persistive,*——*protractive,*——*importless,*——*insisture,*——*deracinate,*——*dividable.* And in the next Act,——*past-proportion,*——*unrespective,*——*propugnation,*——*self-assumption,*——*self-admission,*——*assubjugate,*——*kingdom'd,* &c.

The latter is keyed to a passage in which the Duke expresses his dislike of popular applause:

I cannot help thinking that *Shakespeare,* in these two passages intended to flatter that unkingly weakness of *James the first,* which made him so impatient of the crowds that flocked to see him, especially upon his first coming, that, as some of our Historians say, he restrained them by a Proclamation. Sir *Symonds D'Ewes,* in his Memoirs of his own Life, has a remarkable passage with regard to this humour of *James.* After taking notice, that the King going to Parliament, on the 30*th of January,* 1620–1, "spake lovingly to the people," and said, "*God bless ye, God bless ye;*" he adds these words, "*contrary to his former hasty and passionate custom, which often, in his sudden distemper, would bid a pox or plague on such as flocked to see him.*"

The editor of the New Arden *Measure for Measure* notes that this has been accepted since Malone's time and refers to Malone's chronology of Shakespeare's plays, but he does not mention that Malone gave credit where it was due, to Tyrwhitt.

Tyrwhitt was one of the first to advocate old-spelling texts (p. 13), and he suggested to Malone that he print the old orthography in his 1790 *Shakespeare,* something Malone approved of but felt too demanding (*Letters,* I. 138 n.). There are also two observations on conjectural criticism, both eminently quotable. In the first Tyrwhitt calls it, after Johnson, "a frolick of the understanding" and writes that "when it assumes an air of gravity and importance, a decisive and dictatorial tone; the acute Conjecturer becomes an object of pity, the stupid one of contempt" (pp. 19–20). The second observation should serve as a motto for all editors: "In conjectural Criticism, as in Mechanics, the perfection of the art . . . consists in producing a given effect with the least possible force" (p. 44).

Tyrwhitt had taken up permanent residence in London, having

lived in Oxford until 1762, when he became Clerk of the House of Commons, by which time he had already established a reputation for great learning, despite his not having published anything of a scholarly nature. His first publications, both anonymous, were the *Observations and Conjectures* and *Proceedings and Debates of the House of Commons 1620–1*, 2 vols., 1766. He retired from his position as Clerk in 1768 because of ill health, and devoted himself to scholarship, having ample means to do so. A writer in the *GM* who signed himself Verax stressed the fact of Tyrwhitt's generosity, noting his encouragement and support "of young men of promising abilities and application. His love of his family and friends, and his care of his dependents, made them all sharing in his fortune." Verax had heard that "in one year of his life he gave away two thousand pounds; but he had no luxuries, no follies, no vices to maintain" (1787, i. 219). One of the first fruits of Tyrwhitt's leisure was the contributions to the Johnson-Steevens 1773 *Shakespeare*, for Tyrwhitt was one of a very small number of men who became and remained friends with George Steevens. Steevens's great affection for Tyrwhitt is strongly evidenced in one note in the 1793 *Shakespeare*, published some seven years after Tyrwhitt's death. John Monck Mason had taken polite exception to one of Tyrwhitt's notes, and Steevens, defending his friend's interpretation, wrote, "It will be the lot of few cricks to retire with advantage gained over the remarks of my lamented friend, Mr. Tyrwhitt" (IX. 416.6). Tyrwhitt befriended the needy Dr. Samuel Musgrave, himself a contributor to the 1778 Johnson-Steevens *Shakespeare*, and was intimate, as will be seen, with Clayton Mordaunt Cracherode, a great collector of books and prints. Upon Tyrwhitt's death in 1786 Malone wrote to Bishop Percy, another of Tyrwhitt's friends, and said, among other things, "I particularly feel his loss, because besides the intercourse with so ingenious and amiable a man, I was sure of always obtaining from him the most accurate information on any point on which I consulted him; and promised myself much pleasure from the approbation of so judicious a critick, if by the very laborious process I have gone through I should be able to make any additions, however small, to what has been already done for the illustration of Shakspeare" (*Letters*, I. 33–34). Malone had already expressed his gratitude for Tyrwhitt's help in the Advertisement to his 1780 *Supplement* and paid other, but posthumous, compliments to him in his *Letter to the Rev. Richard Farmer, D.D.* (1792) and in his *Inquiry* into the authenticity of the Ireland Shakespeare papers and documents

(1796). Adopting the device of the dream vision in the *Inquiry*, Malone found himself on Parnassus in the company of Shakespeare and his contemporaries. Apollo passed sentence on the papers, and it was decreed "when a proper fire had been made of the most baleful and noxious weeds, that all the Copies should be burned by Dr. Farmer, Mr. Steevens, and myself, assisted by Mr. Tyrwhitt [he, too, on Parnassus], whose polite demeanour and thoughtful aspect displayed all that urbanity and intelligence for which he was distinguished in life" (pp. 361–62). Tyrwhitt was dead ten years, but his friends had not forgotten him. Bishop Percy first heard of Tyrwhitt's death from the latter's nephew; in his acknowledgment of the younger Thomas Tyrwhitt's letter, Percy wrote of his dead friend: "He was an honour to his age and country, not more for his extensive erudition, his fine genius and deep and solid judgement, than for the candour, elegance, and probity of his manners, his unassuming modesty and simplicity of character, and distinguished virtues. His memory . . . will be transmitted to posterity for unceasing duration among the first scholars and greatest critics to whom the world has been indebted for the improvements of learning" (*Lit. Illustr.*, VIII. 222). John Nichols reprints two letters, dated 1783 and 1784, from Tyrwhitt to Percy. With the first he sent a copy of the Appendix to his edition of the Rowley poems; in the second, in his capacity as a trustee of the British Museum, he asked Percy's advice about the Museum's possible purchase of the Bibliotheca Yelvertoniana. He had himself found some defects in the collection, but wrote, "it is not my business to state to you the defects of the collection. I rather want to learn from you whether you recollect any articles of such value as may make it advisable to endeavour to purchase them, encumbered as they may be with a heap of rubbish. I am sorry to see not one of our old friends, either poet or romancer, in the catalogue" (*Lit. Illustr.* VIII. 220–21). And it was Nichols in his *Literary Anecdotes* who wrote that to Tyrwhitt's "honour be it remembered, that one of the Trusteeships of the British Museum, an office not infrequently courted by the great and the vain, was conferred on him without the slightest private interest or solicitation" (III. 151). Curiously enough, there is no record in Reed's diaries of his dining in the company of Tyrwhitt anywhere in London in the years from 1762 to Tyrwhitt's death in 1786; the Mr. Tyrwhitt who figures once in the diary was the scholar's brother Robert.[3] Tyrwhitt, it is apparent, knew and was intimate with most of the great Shakespeare scholars of his time. Worth noting, because so many other contributors to Shakespeare studies were members of these institutions, Tyrwhitt was briefly in the Middle Temple, was a Fellow of the Royal Society, and of the Society of Antiquaries.[4] It was he, incidentally, and not Thomas Tyers, who was the "T.T." who reviewed Joseph Ritson's *Select Collection of Old Songs* in the *GM* in November 1784 (pp. 817–18), taking exception to Ritson's strictures on Warton's *History of English Poetry* and on Bishop Percy's *Reliques*.[5] Percy, writing to Malone in 1785, attributed the piece to Tyrwhitt, remarking, "If I am right, give my kindest respects to him and tell him I shall gratefully consider it as *absentis pignus amici.*—Pray what [is] his excellent Pen employ'd about? He can never be wholly unoccupied, and whatever he bestows the least Attention on, will ever be interesting" (*Letters*, I. 28–29). Tyrwhitt found that the editor of the *Select Collection* in his Preface had "very illiberally and unfairly indulged himself in an abuse of some of the first critics of the present age, and even those to whom he appears to have been considerably indebted," and he concluded that Ritson reminded him of a couplet in Pope, " 'Ah, what the use, were finer optics given, / T' inspect a mite, not comprehend the heaven?' "

Tyrwhitt's classical training, with its necessary emphasis upon establishing a text from corrupt manuscripts, where there were any, as well as from corrupt printed editions, came to the fore in his *Observations and Conjectures*, as I have indicated above, for his primary concern was with emendations. Today the number and kind of some, even many, of those conjectural emendations would be decried, although some found favor with later editors of Shakespeare. So, too, would the fact that he was working with only two editions of Shakespeare's plays, the second Folio and Theobald's edition, as he himself admitted (p. 19). Later he was to acquire or at least have access to the first Folio and to some of the quartos, but in the 1766 pamphlet he favored readings from the second Folio. Only two or three times did he attempt paraphrases in this early work; only twice did he exhibit a close acquaintance with Shakespeare's text, if the presence of but two cross-references can be regarded as evidence. And there was very little in 1766 that revealed his vast erudition and knowledge of literature. For in his obituary in the *GM*, Nichols wrote that "besides a knowledge of almost every European tongue, Mr. T. was deeply conversant in the learning of Greece and Rome," and he was, as Nichols also noted, "thoroughly read in the old English writers" (1786. ii. 717). Indeed, in the matter of parallels, his work does not compare at all well with that of so many contributors to the editions, for they adduced parallel after parallel from rare and little-known books, plays, and poems—and other literature. Tyrwhitt cites the *Biographia Britannica*, Chaucer's *Troilus and Crysede*, the *Arabian Nights Entertainment*, Beaumont and Fletcher's *The Sea-Voyage*, and the British Museum MS of Sir Symonds D'Ewes's "Memoirs of his own Life."[6] All these, including the British Museum MS of D'Ewes's journal known by many, could easily have been found in a single note by Steevens or Malone. If one had only the *Observations and Conjectures*, Tyrwhitt's importance in Shakespeare studies would almost surely lie solely in the resurrection of *Palladis Tamia* and in one or two conjectural emendations.

Without any real evidence it is fruitless to conjecture exactly where Steevens and Tyrwhitt met, for the meeting could have taken place any time after 1762 (an earlier acquaintance seems unlikely), although Tyrwhitt was not known as the author of the *Observations and Conjectures* for some time. None of his ninety-three notes to the 1773 Johnson-Steevens *Shakespeare* bears his name, only his initials. For example, Steevens writes in a note in 1773 that "the learned and ingenious author of Considerations [sic] and Conjectures upon some passages in [sic] Shakespeare, printed at Oxford 1766, concurs with me" (IV. 171.4) obviously not knowing the author's identity and even getting the title of the pamphlet wrong in two places. In 1778 he changes all the above to "Mr. Tyrwhitt." By 6 February 1776, at which time they are named in a letter as engaged in an edition of the Rowley poems, the two men had met and become friends.[7] No doubt as a result of this friendship and their common interest in the Rowley affair, Steevens, who now knew who the ingenious author of the *Observations and Conjectures* and of the ninety-three notes in the 1773 edition was, solicited further notes and suggestions from Tyrwhitt for the 1778 *Shakespeare*.

There are sixty-one new notes, i.e., not from Tyrwhitt's *Observations and Conjectures*, in the body of the 1773 *Shakespeare*, as distinct from twenty-nine in Appendix I and two in Appendix II in the tenth and last volume of that edition. Thirty-five of the sixty-one notes in the text are emendations, as are fifteen of those in Appendix I. And, to anticipate, sixty of the one hundred forty new notes in the 1778 edition are emendations, as well as nine of the eighteen in Malone's *Supplement*. Most of Tyrwhitt's concern, it is well to repeat, was with establishing the text, and although this is, of course, the primary duty of an editor, he carried his zeal for conjectural emendation too far. Not to such ridiculous extremes as William Warburton, it is true, but still too far for our more sophisticated editorial principles. He, like almost all his contemporaries, attempted to make better sense of passages that already made sense—although sometimes, it must be admitted, they thought they were being confronted with nonsense. What can be said in Tyrwhitt's defense, however, is that he was almost never peremptory or cocksure about his conjectures and that he treated other Shakespeareans with considerable deference. John Nichols wrote of him that his "mode of criticism is allowed to have been at once vigorous and candid" and that "controversy produced no unbecoming change in the habitual gentleness and elegance of his manners" (Lit. Anecd. III. 150). He may seem somewhat sarcastic at Johnson's expense in the Observations and Conjectures, but the sarcastic bits were cut out, presumably by Steevens, in the notes from that work included in the 1773 and 1778 Johnson-Steevens editions. Possibly, too, it should be pointed out that in very many of his emendations he was adjusting the punctuation and that in a lesser but not inconsiderable number he was reassigning speeches, minor depredations when compared with some of the violence committed upon Shakespeare's text by many of Tyrwhitt's contemporaries.

Approximately one hundred of Tyrwhitt's notes are quoted, wholly or in part, or cited in the New Variorum series. This is exclusive of the Observations and Conjectures of 1766 and of those emendations that find a place solely in the textual apparatus of the New Variorum volumes. In a number of the notes in those volumes Tyrwhitt has pride of place, and in at least three notes, where Capell is given credit for being first with an emendation or an observation, Tyrwhitt had anticipated him—in print.[8] Capell's Notes and Various Readings, although ready before its posthumous publication in 1779–83 by John Collins, and although the "First Part" was printed by itself in 1774, was still later than Tyrwhitt's notes to the 1778 Johnson-Steevens Shakespeare. The most important of these three notes has to do with the locale of act I, scene v of King Lear. Lear opens the scene by saying to the disguised Kent, "Go you before to Gloucester with these letters," letters for Regan, married to the Duke of Cornwall, and thus confusion arose between the Duke of Gloucester's castle and the city of Gloucester. The New Variorum King Lear notes that "Capell, followed by the subsequent editors, has removed this difficulty . . . by supposing that this name refers to the city of Gloucester" and gives his reasons for this supposition (p. 96). King Lear was not among the plays for which notes were provided in the publication of 1774 of the "First Part" of Capell's *Notes and Various Readings*, and hence Tyrwhitt came to the same conclusion independently. He wrote, at II.iv.

> It is plain, I. think, that Lear came to the earl of Glocester's, in consequence of his having been at the duke of Cornwall's, and having heard there, that his son and daughter were gone to the earl of Glocester's. His first words shew this: "'Tis strange that they (Cornwall and Regan) *should so depart from home, and not send back my messenger* (Kent)." It is clear also from Kent's speech in this scene, that he went directly from Lear to the duke of Cornwall's, and delivered his letters, but, instead of being sent back with any answer, was ordered to follow the duke and dutchess to the earl of Glocester's. But what then is the meaning of Lear's order to Kent in the preceding act, scene v. *Go you before* to Glocester *with these letters.*——The obvious meaning, and what will agree best with the course of the subsequent events, is, that the duke of Cornwall and his wife were then residing at Glocester. Why Shakespeare should choose to suppose them at Glocester, rather than at any other city, is a different question. Perhaps he might think, that Glocester implied such a neighbourhood to the earl of Glocester's castle, as his story required (1778. IX. 428.1).

The New Variorum editor quite unaccountably omits any reference to this note.

Some modern editors have not been sufficiently diligent in the matter of Tyrwhitt's notes, seemingly unaware of those in the 1773 Appendices. Thus, in his discussion of the sources of *The Merchant of Venice*, the editor of the New Variorum edition takes cognizance of and partially quotes Tyrwhitt's long note on this matter in the third volume of the 1773 edition but entirely overlooks the addition to the note in Appendix II of that edition, thereby depriving Tyrwhitt of the credit for first calling attention, among other things, to "Harleian MSS. (n. 7333)." But Tyrwhitt's whole note bears quotation:

> Since this note was written, I have found among the Harleian MSS. (n. 7333.) an English translation of the *Gesta Romanorum*, which contains the two stories of the Jew and the caskets. I have also met with a printed copy in the black letter, but not older than 1600, as I guess, for the title-page is lost. This has only the story of the caskets. However it is not improbable that the story of the Jew may have been in some of the former impressions; as R. Robinson says expressly, that the book, as published by him in 1577, contained twenty-one sheets, whereas my copy contains only fifteen.

> Upon the whole, if any English translation of the *Pecorone* can be produced of an earlier date than the Merchant of Venice, it will be very clear, I think, that Shakespeare took his fable from thence, as there the two stories are worked up into one, as they are in the play; but it will scarce be doubted, that *Ser Giovanni*, the author of the *Pecorone*, was obliged to the *Gesta Romanorum* for the materials of his novel (III. 224).

Only with this does one have Tyrwhitt's last and most valuable word on the sources of *The Merchant of Venice*.

While the matter of adjusting priority is a necessary one, and while Tyrwhitt's original contribution to Shakespeare studies gains in value from the recognition that he was the first to make certain observations in print, one's overall estimate of him as a scholar is somewhat lessened by the knowledge that he either ignored or was less than careful in consulting previous editors when advancing his own conjectures and comments. Thus, at that juncture in *Antony and Cleopatra*, where Caesar says "The round world / Should have shook lions into civil streets, / And citizens to their dens," Tyrwhitt correctly noted that "shook" was "the participle past of a verb *active*," but also proposed "into their dens" for "to their dens," evidently unaware that the same suggestion had been made in the editions of Theobald, Warburton, and Johnson. This was not his only lapse, for in at least four notes he was anticipated by Theobald, whose edition he acknowledged having in his *Observations and Conjectures*. For example, Theobald had adduced a parallel of "fadings" in *The Winter's Tale* from *The Knight of the Burning Pestle*; so did Tyrwhitt.[9] From all accounts, Tyrwhitt was the soul of honor, and one assumes he arrived at his conclusions independently, but he was guilty of the kind of lapse that he would not have forgiven the editor of a classical text.

Actually, the greatest part of Tyrwhitt's efforts as a scholar was devoted to his editions of Chaucer and of the Rowley poems, aside, of course, from his classical studies, for it is for these last that he is mainly remembered. His Shakespearean contributions, once the *Observations and Conjectures* had been published, were a minor interest, much of them the result of his growing intimacy with Steevens and others concerned with Shakespeare's plays. In the interval between the 1773 and 1778 editions of Shakespeare, to both of which he contributed, he completed his edition of Chaucer, four volumes in 1775, with a fifth, including a glossary, in 1778. In 1777, when he was presumably working on the Chaucer glossary, he published anonymously his *Poems supposed to have been written at Bristol by Thomas Rowley and others in the Fifteenth Century, with a preface and a glossary,* followed by his Appendix to the edition (1778) in which he proved to the satisfaction of all but the most entrenched Rowleians that the poems were the work of the unfortunate Thomas Chatterton. In a preliminary statement in the *Appendix* he premised "only one *postulatum,* which is, that Poets of the same age and country use the same language, allowances being made for certain varieties, which may arise from the local situation, the rank in life, the learning, the affection of the writers, and from the different subjects and forms of their compositions" (p. 312). Having thus postulated, he had no difficulty proving that the language of the poems attributed to Rowley was different from that of English writers of the fifteenth century. Few other men (Samuel Johnson was one exception) had studied the English language as closely as Tyrwhitt. Few others could bring such knowledge to the text of Shakespeare's plays.

While it is well to repeat that some one hundred of Tyrwhitt's notes, other than the purely textual and those in the 1766 pamphlet, have been included in the New Variorum volumes, there have been some curious omissions, and without the reparation of those omissions a final judgment on Tyrwhitt's contributions cannot be made. One would look in vain for his note on the opening stage direction for IV.ii in *Much Ado about Nothing,* this being one of the places where Capell has been wrongly given credit for explaining a discrepancy in the number of characters listed. Here is Tyrwhitt's explanation:

> The persons, throughout this scene, have been strangely confounded in the modern editions. The first error has been the introduction of a *Town-Clerk,* who is, indeed, mentioned in the stagedirection, prefixed to this scene in the old editions, *(Enter the Constables, Borachio, and the Towne-clerke in gownes,)* but no where else; nor is there a single speech ascribed to him in those editions. The part, which he might reasonably have been expected to take upon this occasion, is performed by *the Sexton;* who assists at, or rather directs, the examinations; sets them down in writing, and reports them to Leonato. It is probable, therefore, I think, that *the Sexton* has been stiled *the Town-clerk,* in the stage-direction abovementioned, from his doing the duty of such an officer. But the editors, having brought *both Sexton and Town-clerk* upon the stage, were unwilling, as it seems, that the latter should be a mute personage; and therefore they have put into his mouth *almost all the*

absurdities which the poet certainly intended for his ignorant *constable*. To rectify this confusion, little more is necessary than to go back to the old editions, remembering that the names of *Kempe* and *Cowley*, two celebrated actors of the time, are put in this scene, for the names of the persons represented; viz. *Kempe* for *Dogberry*, and *Cowley* for *Verges* (1778 II. 343.8).

Tyrwhitt was also first to explain "corporal of his field" in *Love's Labour's Lost* as being "employed as an aid-de-camp is now," quoting from Lord Strafford's *Letters* in evidence (1778, II. 421.7).

No notice has been taken of Tyrwhitt's comment on the Epilogue to *2 Henry IV* where the Dancer says that "our humble author will continue the story, with Sir John in it, and make you merry with fair Katharine of France," despite the possible bearing of these words on the disputed authorship of the French scenes in *Henry V*. "I think this is a proof that the French scenes in *Henry V*. however unworthy of our author, were really written by him," Tyrwhitt wrote. "It is evident from this passage, that he had at this time formed the plan of that play; and how was *fair Katharine to make the audience merry*, but by speaking broken English? The conversation and courtship of a great princess, in the usual style of the drama, was not likely to afford any *merriment*" (1778, V. 614.6). Even though there is doubt that Shakespeare wrote the Epilogue, largely because Sir John is not in the version of *Henry V* we now have, Tyrwhitt's comment deserves to be known and evaluated. He was first to explain that "fleet" in *Antony and Cleopatra*, "is the old word for *float*. See Chaucer's *Canterbury Tales*, 1958, 2399, 4883" (1778, VIII. 243.4) and the first to point out that "comply with his dug" in the First Folio text of *Hamlet* meant "compliment" with his dug and hence Warburton's emendation to "compliment with his dug" was unnecessary. He clinched matters by quoting a prior use of "comply" in this sense in *Hamlet* itself (1778, X. 400.7). And while there is no New Variorum edition of *Henry VIII*, I remark that the New Arden edition of that play neglects any mention of the following note, though all the information therein is present in its discussion of the dating of the play (pp. xxvi–xxvii and Appendix I). Tyrwhitt's note, which follows, should have been quoted or at least mentioned in the introduction to that edition.

This passage, and others of this Prologue in which great stress is laid upon *the Truth* of the ensuing representation, would lead one to suspect, that this play of Henry the VIIIth, is the very play mentioned by Sir H. Wotton, [in his letter of 2 July, 1613, *Reliq. Wotton*, p. 425] under the description of "*a new play,* [acted by the king's players at the Bank's Side] called, *All is True,* representing some principal pieces of the reign of Henry the VIIIth." The *extraordinary circumstances of pomp and majesty,* with which sir Henry says, that play was set forth, and the particular incident of *certain cannons shot off at the king's entry to a masque at the cardinal Wolsey's house,* (by which the theatre was set on fire and burnt to the ground,) are strictly applicable to the play before us. Mr. Chamberlaine, in *Winwood's Memorials,* Vol. III. p. 469, mentions, "the burning of *The Globe,* or playhouse, on the *Bankside,* on St. Peter's-day [1613], which, (says he) fell out *by a peale of chambers,* that I know not on what occasion were to be used in the play." B. Jonson, in his *Execration upon Vulcan,* says, they were two poor chambers. [See the stage-direction in this play, a little before the king's entrance. *Drum and trumpet, chambers discharged.*] The continuator of Stowe's *Chronicle,* relating the same accident, p. 1003, says expressly, that it happened at *the play of Henry the VIIIth.*

In a MS. letter of Tho. Lorkin to sir Tho. Puckering, dated *London, this last of June,* 1613, the same fact is thus related. "No longer since than *yesterday,* while Bourbage his companie were acting at the Globe the *play of Hen. VIII.* and there shooting of certayne *chambers* in way of triumph, the fire catch'd &c." MS *Harl.* 7002 (1778. VII. 178.4)

Subsequent editors of Shakespeare will do well to consider or reconsider Tyrwhitt's notes, particularly in the 1773 and 1778 editions.

Although Tyrwhitt's preoccupation was primarily with emendations, he was also concerned to provide parallels, glosses, and explications, and in the course of these he revealed some part of the erudition for which he was noted as well as some of his areas of interest. I have already mentioned his views on the old orthography in his *Observations and Conjectures;* in 1778 he returns to this. In a note on *The Merry Wives of Windsor,* on the lines "Crier Hobgoblin, make the fairy o-yes. / Eva. Elves, list your names: silence you airy toys," he writes, "These two lines were certainly intended to rhime together, as the preceding and subsequent couplets do; and accordingly, in the old editions, the final words of each line are printed, *oyes* and *toyes.* This therefore is a striking instance of the inconvenience which has arisen from modernizing the orthography of Shakespeare" (I. 395.9). When Pope emended "happily" to "haply" in a line in *The Taming of the Shrew* Tyrwhitt was moved to similar protest: "*Happily,* in Shakespeare's time, signified *accidentally,* as well as *fortunately.* It is rather surprising, that an editor should be guilty of so gross a corruption of his author's language, for the sake of *modernizing his orthography*."[10] Tyrwhitt had scrupulously followed Chaucer's orthography in his edition of that poet's works.

Allied to his interest in orthography was his knowledge of Elizabethan pronunciation, of compound words, and of language and etymology. Protheus, in *Two Gentlemen of Verona*, exclaims, "Oh, how this spring of love resembleth / The uncertain glory of an April day." Tyrwhitt wrote,

> *Resembleth* is here used as a quadrisyllable, as if it was written *resembeleth*. See *Com. of Errors*, act V. sc. the last:
> "And these two Dromios, one in *semblance*." *As you like it*, act II. sc. ii.
> "The parts and graces of the *wrestler*."
> And it should be observed, that Shakespeare takes the same liberty with many other words, in which *l* or *r* are subjoined to another consonant. See *Com. of Errors*, next verse but one to that cited above:
> "These are the parents to these *children*." where some editors, being unnecessarily alarmed for the metre, have endeavoured to help it by a word of their own.
> "These *plainly* are the parents to these children." (I. 139.4)

In *Cymbeline*, Cymbeline says that "nor the time, nor the place, / Will serve our long interrogatories," a reading authorized by the First Folio. "Later editors," wrote Tyrwhitt, "have omitted *our*, for the sake of the metre, I suppose; but unnecessarily, as *interrogatory* is used by Shakespeare as a *quadrisyllable*. See the *Merchant of Venice* near the end, where in the old edition it is written *intergatory*."[11] He noticed Shakespeare's use of "childish-foolish," "senseless-obstinate," and "mortal-staring" in *Richard III* and conjectured, needlessly, that "gallant, springing" in that same play should also be a compound word—as indeed it appears in the 1778 text (VII. 46.1). He similarly wished, again unnecessarily and possibly illogically, to make a compound word of "palsy fumbling" in *Troilus and Cresida* (IX. 36.5). He knew that "puck" seems "to have been an old Gothic word. *Puke, puken; Sathanas. Gudm. And. Lexicon Island*"; he derived "patch" from the Italian "pazzo" (mad) and "defeat," in *All's Well That Ends Well*, from the French "*defaire*" (to free, to disembarrass), in the last thus obviating one of Theobald's emendations; he disagreed with Johnson on the derivation and meaning of "caitiff," deriving it "not from *captif*, but from *chetif*, Fr. poor, miserable"; and he defined the noun "crack" in *2 Henry IV* as "an old islandic word, signifying a *boy* or *child*. One of the fabulous kings and heroes of Denmark, called Hrolf, was surnamed *Krake*. See the story of *Edda*, Fable 63."[12] In 1773, in one note, he derived "for the nonce" from "a corruption of corrupt Latin. From *pro-nunc*, I suppose, came *for the nunc*, and so *for the nonce*; just as from *ad-nunc* came *a-non*. The Spanish *entonces* has been formed in the same manner from *in-tunc*" (V. 239.2). If Tyrwhitt is right, etymological dictionaries are wrong, for they find the original in Old and Middle English.

One of the problems that plagued, and still continues to plague, editors of Shakespeare is the order in which he wrote his plays. Malone was working at his essay on the chronology of the plays, an essay first published in the 1778 Johnson-Steevens *Shakespeare*, and he had recourse to some of Tyrwhitt's notes. Tyrwhitt thought *Twelfth Night* a very late play because there is a reference to an "undertaker" and, he wrote, "at the meeting of the parliament in 1614, there seems to have been a very general persuasion, or jealousy at least, that the king had been induced to call a parliament at that time, by certain persons, who *had undertaken*, through their influence in the house of commons, to carry things according to his majesty's wishes. These persons were immediately stigmatized with the invidious name of *undertakers*." He cited volume and page of the *Parliamentary History* and also quoted Bacon in corroboration (1778, IV. 249.1). Malone accepted Tyrwhitt's argument and put *Twelfth Night* in 1614, making it the last of Shakespeare's plays. Tyrwhitt was mistaken in the date of the play, but his note served to illustrate the pejorative connotations of the term "undertaker." It was he, however, who first noted the allusion to *3 Henry VI* in Greene's *Groatsworth of Wit*, an allusion which not only helps date the play but, more importantly, virtually establishes Shakespeare's authorship of all or part of that play (1778, VI. 565–66). And it was Tyrwhitt's resurrection of Meres's *Palladis Tamia* that made it possible for Malone to establish an end date for eleven of Shakespeare's plays. Tyrwhitt was the first to attempt to date *Romeo and Juliet* on the internal evidence of the Nurse's reference to the earthquake of eleven years before the action of the play (1778, X. 26.6). As a result, in the 1778 essay Malone wrote "It is not without great distrust of my own opinion that I express my dissent from a gentleman, to whose judgment the highest respect is due; but, I own, his argument does not appear to me conclusive" and then went on to give his dissenting reasons (I. [290]–[92]). Years later, Malone's posthumously printed life of

Shakespeare appeared in the prolegomenous matter in the 1821 Boswell-Malone *Shakespeare*, and there he admitted that Tyrwhitt's conjecture was not "so improbable" as he had once supposed and gave the reasons for his change of mind (II. 350–51).

Tyrwhitt, like Malone in his reversal of opinion about the dating of *Romeo and Juliet*, was not so enamored of his own conjectures as to cling rigidly to them. In the *Observations and Conjectures* of 1766 he had proposed to emend Enobarbus's "Think, and die" to "Wink, and die," adducing an exact parallel to his emendation in Beaumont and Fletcher's *Sea Voyage*. The note is reprinted in 1773 and in 1778, but in the latter edition Tyrwhitt adds, "After all that has been written upon this passage, I believe the old reading is right; but then we must understand *think and die* to mean the same as *die of thought*, or *melancholy*" and quotes Holinshed and Beaumont and Fletcher's *Beggar's Bush* in evidence for the meaning given to "think" (VIII. 232.5). In 1773 he proposed to emend Mrs. Ford's "how you drumble" to "how you fumble," if he "was certain there was no such word as *drumble*" (I. 264.5), but withdrew the note in 1778 when Steevens showed that "drumble" was indeed a word. Again in 1773 he had offered an emendation on a line in *Timon of Athens*; in 1778 he added, "I have repeated this conjecture, in the words in which it was sent to be inserted in the last edition, merely as it serves to introduce the following explanation of the passage, being now convinced myself that no alteration should be attempted" (VIII. 422.5). The "following explanation" was Johnson's, one that Trywhitt could not accept in 1773.

Tyrwhitt, on the other hand, thought well enough of his notes so as to be on the lookout for matter to add to them. In one note in the *Observations and Conjectures* he had emended the "courtiers' knees" of Mercutio's Queen Mab speech to "counties' knees," invoking Shakespeare's use of "County" Paris in the same play. The note is reprinted in the 1773 edition and Tyrwhitt, signing himself "T.T.," writes in the first Appendix that "the following instances" should be added, adducing parallels from *Much Ado about Nothing* and *All's Well That Ends Well*. He also cites uses of the word in Holinshed and in the Burleigh papers but concludes that "perhaps, it is as probable that the repetition of the *Courtier*, which offends us in this passage, may be owing (not to any error of the press, but) to the players having jumbled together the varieties of several editions, as they certainly have done in other parts of the play" (X. 33). In 1773 Steevens had accepted Tyrwhitt's emendation, in *Love's Labour's Lost*, of Si

Nathaniel's "And such barren plants are set before us, that we thankful should be, / Which we taste and feeling are for those parts that do fructify in us more than he," an emendation which simply put "Which . . . are" in parentheses and added "of" before "taste." There was no note by Tyrwhitt. In 1778, however, one gets his explanation:

> This stubborn piece of nonsense, as somebody has called it wants only a particle, I think, to make it sense. I would read [the emendation, as above].
>
> Which in this passage has the force of as, according to an idiom of our language, not uncommon, though not strictly grammatical. What follows is still more irregular; for I am afraid our poet, for the sake of his rime, has put he for him, or rather in him. If he had been writing prose, he would have expressed his meaning, I believe, more clearly thus—that do fructify in us more than in him." (II. 437.8)

Tyrwhitt's reading has been followed by almost all later editors.

Tyrwhitt's first venture into Shakespearean studies was prompted by his reaction to Johnson's 1765 Shakespeare, and as a result most of his observations and conjectures in 1766 had one of Johnson's notes as a point of departure, a practice which continued sporadically in 1773 and 1778. Hence, some of Tyrwhitt's notes exist solely to correct Johnson, although in the process of correcting Johnson he was forced to conjectures of his own. The following examples are from the 1778 edition. Johnson thought Shakespeare had "entangled" himself in geography by having the Prince of Morocco in The Merchant of Venice boast of having slain the Sophy of Persia. Tyrwhitt wrote, "It were well, if Shakespeare had never entangled himself with geography worse than in the present case. If the prince of Morocco be supposed to have served in the army of sultan Soliman (the second, for instance), I see no geographical objection to his having killed the Sophy of Persia. See D'Herbelot in Soliman Ben Selim" (III. 154.3). Helen, of All's Well That Ends Well speaks of "A counsellor, a traitress, and a dear," and Johnson wrote that "it seems that traitress was in that age a term of endearment." Tyrwhitt could not conceive how "traitress (spoken seriously) was in that age a term of endearment" and suggested that "enemy," two lines above in the same speech, might just as well be thought a term of endearment (IV. 14.3). Modern editors are of two—or more—minds about the word and the passage in which it appears. Hotspur's description of the fop who demanded his prisoners, "his chin, new reap'd, / Shew'd like a stubble land, at harvest-

home," was glossed by Johnson as "that is, at a time of festivity."
Tyrwhitt disagreed: "If we understand *harvest-home* in the general sense of a *time of festivity*, we shall lose the most pointed
circumstance of the comparison. A *chin new shaven* is compared
to a *stubble-land at harvest-home*, not on account of the festivity
of that season, as I apprehend, but because at that time, when the
corn has been but just carried in, the stubble appears more even
and upright, than at any other" (V. 276.8). Johnson thought
Falstaff's reference to himself in the same play as "a pepper-corn,
a brewer's horse" meant he was as lean as these things, but
Tyrwhitt mantained that, "in assertions of this sort, Falstaff does
not mean to point out any *similitude* to his own condition, but
on the contrary some striking *dissimilitude*" and pointed to an
earlier passage in which Falstaff was doing the same thing (V.
369.5). Johnson was wrong; Tyrwhitt was partially right. Johnson
saw a "conceit" alluding to venereal disease in Henry V's reference to "twenty French crowns"; Tyrwhitt saw no necessity for
this interpretation. For him "the conceit here seems to turn
merely upon the equivocal sense of *crown*, which signifies either
a *coin*, or a *head*" (VI. 112.6). Modern opinion upholds Tyrwhitt's explanation.

   It must not be thought that Tyrwhitt was deficient in a sense of
humor or that he would balk at the indelicate or improper. One
would wish to know more about him, but unfortunately, and
largely because of his retiring nature, there is very little biographical and, especially, anecdotal information about him. When a
too enterprising publisher reprinted what he alleged was Tyrwhitt's edition of Chaucer, Tyrwhitt wrote a letter to the GM in
June 1783 in which he disclaimed any part in the edition. He had
derived no profit from his own edition. Hence he wrote, "A
certain philosopher, when his gouty shoes were stolen, only
wished, that they might fit the thief as well as they fitted himself;
and for my own part I shall be contended, if my book shall prove
just as lucrative to Mr. Bell, as it has been to me." He deprecated
the practice of reprinting books without the author's or editor's
knowledge; at the same time he hoped that the young readers for
whom Bell's reprint was intended would enjoy the picture at the
beginning of each volume and would be unconcerned with
everything else (p. 461). Another editor might have breathed fire
and brimstone; Tyrwhitt wished Mr. Bell well. While almost
nothing is known about Tyrwhitt's social life, it is at least clear
that he occasionally took tea with the famous Dr. William
Heberden, the elder ("ultimus Romanorum" Dr. Johnson called

him), and Mrs. Heberden, for in the *GM* for 1785 there is an "Epigram, By Mr. Tyrwhitt, on a Tea-Chest of Mrs. Heberden's, Made of Olive-Wood which was Found at Athens By Mr. Stuart." Six lines of Greek are followed by an English translation by Anonymous:

> In Attic fields, by fam'd Illissus flood,
> A tree to Pallas sacred once I stood.
> Now, torn from thence, with graceful emblems drest,
> For Myra's tea I form a polish'd chest.
> Athens, farewell—nor yet do I repine
> For my Socratic shades and patroness divine.
>
> (ii. 559)

Heberden was Tyrwhitt's physician as well as his friend.

Perhaps it may be best to conclude this analysis of Tyrwhitt's contributions by quoting two more notes. The first shows him in a rare light, that of literary critic, of a sensitive reader reacting emotionally to the power of Shakespeare's artistry. The Duke of Albany asks that the bodies of Goneril and Regan be produced, "be they alive or dead," and when the corpses of the sisters are brought out, he exclaims, "This judgment of the heavens, that makes us tremble, / Touches us not with pity." Tyrwhitt's is the only note on these lines in the 1778 *Shakespeare*. "If Shakespeare had studied Aristotle all his life," he wrote, "he would not perhaps have been able to mark with more precision the distinct operations of *terror* and *pity*" (IX. 558.1). Much as one is glad to see Tyrwhitt reacting in such a fashion and writing such a note, it would be a mistake to conclude with quotation of this note on *King Lear*, for, except for his many conjectural emendations, he ought properly to be remembered for notes like that on the source of *The Merchant of Venice*, one of his longest, only part of which I quote,

> The two principal incidents of this play are to be found separately in a collection of old stories, which were very popular, at least five hundred years ago, under the title of *Gesta Romanorum*. The first *Of the bond*, is ch. xlviii. of the copy, which I chuse to refer to, as the completest of any which I have yet seen. MS. Harl. n. 2270. A knight there borrows money of a merchant, upon condition of forfeiting *all his flesh* for non-payment. Then the penalty is exacted before the judge; *the knight's mistress*, disguised, *in forma viri & vestimentis pretiosis indula*, comes into court, and, by permission of the judge, endeavours to mollify the merchant.

The other incident, *of the caskets*, is in ch. xcix. of the same collection. A king of Apulia sends his daughter to be married to the son of an emperor of Rome. After some adventures, (which are nothing to the present purpose) she is brought before the emperor; who says to her, "Puella, propter amorem filii mei multa adversa sustinuisti. Tamen si digna fueris ut uxor ejus sis cito probabo. Et fecit fieri tria vasa."

The choice is then made clear to the young girl.

From this abstract of these two stories, I think it appears sufficiently plain that they are the REMOTE originals of the two incidents in this play. I can hardly suppose that they were the originals which Shakespeare immediately copied, for this reason principally, because I doubt whether they have ever appeared in print. They certainly are not to be found in an edition of the *Gesta Romanorum*, which I have myself, printed as late as 1521; nor in some much older editions, which I have occasionally examined. There is a book of one Richard Robinson, mentioned by Tanner, Biblioth. Brit. Hib. p. 476. which might possibly afford some light to this subject. The title, as given by the author himself, is, A Record of ancient Hystoryes, in Latin, Gesta Romanorum (autore, ut supponitur, Johanne Leylando, Antiquario) translated by me, perused, corrected, and better'd. London, MDLXX-VII. 12mo. This book is there said, to have had six editions between 1577 and 1601; but I have never been able to meet with a copy of it. The supposition that Leland was the author of *Gesta Romanorum* is certainly groundless; but it is not impossible, that a copy of that book (differing from the printed copy, and, perhaps, containing the two stories which I have here abridged from the Harleian MS.) might have been found among Leland's manuscripts, and translated by Mr. R. Robinson as an original. (1773, III. 224–26)

What stands out, and was intended to stand out, as witness the upper-case letters, is the word "REMOTE" in the sentence, "From this abstract of these two stories, I think it appears sufficiently plain that they are the REMOTE originals of the two incidents in this play." However, this note should be supplemented by what Tyrwhitt himself added in Appendix II as a corrective (above pp. 31–32). The revised note in 1778 (III. 257–58) substitutes the following for everything after the first sentence of the last paragraph in the quoted 1773 version:

That *of the Caskets* Shakespeare might take from the English *Gest. Romanorum*, as Mr. Farmer has observed; and that *of the bond* might come to him from the *Pecorone;* but upon the whole I am rather inclined to suspect, that he has followed some hitherto unknow novelist, who had saved him the trouble of working up the two stories into one.

There can be no better way to see the scholarly mind at work than by reading these notes.

Tyrwhitt contributed eighteen notes to Malone's *Supplement*. Those on the poems have been mentioned above. The longest, however, of all his notes appears as an answer to Bishop Warburton's entirely too long and unnecessary dissertation on the romances of chivalry which he believed to be somewhere in the background of Don Armado in *Love's Labour's Lost*. Since Tyrwhitt's note is almost seven closely printed pages long, I shall quote only some bits and pieces of it. He starts by stating that there is general agreement that Warburton's note is "misplaced" and then continues by saying "I should humbly advise the next editor of Shakespeare to omit it. That he may have the less scruple upon that head, I shall take this opportunity of throwing out a few remarks, which, I think, will be sufficient to shew, that the learned writer's hypothesis was formed upon a very hasty and imperfect view of the subject" (I. 373). Since Warburton had neglected the logical first step, i.e., a definition of his terms, Tyrwhitt repaired the omission:

> A romance of chivalry therefore, according to my notion, is any fabulous narration, in verse or prose, in which the principal characters are knights, conducting themselves, in their several situations and adventures, agreeably to the institutions and customs of chivalry. Whatever names the characters may bear, whether historical or fictitious; and in whatever country, or age, the scene of the action may be laid, if the actors are represented as knights, I should call such a fable a Romance of Chivalry. (I. 375)

Having divided Warburton's argument into three parts and with his definition as a base of operations he proceeded to tear him apart, bit by bit. Warburton had argued that most of these romances took place in Spain. Tyrwhitt wrote, "I am sensible of the impropriety of asserting any thing positively, without an accurate examination of many more of them than have fallen my way. I think, however, I might venture to assert, in direct contradiction to Dr. W. that the scene of them was *not generally* in Spain" (I. 375). He cited Percy, "my learned friend, the Dean of Carlisle," as having "taken notice of the strange mistake of Dr. W. in supposing that the feats of *Oliver* were recorded under the name of *Palmerin de Oliva*; a mistake, into which no one could have fallen, who had read the first page of the book" (I. 376). And after further exposing the errors of Warburton's argument, he concluded roundly with "And so much for Dr. W.'s account of the origin and nature of romances of chivalry." Malone added that "No future editor of Shakespeare will, I believe, readily consent to omit the dissertation here referred to. Mr. Tyrwhitt's judicious observations upon it have given it a value which it certainly had not before; and I think I may venture to foretel, that this futile performance, like the pismire which Martial tells us was accidentally encrusted with amber, will be ever preserved, for the sake of the admirable comment in which it is now inlaid" (I. 380). Warburton's dissertation and Tyrwhitt's judicious observations are enshrined in editions through Boswell-Malone and, doubtless, in later editions.

Richard Farmer had called attention to an old play on the subject of Richard II and had cited Camden's *Annals* and an account of a trial as reported by Sir Francis Bacon as evidence of its existence and subject matter. Tyrwhitt was able to show, by quoting a more extensive account of the same trial in "*State Trials,* vol VIII, p. 60," that the principal subject matter had to do with Henry IV, and only with the deposing of Richard II. "Philips, the player," who was paid to put on the play, was identified by Tyrwhitt as "*Augustine Philippes* . . . one of the patentees of the Globe play-house with *Shakespeare* in 1603; but the play here described was certainly not Shakespeare's HENRY IV, as that commences above a year after the death of *Richard*" (I. 381).

Tyrwhitt also contributed five notes on *Pericles, Prince of Tyre* and two on *The Puritan.* Three of the five on *Pericles* are emendations; all are accepted by the editor of the New Arden edition, although the third of these had appeared silently in Rowe's edition.[13] More important, possibly, than the three emendations, is Tyrwhitt's learned note on the origins of the story of Appollonius, King of Tyre, in which he is first to name the *Pantheon* of Godfrey of Viterbo in the line of descent (II.[3].1). The fifth contribution is not really a note, but rather Tyrwhitt's transcript and conjectural reconstruction of a fragment of a MS poem on Apollonius in Farmer's possession (II.[3].1 and 158 n.). The first of two notes on *The Puritan* is an attempt at dating it, Tyrwhitt demonstrating from internal evidence (an allusion to the peace with Spain) that one of the dates given for the play, 1600, was a mistake, though there was not "the same objection" to 1607, although a reference to Sunday, the 13th of July, in the play disposed him to think the right date was 1608 since 1608 was the only year between 1603 and 1614 when the 13th of July fell on a Sunday (II. 533.1). *The Puritan* was entered at Stationer's Hall on 6 August 1607, so that the ingenious surmise is mistaken, since the play was published "immediately after."[14] But Tyrwhitt was able to provide Steevens with a close parallel from the French of Froissart for the words "nothing was so hot, nor too dear for me" (II. 538.3).

Tyrwhitt's last contributions were five notes for the 1785 *Shakespeare*. The pattern, or proportion, is familiar: three are emendations, one is a correction of Dr. Johnson, and the fifth is a reconsideration of an earlier note. Only one of the emendations has gained attention. Tyrwhitt saw no need for the entrance of the Soothsayer toward the end of II.iv in *Julius Caesar*, reasoning that "all he is made to say, should be given to Artemidorus; who is seen and accosted by Portia, in his passage from the first stand, p. 54, to one more convenient, p. 55" [when the Soothsay enters] (VIII. 55.2). Rowe had substituted Artemidorus for the Soothsayer long ago; both he and Tyrwhitt were wrong, although the latter's note is quoted in the New Variorum.[15] Johnson objected, of the Duke's reference in *The Merchant of Venice* to "Bellario, a learned doctor, / Whom I have sent for to determine this," that "the doctor and the court are here somewhat unskilfully brought together. That the duke would, on such an occasion, consult a doctor of great reputation, is not unlikely; but how should this be foreknown by Portia?" Tyrwhitt could not "see any necessity for supposing that *this* was *foreknown by Portia*. She consults Bellario as an eminent lawyer, and her relation. If the Duke had not consulted him, the only difference would have been, that she would have come into court as an advocate perhaps, instead of a judge" (III. 230.8).

Of most interest, and worthy of final place, is Tyrwhitt's reconsideration of a note on *Measure for Measure*. In his *Observations and Conjectures* he had suggested that Shakespeare was flattering King James in the play (p. 25). In the first Appendix in the 1773 *Shakespeare* he returned to the same idea, prompted by the lines spoken by Angelo, "as these black masks / Proclaim an enshield beauty ten times louder, / Than beauty could displayed." He suggested that "enshield" be emended to "enshell'd" or "in-shell'd" as in *Coriolanus*, giving volume and page number, and then wrote:

THESE *Masks* must mean, I think the *Masks of the audience*; however improperly a compliment to them is put into the mouth of Angelo. As Shakespeare would hardly have been guilty of such an *indecorum* to flatter a common audience, I think this passage affords ground for supposing that the play was written to be acted at court. Some strokes of particular flattery to the king have been pointed out in the *Observations and Conjectures printed at Oxford*, 1766; and there are several other general reflections, in the Character of the duke especially, which seem calculated for the royal ear (II. 56).

The note is signed "T.T.". In 1778 the note is reprinted, "I" is substituted for the circumlocution above, and the note is signed "Tyrwhitt." In 1783 Joseph Ritson published his *Remarks* on the 1778 *Shakespeare* and labeled Tyrwhitt's suggestion about the masks "ingenious, but not decisive," adding that Isabella held a mask in her hand, so that "*these black masks* will, in that case, onely [sic] *be such masks as these*, or *this kind of masks*" (p. 20). He also upheld "enshield" as a contraction of "enshielded." Hence it was that Tyrwhitt, in the 1785 edition, added the following note:

I do not think so well of the conjecture in the latter part of this note as I did some years ago; and therefore I should wish to withdraw it. Not that I am inclined to adopt the idea of the Author of REMARKS, &c. p. 20. as I see no ground for supposing, that Isabella *had* any *mask in her hand*. My notion at present is, that the phrase *these black masks* signifies nothing more than *black masks*; according to an old idiom of our language, by which the demonstrative pronoun is put for the prepositive article. See the *Glossary to Chaucer* Ed. 1775. *This, These*. Shakspeare seems to have used the same idiom not only in the passage quoted by Mr. Steevens from *Romeo and Juliet*; but also in *First Henry* IV. act I. scene 3.

———and but for *these* vile guns
He would himself have been a soldier.

With respect to the former part of this note, though the *Remarker* has told us that "*enshield* is CERTAINLY put by contraction for *enshielded*;" I have no objection to leaving my conjecture in its place, till some authority is produced for such an usage of *enshield* or *enshielded*. (II. 68.1)

Isabella is *not* provided with a mask, and the exact meaning of Angelo's reference to "black masks" is still not clear. The glossary to Chaucer mentioned in Tyrwhitt's note is his own, of course, and there, under "This," one finds "*pron. demonst. Sax. is some-* times put for the prepositive article." The New Arden editor, citing Tyrwhitt's 1778 note, seems to have been unaware of Tyrwhitt's later reversal, further evidence of the relative neglect of the entire body of his contributions. And surely it is fitting tribute to Tyrwhitt that no authority has been produced "for such an usage of *enshield* or *enshielded*," *OED* giving only the passage in *Measure for Measure*.

Although Tyrwhitt died in 1786, remarks that he had made to Steevens found their way into Malone's edition of 1790 and Steevens's of 1793. When the Host in *The Merry Wives of Windsor* queries, "said I well, bully Hector?" Malone inserts a note, marked with an asterisk and interrupting the numbered notes, that reads,

> Mr. Tyrwhitt observes, that a similar phrase is given to the *host* in the *Pardoneres Prologue*. CANT. TALES, v. 12246, edit. 1775 [Tyrwhitt's edition]; and supposes from this, and other circumstances of general resemblance, that Shakspeare when he drew his *host of the Garter,* had not forgotten his Chaucer. But the passage (as he remarked to Mr. Steevens) not being in any of the ancient printed editions, I imagine this phrase ["said I well"] must have reached our author in some other way; for I suspect he did not devote much time to the perusal of old MSS. (I. ii. 207.*)

One of the passages that gave difficulty in that much controverted play *Titus Andronicus* was Marcus's reference to a "bloody battle-axe, / Writing destruction on the enemy's castle." Theobald emended to "casque"; Warburton cited Shelton's translation of *Don Quixote* in evidence that a particular kind of helmet was called a "castle"; and Benjamin Heath, in his *Revisal of Shakespeare's Text*, 1765, stated that "castle" in Shelton's translation of *Don Quixote* was an error of the press for "casque." Steevens cited "Grose's Treatise of ancient Armour" in evidence that a "castle" derived from "casquetel" and did signify a "close helmet." He also quoted Holinshed on the entrance into a tournament of "sir Thomas Knevet in a *castell* of cole blacke," evidently having thought that a clincher. But he added that "a remark . . . of my late friend Mr. Tyrwhitt, has taught me to suspect the validity of my quotation from Holinshed; for one of the knights in the tournament described, made his entry in a *fountain*, and another in a *horse-litter*. Sir Thomas Knevet therefore might have appeared in a building formed in imitation of a *castle*" (XIII. 309.9). Tyrwhitt's caution was a wise one, for the editor of the New Arden *Titus Andronicus* states that "there is no reason to think this is corrupt, or that it has any but normal meaning" (p. 4). If there are further remarks by Tyrwhitt printed in 1790 or 1793, or even later, they have escaped my vigilance, but the "castle" in *Titus Andronicus* remains a "castle."

Perhaps Malone's account of Tyrwhitt's death and his characterization of him in a letter to Bishop Percy may best serve as his epitaph.

> Your lordship has heard before now what a loss we have all sustained by the death of poor M[r] Tyrwhitt. He was carried off after an illness of little more than a fortnight. His immediate complaint was a dysentery; but he had something wrong within, it should seem, which he concealed from every one except his brother. It being necessary to give him a clyster, he was exceedingly averse to the operation, and at last after much entreaty to assign some reason, he told the physician that he had long had a complaint called I think *collapsus ani*: he had this malady for 20 years it seems—and it was sometimes attended with troublesome consequences.—He persevered to the last in starving his disorder, which they say was the worst thing he could have done, as it probably tended to exasperate the parts affected. His friend D[r] Heberden not being in town, he was attended by D[r] Gisborne. He has left a fortune behind him that quite astonished me; near one hundred thousand pounds. He has disposed of it I am told, by a will written with the greatest accuracy with his own hand last June, very honourably and justly among his relations. All his Mss he has left to the Museum, and all such of his books as they are not already possessed of. To that repository he is an irrep[ar]able loss; having been indefatigable, since he was appointed a Curator, in getting it into much better order than he found it in. (*Letters*, I. 32–3)

Perhaps, too, some lines "inscribed on an urn, in the Gardens of the Bishop of Durham, at Mongewell, in Oxfordshire," written in 1800 and printed in the 1807 GM (ii. 1147) and there titled "To the Memory of my two highly-valued friends, T. Tyrwhitt, Esq. and the Rev. C. M. Cracherode, M.A." should be quoted:

> In this once favor'd walk, beneath these elms,
> Whose thicken'd foliage, to the solar ray
> Impervious, casts a venerable gloom,
> Oft in instructive converse we beguil'd
> The fervid time, which each returning year
> To Friendship's call devoted!
> Such things were, but are,
> Alas! no more!

Clayton Mordaunt Cracherode, bibliophile, matriculated a Christ Church in June 1746, aged sixteen, and proceeded to th B.A. in 1750 and the M.A. in 1753; in May 1747 Tyrwhitt, age seventeen, matriculated at Queen's College and proceeded to th

B.A. in 1750 and to the M.A. in 1756. The two remained friends all their lives, Tyrwhitt predeceasing Cracherode by thirteen years. Shute Barrington, Bishop of Durham, was educated at Eton, as was Tyrwhitt, took the degree of B.A. at Merton College and proceeded M.A. in 1757. He outlived his two friends by many years, dying in 1826. But for some years the three walked in the gardens at Mongewell and beguiled the time in instructive converse, possibly some of the time, prompted by Tyrwhitt, turning their attention to Shakespeare.

2

George Tollet, Gentleman-Farmer

George Tollet (1725–79) was admitted to Eton College in 1742, the register of admissions making a tentative identification of him as the son of George Tollet, commissioner of the navy, by his wife Elizabeth Oakes, of the Isle of Man. From Eton he, like so many of his schoolmates, went on to King's College, Cambridge, matriculating as a Fellow Commoner in 1744. He was admitted to Lincoln's Inn on 2 July 1745 and was called to the bar in 1751. At some time after that last date he retired to Betley Hall, Staffordshire, which had been purchased by his father, and there he seems to have settled down to the life of a bachelor country gentleman. William Cole, Tollet's contemporary at Cambridge, described him in his *Athenae Cantabrigienses* as "a shy, reserved man, of no genteel appearance and behaviour." Cole went on to remark,

> He was much acquainted with the late Mr. Ewin, father of Dr. Ewin, whose sister told me, 1780, that the acquaintance began when she went to Stratford-le-Bow school, where Mr. Tollet's aunt (a little, crooked woman, but a sharp wit, and author of some poems in print) took notice of her. Mr. Tollet has many notes in Mr. *Steevens's* edition of Shakespeare; in the first volume of which he has an ingenious dissertation on the figures of some pantomimes in his house at Betley, in Staffordshire, a print of which morris-dancers is at the head of it, and sent to me by Mr. Steevens in September, 1780; who was also a Fellow Commoner of the same college, but came thither the year after I left it, viz., in 1753, as he told me at Dr. Lort's chambers in Trinity College. Mr. Tollet died Oct. 22, 1779. (*Lit. Illustr.* VIII. 584)

Possibly because he was shy and reserved and associated with townspeople, almost nothing is recorded of Tollet's years in Cambridge. Although he was an Eton boy, as was William Cole, Cole was the only one at Cambridge who seems to have remembered him. Cole (1714–82) was eleven years Tollet's senior and was himself of King's College, having migrated there in 1736 from

Clare Hall. A gregarious antiquary who had become a Fellow of the Society of Antiquaries in 1747, Cole knew many of the famous or soon-to-become-famous scholars of his time, and it is likely, though not demonstrable, that he influenced Tollet in the latter's decision to communicate some of his thoughts on Shakespeare to Steevens for the 1773 Johnson-Steevens *Shakespeare*. As will be seen, Tollet had had thoughts about either editing Shakespeare's plays or writing an essay or book upon them. It is, of course, equally possible that Tollet read Steevens's 1766 advertisement "To the Public," announcing a revision of Johnson's edition, and hence abandoned his own project in favor of one which gave promise of greater value, if only because of the combined efforts of a number of scholars headed by Johnson and Steevens. I assume, too, that Tollet was aware that London was a more logical place in which to do scholarly work than Betley Hall.

Perhaps it is a measure of Tollet's almost anonymous existence that the compilers of *Alumni Cantabrigienses* were not sure he was "the Shakespearean critic." Tollet would almost surely have been forgotten except for two things: his aunt Elizabeth was a poet and a friend of Newton's and "he contributed some notes [I am quoting the *DNB*] to Johnson and Steevens's edition of Shakespeare." Actually, the modest "some" of the *DNB* account amounts to over four hundred notes in the 1778 edition added to the fifteen contributed to the 1773 edition, making Tollet one of the greatest single contributors to the commentary on Shakespeare in the eighteenth century, always excepting the editors of the various editions. His notes are on all the plays of the accepted canon except *Julius Caesar, Titus Andronicus* (which many thought uncanonical), and *Romeo and Juliet* (hardly bachelor fare). There are three new notes and an addition to an earlier note posthumously printed in Malone's *Supplement* (1780). "Shortly before his death," the *DNB* continues, "he complained that many of his valuable suggestions were appropriated by the editors in the second issue [1778] of their work without acknowledgment." Since he is given credit by name for over four hundred notes in the 1778 *Shakespeare*, one of them, ten pages long, describing the figures of morris-dancers on a painted glass window at Betley and reproducing them in a folded insert titled "Morris Dancers. From an Ancient Window in the House of George Tollet Esq. at Betley in Staffordshire," this statement may be discounted almost entirely. The only possible reason for a statement such as is attributed to him is that thirty-three of the communications to

Steevens are mentioned, not as separate notes signed with his name, as are all the others, but as part of Steevens's notes. But Steevens mentions Tollet by name as his source and even quotes him. Given a man jealous of his contributions, if Tollet was such, the whole matter becomes more readily understandable.

Tollet's identity was not known to George Steevens in 1773, for in the Appendix to that edition, after quoting a note by Tollet on "Maid Marian," he wrote, "This gentleman, who is only known to us through several ingenious and valuable remarks (communicated by letter in the course of the work) will please to accept our thanks as well for his intentional as for his real kindness" (Mm5^{r-v}). But writing to Garrick on 31 July 1774 Steevens, who had sent a "proof of an unfinished plate," told him that "the drawing was made from a window about three hundred miles off, and contains all his figures in an ancient morrice-dance. I coloured this proof from the original with such wretched paint as I could procure at a country shop."[1] Since there are two notes by Tollet in volume I, he must have been among the first to respond to Steevens's appeal in 1766 for contributions to the revision of Johnson's 1765 edition. However, the first of Tollet's communications to appear as part of a note by Steevens in 1778 is handsomely acknowledged, Steevens writing, "Since the first appearance of this edition [in 1773], my very industrious and learned correspondent, Mr. *Tollet,* of *Betley,* in *Staffordshire,* has enabled me to retract a too hasty censure on *Bailey,* to whom we were long indebted for our only *English Dictionary*" (I. 79.3). Possibly Tollet was not content when, in other notes, Steevens wrote that he received "the original hint for this note" from Mr. Tollet (V. 363.4) or that "for this information" he was "indebted" to "Mr. Tollet who quotes" and then quoted Tollet (V. 376.7). In one note Tollet would seem to have reason to be annoyed. In 1773 he had explained the word "siege" of Stephano's question to Trinculo in *The Tempest,* "how cam'st thou to be the siege of the moon-calf," as "a *stool of easement,* as Dr. Ph. Holland phrases it, in his translation of *Pliny's Natural History*" (I. 52.2). In the 1778 edition his note is replaced by Steevens's: "Siege signifies *stool in* every sense of the word, and is here used in the dirtiest." He thereupon gives a very pertinent example of the word as so used in Holinshed (I. 60.5). Tollet, it is clear from one note, had for some years been thinking about and writing down a commentary on Shakespeare, for he writes, "Before I saw Dr. Johnson's edition of Shakespeare [1765], my opinion of this passage was formed and written" (1778, X. 548.9). It is also apparent from one com munication that he studied not only the text of Shakespeare's plays but also the prolegomenous matter in various editions, for in a note by Steevens on Lewis Theobald's preface to his own edition of Shakespeare Tollet is given credit for spotting a possible source in Spenser for a Latin distich quoted by Theobald (I. 130). But all this is by the way; what is important are Tollet's notes.

Since in most of his notes Tollet gives the date of edition and page number, and sometimes book size, for his citations or quotations, one must conclude either that he had the very books or that he had copied down the information from elsewhere. Given his solitary bent, the former explanation is infinitely more plausible. Since he led the retired life of a country gentleman, he almost surely had little access to libraries other than his own. Although Betley was a market town and Tollet might have picked up bargains from itinerant booksellers, he must have accumulated the greatest part of his collection in the Cambridge and London years. That he was not entirely wrapped up in his books is clear from his sending Steevens "specimens of three kinds of heath which [grew] in his own neighbourhood" in order to vindicate Sir Thomas Hanmer's explanation of a passage in the first scene of The Tempest (I. 8.5).[2] In two notes he shows further knowledge and observation of plants, explaining that "pricking goss" in The Tempest meant "the low sort of gorse that only grows upon wet ground, and which is well described by the name of whins in Markham's Farewell to Husbandry. It has prickles like those on a rose-tree or a gooseberry" (I. 94.2). Here, as in the next note, he is able to adduce a published authority to back up his personal knowledge and observation. No little print was expended on various commentators' efforts to explain the lines, "So doth the woodbine the sweet honey-suckle / Gently entwist," in A Midsummer Night's Dream. Tollet quoted Bacon's Natural History on the existence of two kinds of honeysuckle. "The distinction," he wrote, "however, may serve to shew why Shakespeare and other authors frequently added wood-bine to honey-suckle, when they mean the plant and not the grass" (III. 91.2). From the corpus of over four hundred notes one could very reasonably characterize Tollet not only as a bookish man, for he definitely was that, but also as a man who knew something about a good many subjects. His knowledge of law might be taken for granted, and so, too, possibly, his acquaintance with many aspects of country life— husbandry, botany, hunting, natural history, and local history. One would expect him to be familiar with the Bible, and he was.

He evidently knew something about heraldry, and was much interested in antiquities. He was fairly well read in poetry, largely English poetry of the late-sixteenth and early-seventeenth centuries.

The Preface to the Reverend Stebbing Shaw's *History and Antiquities of Staffordshire*, two volumes in three, 1798 contains the information that "G. Tollet, esq. (brother to the late C. Tollett of Betley, esq.) an ingenious antiquary, was possessed of various MSS. relating to the county, particularly the curious copy of Erdeswick, with additions by Mr. Hurdman, of Spot Grange 1689, and of Stone 1696; he had also taken great pains to compile much useful matter himself, all of which I have been favoured with the use of, by G. Embury Tollet, esq. (to whom the late Mr. Tollet devised his estate) as well the contribution of a plate" (I.viii). While it is not clear to me which Tollet contributed the plate, a contemplated "View of Betley Hall, &" which would have found a place in a third, never published, volume (see I. xxiv), there is no doubt about the identity of the author of two letters in the second volume. They throw additional light on Tollet's activities.

Betley, 15th March, 1768.
　　The bearer hereof to Stafford will there subscribe for me to the general history of Staffordshire.
　　In my opinion, the edition would be more complete if it contained a transcript at large of Domesday Book for the county, as Morton's History of Northamptonshire, and Leycester's Historical Antiquities of Cheshire, both have for those counties. Do you design any such thing, or would you print it if a transcript were procured for you? You will see in the postscript where probably one might be obtained without any great expence. I hear Mr. Loxdale, an attorney at Shrewsbury, and Mr. Bowen, a herald there, have some manuscript collections upon this county. I have a manuscript of Erdeswick's Survey of Staffordshire,[3] with several additions about the succession of families, by John Hurdman, formerly of Stone. You are welcome to a sight of it here, or to examine it with any of your manuscripts; but there are reasons why I should be cautious of letting it go out of my hands. I dare say either of the Mr. Wrights, at Church Eaton, will attend you here at your best leisure. In the mean time, I should be glad to know your intention about a transcript of Domesday Book for the county; and am, sir, your very humble servant,
　　　　　　　　　　　　　　　　　　　　GEORGE TOLLET.

In a postscript he added a number of bibliographical references pertinent to the project (II.i.xvii).

The second letter is even more revealing, showing Tollet to be, at the very least, an amateur archaeologist.

Sir, Betley, March 26, 1769.

Since I wrote to you, I have seen Mr. Unett, of Stafford; and I find there are among Dr. Wilkes's papers transcripts of Domesday-book Staffordshire, and of Hurdman's continuation of Erdeswick's Survey of Staff. I have since obtained a copy of this part of Domesday from Oxford, which I meant as a present for your work; but I do apprehend yours is a better transcript; however, you are welcome to collate mine with yours, if you think proper. We have no botanist hereabouts that I know of. I asked an apothecary here, whether there were wild un-cultivated plants hereabouts that were uncommon, and he replied there were not; but as his assertion may not be true, you will be welcome to stay a week with me in the proper time of observing them, if you are so inclined. But we may meet before then, if it is convenient to you. I mean to open an old sepulchral barrow on Maer-heath, near Madeley and Whitmore, and this shall be done whenever you and Mr. Unet will fix the time.

I send herewith some things found at Harecastle in digging the subterraneous canal; and I have heard of much more curious ones picked up there; but they were gone and disposed of elsewhere at a distance, or destroyed. I will make enquiry again, and remain, your most obedient, humble servant.

GEORGE TOLLET.

P.S. I should like to know, (by the post if you please) how far Dr. Wilkes has gone in relation to fossils, and whether further than Dr. Plott. I believe I could get some information on this subject from Mr. Platt of Oxford, if you deem it necessary, of some things he collected or made observations on in Staffordshire. (II.i.xx)

Since Tollet died in 1779, his name does not appear in the list of subscribers to Shaw's work, but Charles Tollet and George Em-bury Tollet each subscribed for a copy, the latter for one on large paper.

Before proceeding to analyze Tollet's notes, I wish to charac-erize him as much as possible from the admittedly tenuous evidence of his notes. He was essentially a modest, courteous man, possibly even courtly. Thus, when he is about the describe the figures on his stained-glass window at Betley Hall in the long note on "Maid Marian" appended to 1 *Henry IV* in 1778 he begins by saying, "I shall endeavour to explain some of the characters [there were eleven in four rows], and in compliment to the lady [i.e., the figure of Maid Marian] I will begin the descrip-ion with the front rank, in which she is stationed" (V. 426). With the strain of courtliness goes a certain delicacy of expression. In a scene in *Henry VIII* a porter speaks of "some strange Indian with the great tool," and George Steevens, under the guise of "Collins," one of his pseudonyms, quoted a parallel from Beaumont and Fletcher's and Shakespeare's *Two Noble Kinsmen*, "The Bavian with long tail and eke long tool" (VII. 315.4). Tollet wrote, referring to his description of the figures in his stained-glass window, "Fig. I. in the print of the Morris-dancers, at the end of *King Henry IV*, has a bib which extends below the doublet; and its length might be calculated for the concealment of the phallic obscenity mentioned by Beaumont and Fletcher, of which perhaps the *Bavian fool* exhibited an occasional view for the diversion of our indelicate ancestors." Others of his notes also attest to his dislike of the gratuitously indelicate.

Tollet's personal modesty manifests itself in a few notes where he is able to correct some previous editor or critic of Shakespeare. Dr. Johnson declared in the Preface to Shakespeare that "the art of writing notes is not of difficult attainment. The work is performed, first by railing at the stupidity, negligence, ignorance, and asinine tastelessness of the former editors." Tollet, catching Johnson in an error, did not rail; he simply wrote, "Dr. Johnson's explanation cannot be right, because," and he gave his reason (VII. 233.6). Similarly, where Richard Farmer proposed an emendation in a particularly difficult passage in *Henry VIII* and Tollet disagreed he did so in these terms: "Dr. Farmer has displayed such eminent knowledge of Shakespeare, that it is with the utmost diffidence I dissent from the alteration which he would establish here" (VII. 284.7). This same diffidence is seen in the last sentence of his ten-page dissertation, bristling with erudition, on the Morris-dancers, for there he writes, "Such are my conjectures upon a subject of much obscurity; but it is high time to resign it to one more conversant with the history of our ancient dresses" (V. 434). In 1807 Francis Douce wrote a "Dissertation on the Ancient English Morris Dance" and praised Tollet for his learning as displayed in his explanation of the Morris-Dancers and for his "many other valuable communications." He either did not think it necessary to acknowledge Tollet's long note as the source for nine works he quotes or cites or he came upon the works independently.

Tollet's observation of plants has already been mentioned. He seems to have been equally observant of the works of man. The Chorus to act II of *Henry V* personified Expectation, which "hides a sword from hilts unto the point / With crowns imperial, and Tollet is reminded that "in the armoury in the Tower of

London, Edward III. is represented with two crowns on his sword, alluding to the two kingdoms, France and England, of both of which he was crowned heir," and he conjectures that "perhaps the poet took the thought from this representation." The Fool points to King Lear and says, "That's a sheal'd peascod," and Tollet who, as a Templar, must have taken in all the sights of London, recalls that "the robing of Richard IId's effigy in Westminster Abbey is wrought with *peascods open* and the *peas out;* perhaps in allusion of his being once in full possession of sovereignty, but soon reduced to an empty title."[4]

But it was in the country that Tollet spent most of his life. He knew what "unbolted mortar" was and could therefore, as others evidently had not, explain that phrase in its appearance in *King Lear:* "*Unbolted* mortar is mortar made of unsifted lime, and therefore to break the lumps it is necessary to tread it by men in wooden shoes. This *unbolted* villain is therfore this *coarse* rascal" (IX. 417.5). Tollet knew the ways of a butcher with a calf, for when Henry VI says, "And as the butcher takes away the calf, / And binds the wretch, and beats it when it strays, / Bearing it to the bloody slaughter-house," Tollet is ready with a note based on personal observation: "It is common for butchers to tie a rope or halter about the neck of a calf when they take it away from the breeder's farm, and to beat it gently if it attempts to stray from the direct road. The duke of Gloster is borne away like a calf, that is, he is taken away on his feet; but he is not carried away as a burthen on horseback, or upon men's shoulders, or in their hands" (VI. 351.1). Tollet's seems an entirely probable explanation of the Folio text, and his note continued in editions through the Boswell-Malone of 1821. And Tollet knew all about Maypoles. He knew that "by an ordinance of the Rump Parliament in April 1644" they were taken down by constables and church wardens, but that they were erected again after the Restoration. "I apprehend," he continued, "they are now generally unregarded and unfrequented, but we still on May-day adorn our doors in the country with flowers and the boughs of birch, which tree was especially honoured on the same festival by our Gothic ancestors" (V. 431).

The first notice of the Morris dancers on the stained-glass window at Betley came in a note in the 1773 Appendix. Tollet wrote,

> After the Reformation took place, Maid Marian, her morrice dancers and other attendants, were by some considered as a lewd lascivious rout: and if *Maid Marian might be the deputy's wife,* the

hostess might *be the alderman's wife,* i.e. *might precede Maid Marian in lewdness.*

On a glass window in my house is painted an ancient representation of the celebration of May-day. On a pole are fixed a flag and a pendant. *Marian* with a crown on her head is in front, with the figure of a friar at her left hand, and behind her is a man upon a hobby-horse, or rather within a pasteboard hobby-horse. Eight anticks, in motley dresses, attend in various dancing postures. I would have sent a drawing could such a thing have been executed in my neighbourhood. (V. 320)

Betley and its environs could not boast an artist capable of drawing the figures, some indication of its cultural isolation. Indeed, when forced to it, Tollet himself did a minor job of copying for a note on Falstaff's "Welsh hook" in 1 *Henry IV* as, we are told by Steevens, the representation of that weapon "was copied by him from Speed's *History of Great Britain,* p. 180" (V. 333.9). But there had, from time to time, to be visitors, and we learn from the much expanded note on the Morris dancers in the 1778 edition that "a gentleman of the highest class in historical literature [Steevens] apprehends, that the representation upon my window is that of a Morris dance procession about a May-pole" (V. 433). And thus one gets a picture of this shy, bookish bachelor living a secluded but by no means hermitlike existence, writing his letters with their suggestions on Shakespeare's plays to Steevens in London and so in some measure satisfying his long-held desire to make known his views on Shakespeare. Possibly he was musical; at least he demonstrates a close acquaintance with recorders and German flutes, for he discriminates nicely between them in a note on *Hamlet* (X. 308.3).

Tollet's chief concern in his communications to Steevens was with the explication of Shakespeare's text rather than with its establishment. He, unlike Thomas Tyrwhitt and others, was reluctant to emend, with the result that there are only seven conjectural emendations in his more than four hundred notes. Theobald had termed one passage in *Othello* "stubborn nonsense" as it appeared in texts up to his edition, and succeeding editors continued to try their luck with it. Othello's reference to his "defunct, and proper satisfaction" attracted the emendators, Tollet among them. His note, a small part of which is quoted in the New Variorum edition, reads in full:

I would propose to read, In my *defenct,* or *defenc'd,* & c. i.e. I do not beg her company merely to please the palate of my appetite, nor to comply with the heat of lust which the young man *affects*, i.e. loves and is fond of, in a gratification which I have by marriage *defenc'd*, or inclosed and guarded, and made my own property. *Unproper beds*, in this play, mean, beds not peculiar or appropriate to the right owner, but common to other occupiers. In the *Merry Wives*, &c. the marriage vow is represented by *Ford* as the ward and *defence* of purity or conjugal fidelity. "I could drive her then from the ward of her purity, her reputation, and a thousand other her *defences*, which are now too strongly embattel'd against me." The verb *affect* is more generally, among ancient authors, taken in the construction which I have given to it, than as Mr. Theobald would interpret it. It is so in this very play, "Not to *affect* many proposed matches," means not to *like*, or *be fond of* many proposed matches.

I am persuaded that the word *defunct* must be at all events ejected. *Othello* talks here of his *appetite*, and it is very plain that Desdemona to her death was fond of him after wedlock, and that he loved her. How then could his conjugal desires be dead or *defunct*? or how could they be *defunct* or discharged and performed when the marriage was not consummated? (X. 467.4)

And where Polonius acknowledges that a cloud is "backed like a weasel" Steevens relayed Tollet's note suggesting "beck'd," i.e., "snouted" with its accompanying parallels from Holinshed, Francis Quarles's *Virgin Widow*, and a use of "beaked" in Milton's *Lycidas*, "i.e. prominent like the *beak* of a bird or a ship" (X. 309.4).

Tollet's notes are not ignored in the New Variorum volumes, although one could wish that some had not been so shortened or otherwise dispatched in short order. Troilus, for one example, gives as one simile for steadfastness in love to be as true "as plantage to the moon," using a word (plantage) that made a minor but noticeable ripple in editorial waters. The New Variorum editor quotes or cites Theobald, Hanmer, Warburton, Heath, Johnson, Steevens, and Farmer, of eighteenth-century commentators, and, finally, as if in an afterthought, remarks that "Tollet (Var. '73) suggested that Sh. coined the word" (pp. 161–62). *OED* defines the word as 1) "The cultivation of plants; planting," with its earliest use in 1632, and 2) "Plants in the mass; vegetation, herbage," with its earliest use in Shakespeare's play, sufficient vindication of Tollet's suggestion. But Tollet's note needs to be quoted in full:

It is to be considered, that Shakespeaere might think he had a right to form or new create a word as well as others had done before him. The termination of words in *age* was very common in the time of our poet.

In Holland's translation of *Pliny*, tom. ii. p. 12, we meet with the word *gardenage* for *the herbs of the garden;* and p. 96 he says, "Here an end of gardens and *gardenage.*" Shakespeare uses *guardage* for *guardianship.* Holland uses *guardenage* in the same sense; and *hospitage* is a word we meet with in Spenser. (1773, IX. 75.2) [OED gives "horticulture" as a primary meaning and "garden-stuff" as a secondary.]

How much more edifying is Tollet's note than the New Variorum editor's virtual dismissal of it. Nor does the editor of the New Variorum *Othello*, the play in which "guardage" appears, make any reference to Tollet, quoting an edition of 1879, i.e., "Guardianship, used by Shakespeare nowhere else." To Tollet's credit it should be added that he corrected himself in 1778, having discovered that "*plantage* is the French word for a *plantation*, a *planting*, or *setting*. See Boyer's and Cotgrave's Dictionaries. In the French translation of Dr. Agricola's *Agriculture, Plantage a rebours* is frequently used for *planting reverse*" (IX. 83.6).

Although much of Tollet's commentary has appeared in the New Variorum volumes it may be well to examine some other examples of neglect of that commentary. Tollet was first to cite "Lyte's Herbal" in explanation of "love-in-idleness" in *A Midsummer Night's Dream* as the flower called "pansies, or heart's-ease," and although the New Variorum editor himself cites Lyte he ignores Tollet. Tollet also knew why the flower was described by Oberon as "purple with love's wound," i.e., "because one or two of its petals are of a purple colour" (III. 44.5), another bit of information for which he is given no credit. In the same play he explained Lysander's "fiery o's" as follows: "D'Ewes's *Journal of Queen Elizabeth's Parliaments*, p. 650, mentions a patent to make spangles and *oes* of gold; and I think haberdashers call small curtain rings, O's, as being circular" (III. 77.1). Steevens said "Shakespeare uses O for a circle" in his note in 1778; by 1793 he was able to come up with a quotation from John Davies of Hereford, "Which silver oes and spangles over-ran," plainly resulting from Tollet's lead. In *Antony and Cleopatra*, when Antony turns on Cleopatra and calls her a "triple-turn'd whore," it was Tollet who first explained that "she was first for Julius Caesar, then for Pompey the great, and afterwards for Antony" (VIII. 263.1). The New Variorum quotes Johnson's mistaken note and then Malone's; the latter reads, "Cleopatra was first the mistress of Julius Caesar, then of Cneius Pompey, and afterwards of Antony" (p. 293). No mention of Tollet. If he is right, then a tiny bit of the credit Malone has deservedly earned should go to Tollet.

In the masque in *The Tempest* Iris speaks of "broom groves, / Whose shadow the dismissed batchelor loves," and Tollet wrote that "disappointed lovers are still said to wear the *willow*, and in these lines *broom groves* are assigned to that unfortunate tribe for a retreat. This may allude to some old custom. We still say that a husband hangs out the broom when his wife goes from home for a short time; and on such occasions a *broom* besome has been exhibited as a signal that the house was freed from uxorial restraint, and where the master might be considered as a temporary bachelor. *Broom grove may signify broom bushes.* See *Grava* in Cowel's Law Dict." (I. 86.3). While the New Variorum gives almost two pages to comments on "broom groves," there is a curious omission of Tollet's note, curious in that his description of the then still prevalent rural customs seems to explain the "dismissed batchelor," words other commentators passed over in silence. Another ingenious conjecture is Tollet's suggestion that the "signior" in Berowne's "This signior Junio's giant-dwarf, Dan Cupid" means "senior" and not "the Italian title of honour." Theobald had seen an allusion to Beaumont and Fletcher's *Bonduca*, and John Upton asserted that the painter Julio Romano had depicted Cupid as a giant-dwarf. Tollet's note deserves as much attention as the overly ingenious attempts at explication quoted in the New Variorum, none of which proves satisfactory to the editor. Tollet wrote,

> There is no reason to suppose that Beaumont's and Fletcher's *Bonduca* was written so early as the year 1598, when this play appeared. Even if it was then published, the supposed allusion to the character of Junius is forced and improbable; and who, in support of Upton's conjecture will ascertain, that Julio Romano ever drew Cupid as a giant-dwarf? Shakespeare, in *K. Rich. III.* act IV. sc. iv. uses *signory* for *seniority*; and Stowe's Chronicle, p. 149. Edit. 1614, speaks of Edward the *signior*, i.e. the elder. I can therefore suppose that *signior* here means *senior*, and not the Italian title of honour. Thus in the first folio, at the end of the *Comedy of Errors*:
> "S. Dro. Not I, sir; you are my *elder.*
> E. Dro. That's a question: how shall we try it?
> S. Dro. We'll draw cuts for the *signior.*" (II. 420.5)

Bonduca, incidentally, is dated 1613. When "that rare Italian master, Julio Romano" was referred to in *The Winter's Tale*, the question rose whether he had been both sculptor and painter of the presumptive statue of Hermione. Tollet's full note follows:

> I wish we could understand this passage, as if *Julio Romano* had only painted the statue carved by another. Ben Jonson makes Doctor Rut in the *Magnetic Lady*, act V. sc. viii. say:
>
> "——all city statues must be *painted*,
>
> Else they be worth nought i'their subtil judgments." Sir Henry Wotton, in his *Elements of Architecture*, mentions the fashion of colouring even regal statues for the stronger expression of affection, which he takes leave to call an English barbarism. Such, however, was the practice of the time: and unless the supposed statue of Hermione were painted, there could be no ruddiness upon her lip, nor could the veins *verily seem to bear blood*, as the poet expresses it afterwards. (IV. 426.7)

The New Variorum editor, after citing or quoting Theobald, Warburton, Heath, Capell, and Johnson, writes that "Tollet calls attention to the following passage in Jonson's *Magnetic Lady*," which he then quotes. No more. Immediately after the quotation from Jonson's play the New Variorum editor quotes Gifford on Sir Henry Wotton's calling the painting of statues an "English barbarism," a view to which he takes exception. But Tollet, obviously, had been well before him. Somewhat similar treatment is accorded Tollet's remarks on "Cherish springs" in Shakespeare's *Lucrece* (1. 950), remarks prompted by Warburton's attempt to emend "the virginal palms of your daughters" in *Coriolanus* to virginal "*pasmes*" or "*pames*," French for "swooning fits," by giving his firm opinion that Shakespeare, in the *Lucrece* line, wrote "*tarish*" springs, French for "to dry up." The editor of the New Variorum *Poems* quotes two sentences from Tollet's remarks that appear in a note by Steevens. Here is the full note.

> After all, I believe the former reading of the passage in *Tarquin and Lucrece* to be the true one. Shakespeare's meaning is, that Time was variously employed, both in destroying old things and in raising up young ones. The next stanza sufficiently proves it:
>
> > "To shew the beldame daughters of her daughter,
> > To make the child a man, the man a child;
> > To chear the ploughman with encreaseful crops,
> > And waste huge stones with little water-drops.
> > To dry the old oak's sap, and *cherish springs*;"
>
> i.e. to dry up the old oak's sap, and consequently to destroy it; and

likewise to cherish springs, i.e. to raise up or nourish the shoots of coppice-wood, or of young trees, groves, and plantations. The word springs is used in this sense by Chaucer, Spenser, Fairfax, Drayton, Donne, and Milton, as well as by the old writers on husbandry, Fitzherbert, Tusser, Markham, and by Shakespeare himself in the Comedy of Errors;
"————shall, Antipholus,
Even in the spring of love, thy love-springs rot?" Again, in Holinshed's Description of England, both the contested words in the latter part of the verse, occur. "We have manie woods, forrests, and parks which cherish trees abundantlie, beside infinit numbers of hedge rowes, groves, and springs, that are mainteined &c." Thus far Mr. Tollet. (VII. 476.3)

Johnson, it may be noted, had suggested "perish" springs, and both Farmer and Steevens had adduced examples to support that emendation. It remained for Tollet to explain the old reading, really clinching the matter. What is particularly exasperating is that Hyder Rollins, editor of the New Variorum Poems, omits Tollet's reference to the use of "springs" in the arboreal sense in "the old writers on husbandry, Fitzherbert, Tusser, Markham, and by Shakespeare himself in the Comedy of Errors," as well as the very telling quotation from Holinshed.

While a number of notes displaying one or another of Tollet's areas of preoccupation or interest have already been quoted, a few more will further help to establish his quality as a student of Shakespeare's plays. Timon of Athens's fulminations against gold include one on its power over women.

> this is it,
> That makes the wappen'd widow wed again;
> She, whom the spital-house and ulcerous sores
> Would cast the gorge at, this embalms and spices
> To the April day again.

Johnson had explained "to the April day" as "to the wedding day, called by the poet, satirically, April day, or fool's day" (VIII. 406.2); his and Tollet's are the only notes on the phrase in the 1778 edition, nor were any added in later editions up to and including the Boswell-Malone in 1821. Tollet's note affords another fine example of his ability to produce a number of close parallels in defense of his interpretation.

The April day does not relate to the widow, but to the other diseased female, who is represented as the outcast of an hospital.

She it is whom gold *embalms and spices* to the *April day again:* i.e. gold restores her to all the *freshness and sweetness* of youth. Such is the power of gold, that it will

> "——make black, white; foul, fair;
> Wrong, right; &c."

A quotation or two may perhaps support this interpretation. Sidney's *Arcadia*, p. 262, edit. 1633: "Do you see how the spring time is full of flowers, decking itself with them, and not aspiring to the fruits of autumn? What lesson is that unto you, but that in the *April of your age* you should be like *April*." Again, in Stephens's *Apology for Herodotus*, 1607, "He is a young man, and in the *April of his age*." Peacham's *Compleat Gentleman*, chap. iii. calls *youth* "the *April* of man's life." Shakespeare's Sonnet entitled *Love's Cruelty*, has the same thought:

> "Thou are thy mother's glass, and she in thee
> Calls back the lovely *April* of her prime."

Daniel's 31st sonnet has, "——the *April* of my years." Master Fenton "smells *April* and *May*." (VIII. 406.2)

The editor of the New Arden *Timon of Athens* compares *The Merry Wives of Windsor*, evidently unaware that Tollet had done so almost two hundred years earlier, and he gives Knight credit for the parallel from Shakespeare's twenty-third sonnet that was known to Tollet as "Love's Cruelty" from Benson's edition (1640).

Much ingenuity has been employed in the attempt to explain the apparent discrepancies of the time-scheme in *Othello*, with the New Variorum editor devoting over twelve pages of small print to the question, largely quoting Professor Wilson's theory of two time schemes: Historic Time and Dramatic Time. Earlier editors and critics were uneasy when confronted with the discrepancies. Johnson, however, simply commented of one such passage, "This is another passage which seems to suppose a longer space comprised in the action of this play than the scenes include." Steevens tried to explain the passage that troubled Johnson, "but yet Iago knows, / That she with Cassio hath the act of shame / A thousand times committed," but then repeated Tollet's suggestions to him:

Mr. Tollet, however, on this occasion has produced several instances in support of Dr. Johnson's opinion; and as I am unable to explain them in favour of my own supposition, I shall lay them before the public. Act 3, Sc. 3. Othello says:

What sense had I of her stolen hours of lust?
I saw it not, thought it not, it harm'd not me;
I slept the next night well, was free and merry:
I found not Cassio's kisses on her lips.

On *Othello's* wedding night he and Cassio embarked from Venice, where *Desdemona* was left under the care of *Iago.* They all meet at Cyprus; and since their arrival there, the scenes include only one night, the night of the celebration of their nuptials. Iago had not then infused any jealousy into *Othello's* mind, nor did he suspect any former intimacy between *Cassio* and *Desdemona,* but only thought it "apt, and of great credit that she loved him." What night then was there to intervene between *Cassio's* kisses and *Othello's* sleeping the next night well? *Iago* has said, "I lay with *Cassio* lately," which he could not have done, unless they had been longer at *Cyprus* than is represented in the play; nor could *Cassio* have kept away, for the space of a whole week, from *Bianca.*" (X. 613.4)

believe this is one of the earliest attempts to work out a time heme of the events which occurred when all the principals had rived on Cyprus. That there is total neglect of Tollet's note in e discussion of the duration of the action of the play in the ppendix to the New Variorum edition again underlines the cessity for closer study of the early contributors to the explica-n of Shakespeare's works.

Tollet's last contributions, as I have noted above, were to Ma-ne's *Supplement,* 1780. One is an addition to a former note. ppolita, in *A Midsummer Night's Dream,* uses the expression ay'd the bear." Tollet, in 1778, had quoted or cited Holinshed, iny, Plutarch, and Turberville on bear-hunting (III. 96.2); in '80 he added "Shakespeare must have read the *Knight's Tale* in aucer, where are mentioned Theseus's 'white alandes [grey-unds] to huntin at the lyon, or the wild *bere'*" (I. 119). In other note (I. 130) he has recourse to Holland's translation of iny's *Natural History,* a work that he had quoted or cited a mber of times in 1778. The remaining two notes quote Re-nald Scot's *Discovery of Witchcraft:* one, briefly, in a short note the witches in *Macbeth* having spirits in "the likeness of todes d cats,"[5] and the other, also briefly, but in a longer note. eevens had noted that "Shakspeare has been censured for intro-cing Hecate among the vulgar witches, and, consequently, for nfounding ancient with modern superstitions," but he stated at there was authority for his having given "a mistress to the itches" (1778, IV. 547.1). Tollet wrote that "Scot's *Discovery of itchcraft,* book iii. c.2 and c.16 and book xii. c.3 mentions it as the common opinion of all writers, that witches were supposed to have nightly 'meetings with Herodias, and the Pagan gods,' and 'that in the night times they ride abroad with *Diana,* the goddess of the Pagans, etc.'——Their dame or chief leader seems always to have been an old Pagan, as 'the ladie Sibylla, Minerva, or *Diana*'" (I. 157). Tollet's contributions are such that he richly deserves the greater recognition that will, I trust, be his as a result of this study.

3

Sir William Blackstone, Solicitor-General to the Queen

The title-page of Edmond Malone's *Supplement* to the 1778 *Shakespeare* bears the information that there were "*Notes by the Editor and Others.*" At the end of the "Supplemental Observations" on the 1778 edition there is a statement that "all the notes subscribed——E. were communicated to Mr. Steevens by a gentleman so eminent in literature, that his name (were the use of it permitted) could not fail to confer the highest honour this undertaking can receive" (I. 370). In Malone's Advertisement, written last as was usual, he acknowledged that

> Various additional observations by several of the former commentators are . . . inserted in the following Supplement. To these the editor has been enabled to add the annotations of some gentlemen who now first appear as scholiasts on our author; among which every reader, he is persuaded, will be pleased to find the remarks of one of the most eminent literary characters that the present age has produced; a person whose name will be revered, and whose works will be studied and admired, as long as the laws and constitution of England shall have any existence. It is scarcely necessary to observe that by this description the late Sir William Blackstone is pointed; whose notes, in conformity to his own desire, have no other distinction than the final letter of his name. There is now no longer occasion for secrecy; and the editor has only to lament that so unfortunate an event as the death of this gentleman should have left him at liberty to divulge it; a liberty, however, which he should scruple to take were he not confident, that, notwithstanding the very high rank in which the learned and elegant compositions of this great lawyer have deservedly placed him, these amusements of his vacant hours will by no means diminish the lustre of his reputation. (pp. iii–iv)

Blackstone died on 14 February 1780; Malone's volumes were published in May of that year.

Part of the history of Blackstone's involvement in Malone's

Supplement can be traced through four letters now in The Folger Shakespeare Library in Washington, D.C.[1] On 24 July 1778, after the publication of the 1778 Johnson-Steevens *Shakespeare*, Blackstone wrote to Steevens from Wallingford, saying,

> I am much obliged to You for the Favour of Your intended Visit in London, & for Your Letter of the 21st instant, in which I fear You overvalue a few trifling Remarks, which I made with my Pencil in the blank Leaves of my Shakespeare, when I amused myself with reading his Works, soon after Your last publication; to which I am indebted for the Renewal of a Pleasure which I had so often before experienced. I flatter myself with the Hopes of enjoying the same Pleasure once more in my Life, when Your new Edition is published; & shall therefore most thankfully accept of Your obliging Present, promising myself great Satisfaction in tracing out the New Improvements made by so judicious & candid a Critic.

Evidently Blackstone had sent his "few trifling Remarks" on Shakespeare some time before July 21, on which date Steevens wrote back and proposed to visit him.

The next extant letter in the correspondence is from Steevens and is dated 29 April 1779.

> Permit me to return to you my most respectful acknowledgments for your assistance, which confers the highest honour our undertaking can receive. All your notes shall be carefully published; but before I put the last of them (that on Othello, p. 538) into its proper place, let me solicit your opinion of the following remark on the same passage. I had written it before I received yours.

Blackstone had quoted Iago's "I did say so [Enter Othello] / Look, where he comes," and had written,

> This is a most unmeaning sentence, in the mouth of such a speaker, and at such a time. If we can suppose this part of this play to have been taken down by the ear, and so handed to the first editors, a similarity of sounds might perhaps lead to a discovery of the true text. Iago has just got the fatal handkerchief, and is commenting upon it in his hand:
>
> > "In Cassio's lodging will I lose *this* napkin.
> > ———*This* may do something"

But seeing Othello coming, he stops short, and hastily proceeds to conceal it. Possibly then this may be the reading:

"———Hide it!—so—so—
Look where he comes!———"

So, so, is no uncommon interjection with Shakspeare, when a man is surprized in an action which he wishes to conceal. Othello uses it in this play, when interrupted by Emilia in the horrid act of killing Desdemona.

—I did say so;—

As this passage is supposed to be obscure, I shall attempt an explanation of it.

Iago first ruminates on the qualities of the passion which he is labouring to excite; and then proceeds to comment on its effects. *Jealousy* (says he) *with the smallest operation of the blood, flames out with all the vehemence of sulphur* etc.

I did say so;
Look where he comes!

i.e. "I know that the least touch of such a passion would not permit the Moor to enjoy a moment of repose:—*I have just said* that jealousy is a restless commotion of the mind; and look where Othello approaches to confirm the propriety and justice of my observation!"
Permit me to add, that *Cessor! Fr.* has no just title to a place in any part of the works of Shakspeare, though his commentators have more than once attempted to introduce it. As often as I have met with it I have strove to turn it out. It occurs, however, but in three places, and is then appropriated to the Tinker in *Taming of the Shrew*, and the pretended Madman in *King Lear*.

I likewise beg leave to express my gratitude for your enquiries relative to the Exchequer business. I shall not fail to make my defense there as soon as I am call'd on.

I enclose the *Quakers Unmasked* 1664, & have sent for the *Jus Patronatus* out of a Country Catalogue in which it is prized at six-pence.

The reference to "our undertaking" is to Malone's *Supplement* or which Steevens had solicited Blackstone's notes, and it indi-ates, among other things, the degree of progress made on the irst of the two volumes. "Cessor," difficult to make out, is surely Sessa," the only exclamation peculiar to the two plays men-ioned. Blackstone replied almost immediately, on 1 May 1779:

I received Your Favour of the 29th April, & am much obliged to you for the Contents, in every respect.

I readily acquiesce in Your superior knowledge of Shakespeare's
Sentiments as well as Stile, with respect to the Emendation proposed
in Othello 538. You will be so good as to decide, for to You I entirely
leave it, whether You will subjoin to Your own Stricture or my Note
this further Remark.

[paper missing]

Or, totally to omit my original Note, as You in Your Discretion shall
think proper.

The "further Remark," on a separate piece of paper, is missing
but is easily supplied by Malone's *Supplement* where it is
printed. Blackstone had written: "As Mr. Steevens has by his
interpretation elicited some meaning (though, I still think, an
obscure one) out of this difficult hemistic, I readily retract my
amendment: being of opinion that such bold and licentious conjectures can never be warranted, unless where the sense is quite
desperate" (X. 538). Steevens replied two days later:

> I cannot forbear to return my immediate thanks for the honour you
> have done me in taking notice of my very imperfect attempt at
> explanation. I shall insert both your notes with my own between
> them; & I hope you will excuse the trouble I have ventured to give
> you. These observations & will not go to press till a month or six
> weeks hence; so that if you chance to meet with other mistakes (of
> which I fear we have but too many) I will continue to pay the utmost
> attention to your corrections.

With this letter the correspondence would seem to have come to
an end.

No reference is made to meetings between Blackstone and
Malone in Sir James Prior's *Life of Edmond Malone* (London
1870), but it is almost inevitable that they would have met, both
doubtless moving in the same intellectual circles and having the
law and literature as common interests. And, indeed, they knew
each other by 1779 when Malone wrote to Lord Charlemont on
April 5 that "Sir W. Blackstone has written many notes, which
were too late for the last edition [the 1778 Johnson-Steevens], and
some new ones since."[2] Malone, according to Prior, said of
Blackstone's notes on Shakespeare: "The notes which he gave me
on Shakespeare [not to Steevens, as was stated in the *Supplement*, creating a minor problem for a biographer] show him to
have been a man of excellent taste and accuracy, and a good
critick" (p. 431). The reviewer for the *Monthly Review* wrote of
Malone's *Supplement* that "Sir William Blackstone for the first
time appears here as a scholiast. His very judicious notes have r

other distinction than the final letter of his name——E." (October 1780). This reviewer was partly parroting his confrere of the *Critical Review*, who wrote that "among those who now first appear as scholiasts on Shakespeare, we find the name of the late learned Sir William Blackstone, who frequently bestowed his vacant hours on the perusal of the great English poet. His notes, we are told, in conformity to his own desire, have no other distinction than the final letter of his name" (May 1780). Both had been anticipated by the compiler of Blackstone's obituary in the GM for February 1780, who wrote that Blackstone "was a great and able scholar, and was particularly happy in his investigations of the best writers of our own country. The works of Shakespeare in particular had been an object of his attention, and we are happy to inform our readers that his observations on that incomparable Dramatist will soon be given to the world" (p. 103).

Two modern biographies of Sir William Blackstone were published in 1938; both leave room for another and definitive biography, written, preferably, by a scholar trained in methods of biographical research and aware of the problems in the writing of biography. One aspect of Blackstone's intellectual life that cries out for further examination and analysis is his interest in Shakespeare. One of his modern biographers, David A. Lockmiller, presumes that while at Oxford Blackstone "belonged to the Shakespeare club," without any evidence being given as to the existence of such a club, either at Pembroke College or in the University as a whole. L. C. Warden, Blackstone's other modern biographer, is much more forthcoming about his subject's interest in Shakespeare, but his concern about this interest takes curious forms.[3] Early in the biography, seeking to establish that Blackstone, according to some, "made a mistake in not following a literary career" because "his poetry indicated that there was real genius at hand" (p. 33), Warden writes that "Shakespeare found in him an ardent admirer. Before he had gone to Oxford he had read all of the plays of Shakespeare through and had exhibited considerable insight into their meaning" (p. 32). One looks in vain for any evidence in support of such statements, especially in a biography of a famous lawyer written by another lawyer. Warden, writing about Blackstone's "years of trial and testing," states that Blackstone "observed the underlying truth of society that the faster a person goes up the faster he goes down" and then continues:

In several of his annotations on Shakespeare, which he was wont to make often during those years of waiting, he notes particularly al-

most every reference Shakespeare used regarding this principle, which every student of England's noted playwright knows were many. Blackstone got great satisfaction out of Shakespeare, especially during his early years at the Bar, probably because there is much in his works to console the disappointed. The young struggling lawyer read over and over the following soliloquy from Hamlet:
"To be, or not to be; that is the question. . . ."
Shakespeare had had great difficulty in making his way, which Blackstone knew. His most cherished ambition, that of becoming a knighted country gentleman, never was realized, due to Bacon's turning on him, more than likely. Thus, in all of his plays from the first to the last there is medicine for the sick at heart. But not only for consolation did Blackstone read Shakespeare, but also for the sheer beauty and greatness of his works. He thoroughly enjoyed good literature and always left it with hesitation. (pp. 73–74)

In a section on Blackstone as teacher, Warden notes the influence of the Bible upon him, and then adds,

The Bible however was not his only guide. The luminous pages of Pope and Addison with their smooth and pleasing style were covered again and again. Shakespeare was a frequent visitor to Blackstone's study; enjoying the plays as such very much, Blackstone fed upon the master's style and language. The net result of it all being that Blackstone was putting the law in a new garb, dressing her up for her coming out party, for as he penned those lectures that summer, he employed the parables of Christ, the smooth style of Addison, the clarity of Pope, and the versatility of Shakespeare. (p. 154)

The first evidence of Blackstone's scholarly interst in the problems of Shakespeare's text and its explication dates back to 1746 when he was twenty-three years old and had just been called to the bar. He had bought a copy of the 1745 Shakespeare, a reprint of Sir Thomas Hanmer's 1744 edition, one in which the anonymous editor had been at pains to isolate Hanmer's emendations and he had jotted down some "Cursory Observations on Shakespeare, with a particular View to Sr T.H.'s Emendations." These have been reprinted in The Shakespeare Society's Papers, vol. no. 24 of the Publications (1844) and were known to and used by the Furnesses in some of the New Variorum volumes. There are fourteen observations, ranging from a one-word query, i.e. "base" as a conjectural emendation for "It was a bare Petition State" in Coriolanus, to an explicatory note of over eight lines print on one of Hanmer's emendations in Julius Caesar. Two of the fourteen notes were revised later and appeared in Malone

Supplement. In 1746 Blackstone had observed of Hanmer's emendation of "ministers" for "masters" in *The Tempest's* "(Weak masters thou ye be)" that "it hardly seems consistent that Prospero, while he is recounting the mighty Feats he had performed by yᵉ Aid of these Elves, should call them weak Ministers. The Common Reading carries with it a fine Sense, that those Beings are so powerful when acting under yᵉ Directions of another; yet, when left to themselves, they are weak, and unable to perform any thing" (pp. 96–97). In 1780 the note, ignoring Hanmer's emendation, reads, "That is; ye are powerful auxiliaries, but weak if left to yourselves;—your employment is then to make green ringlets, and midnight mushrooms, and to play the idle pranks mentioned by Ariel in his next song;—yet by your aid I have been enabled to invert the course of nature. We say proverbially, 'Fire is a good *servant*, but a bad *master*' " (I. 86). The second note is an original observation on the elective system in Denmark and is keyed to the people's cry of Laertes for king. Blackstone noted that "in Denmark, as in all Gothic Constitutions, yᵉ Kingdom was, till of late years Elective. To this Shakespeare alludes, p. 425 & 433, Act V., Sc. 3 & 6. Why, then, is Antiquity forgot [Shakespeare's words], etc., by this popular Choice of Laertes? The Danes usually paid such respect to the Memory of their Princes, that they generally elected yᵉ nearest of Blood to yᵉ deceased Monarch that appeared worthy of yᵉ Crown; and seldom a Stranger to his Family, as was Laertes" (p. 100). The 1780 revised version is quoted in full below (pp. 83–84); the traces of the original observation are clearly discernible.

In *The Dunciad*, in his parody of the Honors List, Alexander Pope gives pride of place to the Queen of Dulness's "Children first of more distinguish'd sort, / Who study Shakespeare at the Inns of Court" (B version, 567–68). James Sutherland, editor of *The Dunciad* in the Twickenham edition, notes that "if the line had any particular reference in 1742 [the date of publication of the final version of the work], it could hardly have been to [Thomas] Edwards," author of *The Canons of Criticism*, as William Warburton, in his capacity as editor of Pope's works, had stated. "Pope," Sutherland continues, "was probably thinking generally of legal dabblers in Shakespearian criticism, the literary lawyers who studied Shakespeare rather than Coke upon Littleton. Cf. the Templar in the *Spectator* club, who was placed in the Inner Temple by his father 'to study the laws of the land, and is the most learned of any of the house in those of the stage,'—*Spectator*, No. 2." What Professor Sutherland might have added, although it was probably not in his province to do so, was that the history of Shakespearian editing and criticism would have been a far different thing in the eighteenth century if it had not been for the efforts of a number of men who studied Shakespeare at the Inns of Court. Nicholas Rowe, the father of modern Shakespeare editing, whose edition of the plays was published in 1709, was of the Middle Temple. Other names that come immediately to mind as the great editors of the period are those of George Steevens, who settled in chambers in the Temple briefly before taking up his home in Hampstead, and of Isaac Reed of Staple Inn. Reed was followed by the greatest of the eighteenth-century editors of Shakespeare, Edmond Malone, who had entered the Inner Temple in 1741. Malone's edition appeared in 1790; when he died in 1812 he was engaged in a revision of that edition, helped by James Boswell, the younger, himself of the Inner Temple. Others who should be named are Lewis Theobald, "attorney," author of *Shakespeare Restored*, a work that won him the dubious honor of being the hero of the first version of *The Dunciad*. And Theobald was, of course, one of the abler eighteenth-century editors of Shakespeare. Thomas Edwards, mentioned above, was of Lincoln's Inn. Sir John Hawkins, who practiced in the courts of Common Law, contributed twenty notes to the Appendix of Johnson's *Shakespeare* (1765), added a few more for the 1773 and 1778 Johnson-Steevens variorums, and helped materially with the Glossary of the second edition of the so-called Oxford *Shakespeare*, published in 1770–71. Tyrwitt was called to the bar at the Middle Temple, as was Benjamin Heath, a well-to-do amateur of letters whose *Revisal of Shakespeare's Text*, published in 1765 a few months before Johnson's edition and overshadowed by that work, deserves to be better known than it is. Later in the century the formidable Joseph Ritson, conveyancer, took chambers in Gray's Inn. Benjamin Way, of the Inner Temple, made Thomas Edwards's MS notes available to Steevens, and George Tollet, of Lincoln's Inn, contributed a considerable number of notes to Steevens's editions, as has been seen. To these names must be added that of Sir William Blackstone.

There are eighty-nine notes by Blackstone covering all the volumes of the 1778 *Shakespeare* to which Malone's volumes were a supplement; all eighty-nine are on the plays of the accepted canon, the poems and the apocryphal plays not having been printed in the 1778 edition but being added by Malone. While it is useless to conjecture at the absence of any notes on a few plays, one cannot help wondering why the powerful tragedy of Lear elicited no comment. Lewis Warden writes, with more fiction than fact, that Blackstone "had read King Lear [sic] over and had been touched very much by the stirring denunciation Shakespeare brought down on the ungrateful daughters of the King. He liked the story and the play, for he was fond of Shakespeare in any garb but in this particular play he liked especially the message of life that was portrayed. By his nature anyway he was always a grateful person and naturally held in disrepute anyone who was otherwise."[4] Possibly the fullness of commentary already in existence on *Lear* was a deterrent, for the *Supplement* has only a meagre fifteen notes on that play, three by Steevens and the rest by Malone. But one's concern must be with the notes that were written, not with those that might have been written.

Immediate interest attaches to the thirteen notes which reveal Blackstone's legal background. The very first of these, and it must be understood that all the notes in the *Supplement* are keyed to volume and page of the Johnson-Steevens 1778 *Shakespeare*, is an addition to a statement by Steevens in the prolegomenous matter to the effect that "Their caution against prophaneness is, in my opinion, the only thing for which we are indebted to the judgment of the editors of the folio" (I. 167). Blackstone's note reads, "I doubt whether we are so much indebted to the judgment of the editors of the folio edition, for their caution against prophaneness, as to the statute 3 Jac. I. c. 21. which prohibits under severe penalties the use of the sacred name in any plays or interludes. This occasioned the playhouse copies to be altered, and they printed from the playhouse copies." When Shallow, in *The Merry Wives of Windsor*, threatens that "The council shall hear it; it is a riot," Blackstone adds to Dr. Zachary Grey's note quoting "a statute made in the reign of K. Henry IV. (13, chap. 7.)" the information that "by the council is only meant the court of star-chamber, composed chiefly of the king's council sitting in *Camera stellata*, which took cognizance of atrocious riots" (I. 224). Compare Blackstone's *Commentaries*, Book IV, Chapter 19, "Of Courts of Criminal Jurisdiction," in the definition of "the court of star-chamber, *camera stellata* . . . consisting of divers lords, spiritual and temporal, being privy counsellors. . . . Their jurisdiction extended legally over riots." Blackstone's comment on Vincentio, Duke of Vienna's, reference to "the terms / For common justice" in *Measure for Measure* is that "Terms mean the technical language of the courts. An old book called *Les Termes de la Ley* (written in Henry the Eighth's time) was in Shakespeare's days, and is now, the accidence of young students in the law" (II. 6). In other notes he cites "the stat.[ute] 1. Edw. VI. c. 2." on the "characts [inscriptions]" that must appear on "the seals of office of every bishop" (II. 137); he cites "a statute of 3 Hen. VII. c. 14. which "directs certain offences committed in the king's palace, to be tried by twelve *sad* [grave] men of the king's household" (III. 95); and he cites 33 Hen. VIII. c. 9 as the statute prohibiting, among other games, "slide-thrift" or "shove-groat," an allusion that had been explained by Steevens, i.e., "a shove-groat shilling" was "a piece of polished metal made use of in the play of shovel-board" (V. 505). In Book IV of the *Commentaries*, Chapter 13, Blackstone cites the same statute, "which prohibits to all but gentlemen the games of tennis, tables, cards, dice, bowls and other unlawful diversions there specified, unless in the time of Christmas, under pecuniary pains and imprisonment." Blackstone explained that "*drawn* in the sense of *embowelled*, is never used but in speakng of a *fowl*. It is true, *embowelling* is also part of the sentence in high treason, but in order of time it comes after *drawing* and *hanging*" (VII. 142), a nice distinction for the treasonous. A much more detailed and terrible description of the punishment meted out for treason occurs in Book IV of the *Commentaries*, Chapter 6, "Of High Treason." There "drawn" is described as "not to be carried or walk; though usually (by connivance, at length ripened by humanity into law) a sledge or hurdle is allowed, to preserve the offender from the extreme torment of being dragged on the ground or pavement." In another note, knowledge of canon law is displayed, for when Queen Katherine cries out in *Henry VIII*, "I utterly abhor, yea, from my soul / Refute you for my judge," Blackstone explains that "abhor" and "refute" are not "mere words of passion, but technical terms in the canon law—*Detestor* and *Recuso*. The former in the language of the canonists, signifies no more, than I *protest* against" (VII. 241). And of Iago's "a voice potential / As double as the duke's" Sir William wrote, "The chief justice [invoked by Dr. Johnson as having a double voice and refuted by Tollet] has no double voice. If the court is equally divided, nothing is done" (X. 442).

Two of Blackstone's legal notes deserve full quotation. In one he comments on the Duke of Buckingham's reference to "loath'd bigamy" in *Richard III* that "bigamy, by a canon of the council of Lyons, A.D. 1274 (adopted in England by a statute, in 4 Edw. I. was made unlawful and infamous. It differed from polygamy, or having two wives at once; as it consisted in either marrying two virgins successively, or once marrying a widow" (VII. 100). This comes, virtually verbatim, from the *Commentaries*, Book IV, Chapter 13, "Of Offences Against the Public Health, and the Public Policy or Economy," the section that treats of felonious offenses with regard to the state of holy matrimony. We learn that "Her Grace the Duchess of *Kingston*, on quoting our author's [Blackstone's] *Commentaries*, on her trial for bigamy, in the House of Lords, before her Peers, in the month of *April*, 1776, thus speaks of Sir *William* and his *Commentaries*: 'according to the testimony of the learned judge *Blackstone*; whose works are as entertaining as they are instructive,'" evidence that others than lawyers had recourse to the *Commentaries*.[5] In the second note Blackstone tangles with a passage that had plagued editors of Shakespeare from Sir Thomas Hanmer to George Steevens and which had also tried the ingenuity of John Upton and William Kenrick. Macbeth is the speaker, responding to Duncan's "More is thy due than more than all can pay."

> The service and the loyalty I owe,
> In doing it, pays itself. Your highness' part
> Is to receive our duties: and our duties
> Are to your throne and state, children, and servants;
> Which do but what they should, by doing every thing
> Safe toward your love and honour.

Dr. Johnson, in a note reviewing his and the emendations of Hanmer and Warburton, frankly gave up: "I am afraid none of us have hit the right word" [instead of "safe," which is, incidentally, the accepted reading]. Here is Blackstone's solution:

> Safe (i.e. saved) toward *you* love and honour; and then the sense will be—"Our duties are your children, and servants or vassals to your throne and state; who do but what they should, by doing every thing with a saving of their love and honour toward you." The whole is an allusion to the forms of doing homage in the feudal times. The oath of allegiance, or *liege homage*, to the king was absolute and without any exception; but *simple homage*, when done to a subject for lands holden of him, was always with a *saving* of the allegiance (the *love* and *honour*) due to the sovereign. "*Sauf la foy que jeo doy a nostre seignor le roy.*" as it is in Lyttleton. And though the expression be somewhat stiff and forced, it is not more so than many others in this play, and suits well with the situation of Macbeth, now beginning to waver in his allegiance. For, as our author elsewhere says,

When love begins to sicken and decay,
It useth an enforced ceremony. (IV. 471)

The reference in the quoted lines is to a passage in *Julius Caesar.*

The eighteenth century might, from the point of view of a textual critic, be called the age of emendation. One has only to read the flights of fancy of William Warburton in his edition of Shakespeare's plays to see emendation run rampant. Dr. Johnson wrote in the Preface to his edition: "As I practised conjecture more, I learned to trust it less; and after I had printed a few plays, resolved to insert none of my own readings in the text. Upon this caution I now congratulate myself, for every day encreases my doubt of my emendations." But Johnson suggested a considerable number of emendations, confining them, however, to his footnotes and not inserting them in the text. Emendation was, however, and continues to be a constant temptation, and Blackstone succumbed no fewer than eighteen times, that is, in roughly one out of every five of his notes. One is of considerable interest as revelatory of Blackstone's larger critical preoccupations. Toward the end of *Two Gentlemen of Verona* Valentine has a speech which ends with the surprising statement, "And, that my love [for Protheus] may appear plain and free, / All, that was mine in Silvia, I give thee" (I. 212). "Transfer these two lines to the end of Thurio's second speech in page 214," writes Blackstone, "and all is right. Why then should Julia faint? It is only an artifice, seeing Silvia given up to Valentine, to discover her to Protheus, by a pretended mistake of the rings. One great fault of this play is the hastening too abruptly, and without due preparation, to the denoüement, which shews that, if it be Shakespeare's, (which I cannot doubt) it was one of his very early performances." Consciously or unconsciously, Blackstone is echoing Dr. Johnson's General Observation on *As You Like It* where Johnson writes that "by hastening to the end of his work" Shakespeare "lost an opportunity of exhibiting a moral lesson." And Blackstone's confidence in the canonicity of the play is also one he shared with Johnson.

Four emendations have to do with punctuation and need not detain us. Macduff's "This avarice / Sticks deeper; grows with more pernicious root / Than summer-seeming lust" had prompted Warburton to suggest "summer-teeming lust" and Johnson to acknowledge that when he was "younger and bolder" (before 1745, that is)[6] he had "corrected it thus: Than fume of seeming lust." Blackstone writes, "Read—summer-*seeding*. Th allusion is to plants; and the sense is, 'Avarice is a perennial weed; it has a deeper and more pernicious root than *lust*, which is a mere annual, and lasts but a summer, when it sheds its seed and decays'". (IV. 577), thus revealing himself as a gardener as well as a textual critic. The elder Furness, editor of the New Variorum *Macbeth*, noting that Blackstone had been anticipated in this by Heath in 1765, confessed he had been "unable to find where Steevens obtained this note of the eminent Justice's; it is not in the list published by the Shakespeare Society" (p. 284). In another note Blackstone suspects a compositorial transposition of words in Apemantus's "That I had no angry wit to be a lord" in *Timon of Athens*, suggesting either "Angry that I had no wit,—to be a lord" or "Angry to be a lord,—that I had no wit" (VIII. 333). When King Claudius tells Laertes that if Hamlet escapes his "venom'd stuck, / Our purpose may hold there" (i.e., the poisoned wine), Blackstone is uneasy and suggests "*tuck*, a common name for a rapier" instead (X. 369). The last note contributed by Blackstone to the *Supplement* is another emendation. Othello's "I have another weapon in this chamber, / It is a sword of Spain, the ice-brook's temper" had, in its last phrase, given rise to a number of emendations and explanations. Blackstone's note illustrates again his ingenuity as well as a vein of dry humor. He writes, "If we suppose that the words ['tis ebroes] [his suggestion] were huddled together either in transcribing or composing, thus, ['tisebroes] the compositor in running it over with his eye, might (to make it sense as he thought) add a couple of letters and divide the word thus (th' isebrokes) which is nearly as it stands in the old quarto. I doubt whether *ice-brooks* are usual in the climate of Spain" (X. 618).[7]

Five notes are of especial interest, as they show Blackstone weighing various kinds of evidence in the fascinating puzzle of trying to fix the chronology of Shakespeare's plays. Nicholas Rowe had long ago made a general and unscholarly statement to the effect that "perhaps we are not to look for his beginning, like those of other writers, in his least perfect works; art had so little, and nature so large a share in what he did, that for ought I know, the performances of his youth, as they were the most vigorous, were the best."[8] It remained for Malone, almost exactly sixty years later than the publication of Rowe's *Shakespeare*, to do the necessary scholarly research that resulted in his *Attempt to Ascertain the Order in which the Plays Attributed to Shakespeare were Written*, published in quarto in 1778 and reprinted in the 1778 Johnson-Steevens variorum to which Malone's two volumes were the *Supplement.* Some of Blackstone's criteria for determining the relative chronology of the plays may seem unusual, as witness the very first of these five notes. Of *The Tempest* he wrote, "This play must have been written after 1609, when Bermudas was discovered, and before 1614, when Jonson sneers at it in his *Bartholomew Fair.* In the latter plays of Shakspeare, he has less of pun and quibble than in his early ones. In *The Merchant of Venice,* he expressly declares against them. This perhaps might be one criterion to discover the dates of his plays" (I. 4). Malone had used the same *terminus à quo* and had conjectured 1612 as the date of *The Tempest,* remarking that "it exhibits such strong internal marks of having been a late production." It will be remembered that Blackstone called *Two Gentlemen of Verona* one of Shakespeare's "very early performances" (above, p. 78) because it hastened to the end too abruptly (I. 212). Malone had assigned the play to 1593, sixth in order of appearance among the canonical plays, on the basis of "strong internal marks of an early composition" and its mention by Francis Meres in 1598. Still relying largely on internal evidence, Blackstone suspected that *The Comedy of Errors* and "all other plays where much rhime is used, and especially in long hobbling verses, to have been among Shakspeare's more early productions" (II. 165). Malone had invoked "internal proofs" and the testimony of Meres in assigning the play to 1596. "The borrowing of a line from *Hieronymo,* which was published in 1605," wrote Blackstone, "proves this play [*Much Ado About Nothing*] to be one of Shakspeare's later compositions. As also its being ridiculed by Ben Jonson, in his *Bartholomew Fair*" (II. 266). But Malone added a note to the effect that "*The Spanish Tragedy, or Hieronymo is Mad again . . .* was written many years earlier" than 1605 and that the line borrowed from it would not "serve to ascertain the date" of that play, referring to his essay on the chronology of Shakespeare's plays in volume one of the 1778 Johnson-Steevens variorum Blackstone had no further comment to make.

Moth's reference to "the dancing horse" in *Love's Labour's Lost* had been identified by Zachary Grey as an allusion to a certain Banks's horse which would, according to Sir Kenelm Digby quoted by Grey, "restore a glove to the due owner, after the master had whispered the man's name in his ear . . . and even obey presently his command, in discharging himself of his excrements, whensoever he had bade him." Steevens had collected almost a dozen references to this fabulous equine. Blackstone note reads, "The time when Banks's horse was exhibited will fi the date of this play; which also appears on p. 433 to be about 1597" (II. 394). A note by Warburton on p. 433 calls attention to an edition of this play, dated 1598, bearing the words "presented before her highness [Queen Elizabeth] this last Christmas, 1597," and it was this upon which Blackstone based his opinion. Interestingly enough, Malone dated the play 1591, made no reference to Banks's horse, but remarked that there had to be an edition earlier than that of 1598, for that edition was said to be "newly corrected and augmented."[9] The last of Blackstone's notes on dating is short and to the point. He sees in Camillo's lines in *A Winter's Tale*, "If I could find example / Of thousands, that had struck anointed kings, / And flourish'd after, I'd not do't," an "allusion to the death of the queen of Scots. The play therefore was written in king James's time" (IV. 312). Malone was in some doubts about the date of the play, putting it in 1594, but expressing his opinion that it might belong to 1601 or 1602.[10] No reference is made to the possibility of an allusion to the death of the Queen of Scots. However slight the worth of Blackstone's attempts at dating some of Shakespeare's plays, one can see that he relied rather heavily on internal evidence but certainly not to the exclusion of external.

In two notes Blackstone had recourse to the work of Sir Henry Spelman, a writer on English law with whom he doubtless felt some kinship. The first of these is a fine example of Blackstone at his best. The estimable Mrs. Page, one of the merry wives of Windsor, tells Mrs. Ford that "These knights will hack; and so thou shouldst not alter the article of thy gentry." Warburton had stated that "the unintelligible nonsense of this speech is hardly to be matched" and had emended "hack" to "lack," giving rise to one of his involved explications. Hanmer, Johnson, and Steevens had tried to make sense of the unemended passage. Blackstone suggested,

> These knights will *hack* (that is, become cheap and vulgar) and therefore she advises her friend not to sully her gentry by becoming one. The whole of this discourse about knighthood is added since the first edition of the play; and therefore I suspect this is an oblique reflection on the prodigality of James I. in bestowing these honours, and erecting in 1611, a new order of knighthood, called Baronets; which few of the ancient gentry would condescend to accept. See Sir Hugh Spelman's epigram on them, *Gloss.* p. 76, which ends thus:

> > "——dum cauponare recusant
> > Ex vera geniti nobilitate viri;

> Interea e caulis hic prorepit, ille tabernis
> Et modo sit dominus, qui modo servus erat."

See another stroke at them in *Othello*, vol. X. p. 553. To *hick* and to *hack*, in Mrs. Quickly's language, signifies to *stammer* or *hesitate*, as boys do in saying their lessons. (I. 259)

Here we have knowledge of the editions of the play, suspicion of an historical allusion, an apt quotation, a cross-reference to *Othello*, and a gloss on the key word "hack" in its appearance in another of Shakespeare's plays. Blackstone is quoting from the section "Diatribe de Baronibus" in Spelman's *Archaeologus. In modum glossarii*, published in 1626 and titled *Glossarium Archaiologicum* when it appeared posthumously in 1664, edited by Sir William Dugdale. The second of the notes based on Spelman is on *Othello* (X. 554) and is complementary to that on *The Merry Wives of Windsor* in that Blackstone sees another allusion to "the new order of baronets" and quotes another four lines from Spelman's Epigram, referring back to his note on the earlier play.

A quick look at other notes that show Blackstone's range of knowledge reveal him to know English proverbs, as witness his comment that "we say proverbially, 'Fire is a good *servant*, but a bad *master*'" (I. 101), and "'To sleep like a *town-top*,' is a proverbial expression. A top is said *to sleep*, when it turns round with great velocity, and makes a smooth humming noise" (IV. 162). The latter note arouses the suspicion that Sir William was once a little boy. The editors of the *Oxford English Dictionary*, sub "sleep," 3c. "Of a top," who could only muster up illustrative quotations from 1854 and 1879, would have profited from a knowledge of this note. Grumio's "fire, fire; cast on no water" in *The Taming of the Shrew* reveals Blackstone's knowledge of popular songs. "There is an old popular catch of three parts," he writes, "in these words:

> Scotland burneth, Scotland burneth.
> Fire, fire; ——Fire, fire;
> Cast on some more water." (III. 476)

Similarly, the Earl of Oxford's saying in *Richard III* that "Every man's conscience is a thousand swords" reminds Blackstone of another apt parallel, for he explains Oxford's words as "alluding to the old adage, 'Conscientia mille testes'" (VII. 142).

I have reserved for the last and for full quotation four more

ɔtes. The first two are short. Polonius tells Hamlet that the
ayers have arrived. "Buz, buz," answers the some-points-of-
e-compass-mad Hamlet. Steevens said Hamlet was simply try-
g to interrupt Polonius; Blackstone went back to his Oxford
ays, "Buz used to be an interjection at Oxford, when any one
ɘgan a story that was generally known before" (X. 258). Hamlet's
Imission, "I once did hold it, as our statists do, / A baseness to
rite fair, and labour'd much / How to forget that learning,"
ɔompted Steevens to remark that a statist was a statesman, but it
mained for Blackstone to wrap the matter up properly with the
atement that "most of the great men of Shakspeare's times,
hose autographs have been preserved, wrote very bad hands;
ɩeir secretaries very neat ones" (X. 391). Jack Cade's accusation
ɩat Lord Say had "caused printing to be us'd" (2 Henry VI) was
beled an anachronism by both Johnson and Steevens. Sir
ʔilliam wrote that "Mr. Meerman in his Origines Typographicae
ɑth availed himself of this passage in Shakspeare, to support his
ypothesis, that printing was introduced into England (before
ɩe time of Caxton) by Frederic Corsellis a workman from
aerlem, in the time of Henry VI" (VI. 399). As a most zealous
ɘlegate of the Clarendon Press, one with a keen interest "with
ɞgard to the mechanical part of printing" (his own words, as
ɯoted in the DNB), it should come as no surprise that he knew
ɘrard Meerman's work.

King Claudius proclaims to Hamlet,

> ———let the world take note,
> You are the most immediate to our throne;
> And, with no less nobility of love
> Do I impart to you.

ɘorge Steevens noted that "the crown of Denmark was elective"
ɩnd produced in evidence a passage from Sir Clyomon, Knight of
ɩe Golden Shield, published in 1599 but written between 1570
ɩnd 1583. Blackstone's note on this passage is one of his longest
ɩnd the last that I shall quote.

> I agree with Mr. Steevens, that the crown of Denmark (as in most of
> the Gothick kingdoms) was elective, and not hereditary; though it
> might be customary, in elections, to pay some attention to the royal
> blood, which by degrees produced hereditary succession. Why then
> do the rest of the commentators so often treat Claudius as an usurper,
> who had deprived young Hamlet of his right by heirship of his

father's crown? Hamlet calls him drunkard, murderer, and villai
one who had carried the election by low and mean practices; had
"Popt in between the election and my hopes. . . ." had

> "From a shelf the precious diadem stole,
> And put it in his pocket:"

but never hints at his being an usurper. His discontent arose from h
uncle's being preferred before him, not from any legal right which h
pretended to set up to the crown. Some regard was probably had
the recommendation of the preceding prince, in electing the su
cessor. And therefore young Hamlet had "the voice of the king him
self for his succession in Denmark;" and he at his own deat
prophecies that "the election would light on Fortinbras, who had h
dying voice," conceiving that by the death of his uncle, he himse
had been king for an instant, and had therefore a right to recommen
When, in the fourth act, the rabble wished to choose Laertes king,
understand that antiquity was forgot, and custom violated, by elec
ing a new king in the lifetime of the old one, and perhaps also by th
calling in a stranger to the royal blood. (X. 189)

This, in its latter part, reveals a staunchly English attitude.

One large question remains. How much did Blackstone cor
tribute to the elucidation of Shakespeare's text and to the solu
tion of various other problems connected with the plays? Nc
very much, evidently. His objection to the time references in a
Midsummer Night's Dream is ignored, as is his remark on th
capital letters in the letter to Malvolio in Twelfth Night. But hi
note on the possible allusion to the death of the Queen of Scots i
some words of Camillo's in A Winter's Tale caused Malone t
have second thoughts on his own dating of the play and gave ris
to refutations by the Reverend James Hurdis, by George Cha
mers, and by Francis Douce. The last-named wrote, "If, as M
Blackstone supposes, this is an allusion to the death of the quee
of Scots, it exhibits Shakespeare in the character of a cringin
flatterer accommodating himself to existing circumstances, an
is moreover an extremely severe one." One is left, then, with th
delicately phrased note on the C's, the U's, the T's, and the grea
P's of Malvolio in Twelfth Night, for Blackstone feared that "som
very coarse and vulgar appellations are meant to be alluded to b
these capital letters," and he was the first so to fear. Later editor
he of the Yale edition, for example, followed in his footstep
writing, "Malvolio happens to spell out two Elizabetha
obscenities," although he too does not tell us what they are.

Samuel Johnson, in his 1765 *Shakespeare,* wrote of Antony's "Cry *Havock,* and let slip the Dogs of war" (VII. 56.8): "A learned correspondent has informed me, that, in the military operations of old times, *havock* was the word by which declaration was made, that no quarter should be given." In the 1793 *Shakespeare,* nominally edited by Reed but actually by Steevens, Steevens identifies the anonymous "learned correspondent" as Blackstone. If Steevens is right, and there is no other evidence that Blackstone and Johnson knew each other, although both men had been at Pembroke College, Oxford at different times, this communication marks the *terminus à quo* of Blackstone's *public* interest in Shakespeare. The *terminus ad quem* is to be found in a note by Steevens buried in the second volume of Malone's *Supplement,* a note on "Come cut and long-tail" in *The Merry Wives of Windsor* (p. 688). He writes,

> The last conversation I had the honour to enjoy with sir William Blackstone, was on this subject; and by a series of accurate references to the whole collection of ancient *Forest Laws,* he convinced me of our repeated error, *expeditation* and *genuscission* being the only established and technical modes ever used for disabling the canine species. Part of the *tails* of spaniels indeed are generally *cut* off (*ornamenti gratia*) while they are puppies, so that (admitting a loose description) every kind of dog is comprehended in the phrase of *cut and long-tail,* and every rank of people in the same expression, if metaphorically used. See my note among Mr. Malone's *Supplemental Observations,* p. 92.
> Being now unrestrained from avowing that the notes accompanied by the signature——E. are the productions of the consummate lawyer and polite scholar already mentioned, I must add, with the deepest regret, that but a few weeks ago he taught me to expect a still greater mark of his friendship and condescension. Had his life been spared, he would have examined these volumes before they were entirely printed off, that he might have enriched them with whatever the stores of maturer consideration could supply.—But when I reflect that the general fund of judicial knowledge, and consequently of publick welfare, is diminished by an event which even the wise and great must deplore, perhaps the sigh of subordinate interest and respectful gratitude like mine, would too presumptuously intrude itself among the weightier sorrows of more distinguished mourners.

This tribute, from a man little given to praise, is surely the kindest final comment on Blackstone's notes on Shakespeare.

4

Thomas Holt White, Retired Ironmonger

The usually reliable John Nicholses, père (1745–1826) et fils (1779–1863), both erred in their brief biographical notices of Thomas Holt White, brother of the famous Gilbert White of Selborne. John Nichols, the elder, in his *Literary Anecdotes*, stated that John Evelyn's *Fumifugium* was edited by "Thomas White, Esq., F.R.S., father of Thomas Holt White, Esq. of Enfield" (VIII. 428)."[1] He is in error here, for the father of Thomas Holt White of Enfield was also Thomas *Holt* White, although *not* of Enfield. Nichols repeated the error in his next volume, claiming that the younger Thomas Holt White was the commentator on Shakespeare (IX. 384). John Bowyer Nichols, adding two volumes to his father's six-volume *Illustrations of the Literary History of the Eighteenth Century*, perpetuated the error, stating that Thomas White, brother of Gilbert, was "the father of Thomas Holt White, esq. of Enfield, a commentator on Shakespeare, and a frequent correspondent of the *Gentleman's Magazine* under his initials T.H.W. He also distinguished himself by separate publications. See *Literary Anecdotes*, IX. 384" (VIII. 467). However, the meagre account of Thomas Holt White, the elder (1724–97), in the *DNB*, part of the account of Gilbert, correctly attributes the notes on Shakespeare to the right Thomas Holt White. The younger Thomas Holt White matriculated at Oriel College, Oxford, his uncle Gilbert's college, in 1782 and died in 1841. He eventually resided at Enfield *(Alumni Oxonienses)*. Since, as will be seen, Thomas Holt White contributed four notes to Malone's *Supplement* (1780) and subsequent notes by him ceased with the 1803 *Shakespeare*, it had to be the father, not the son, who was "the commentator on Shakespeare" and the correspondent to the *GM* the latter of which points is made abundantly clear in *The Life and Letters of Gilbert White of Selborne* by Rashleigh Holt-White (New York and London, 1901). Nothing, however, is said in this work of Thomas Holt White's notes on Shakespeare, an omission now to be corrected.

The fullest account of the elder Thomas Holt White is that in *The Life and Letters of Gilbert White.*[2] The essential facts are these: he was born in 1724, educated by Mr. Hampton (father of James, the translator of Polybius), was an "elegant classic," went into a wholesale ironmonger's business, married his partner's childless widow, fathered a daughter and two sons, and in 1776 inherited considerable estates from his "maternal great-uncle in the blood," Thomas Holt. He added "Holt" to his own name, retired from business, and settled in South Lambeth. He was elected a Fellow of the Royal Society in January 1777 and, in collaboration with his brother-in-law, Thomas Parker, contributed papers to the Society.[3] Among his contributions to the GM is a series of articles on "The Trees of Great Britain" which brought praise from at least one reader of that periodical.[4] From the *Life and Letters* one also learns that White knew Anglo-Saxon, that he had intended and was encouraged by Gilbert to undertake a "Natural History and Antiquities" of Hampshire (I. 297–98), that he corrected some of the proofs of Gilbert's *Natural History of Selborne* (II. 182), and that he reviewed his brother's book in the GM for 1789 (II. 184). Besides the series on "The Trees of Great Britain" and the two-part review of Gilbert's book, he is also credited with an account of the great frost of December 1784, an account which appeared in the GM in February 1785 (LIII. 170–71).

White's name does not appear in Isaac Reed's diary; he is not mentioned in Boswell's life of Johnson; and he seems not to have led an active social life. The obituary notice in the GM merely gives his name, omitting "Holt," and his membership in the Royal Society, and even this brief notice is overlooked by Sir William Musgrave in his collection of pre-nineteenth-century obituaries. He has remained an almost entirely forgotten man, and yet, as will be seen, he deserves to be as well known as his famous brother. Indeed, much more is known about Benjamin White, the printer of his brother Gilbert's *Natural History and Antiquities of Selborne*, than about the more accomplished Thomas Holt White.

First evidence of Holt White's interest in Shakespeare comes in our notes in Malone's *Supplement* (1780). When Caliban sings "Nor scrape trencher [so in the 1778 *Shakespeare*], nor wash dish" in *The Tempest*, "White" notes that "It should be remembered, that trenchers, which, in the time of our author, were generally used, were cleansed by scraping only, and were never washed. They were scraped daily, till they were entirely worn away. This practice is again alluded to in Romeo and Juliet: 'Where's Potpan, that he helps not to take away? he shift a trencher! he scrape a trencher!' "[5] The second of White's notes is on As You Like It. Rosalind says to Phebe, "Look upon him [Silvius], love him; he worships you." White writes that "To worship is used in the marriage service in a similar, but more extended, sense: 'With my body I thee worship,'" and adds a contemporary example of the use of the word (II. 701 in Malone). The first of these four notes caught the eye of the irascible Joseph Ritson. In his Remarks (1783) he wrote, " 'It should be remembered,' says one of mr. Malones mushroom assistants in this notable piece of editorial cookry, 'that trenchers, which, in the time of our author, were generally used, were cleansed by scraping ONLY, and were never washed. They were scraped daily,' continues he, 'till they were entirely worn away.'" Ritson then demonstrated to his own complete satisfaction that the assertion was "as ridiculous as untrue" and concluded roundly, "And if mr. White (the trencher-scraper in the note) have been used onely to scrape, and never to wash his trenchers, one cannot well envy his guests the luxury of fouling a plate with him" (p. 235). White, described as one of his "assistants" on the basis of a mere two notes, may have been known to Malone, but he is not mentioned in Prior's biography of Malone. Since Gilbert White's Natural History took the form of a series of letters to "the Honourable Daines Barrington," lawyer, antiquary, and naturalist (1727–1800), and since Gilbert knew Barrington as early as 1768,[6] and since, further, Barrington occupied such a prominent position in London scientific and literary circles, Thomas, as Gilbert's brother, would not have lacked an entree into the company of Malone and other Shakespeareans. Another brother, Benjamin, was already a well-established London publisher, further enhancing Holt White's chances of becoming acquainted with persons in the literary life of the city. Holt White's six notes in the 1785 Shakespeare, edited by Reed, are signed "T.H.W.," all but the last, which mistakenly emerged as "H.T.W." Curiously enough, a note of uncertain authorship in Malone's Shakespear (1790) is attributed to "White," while one other in the same edition is attributed to "T.H.W." The former (V. 202.3) is upon Hotspur's "'tis a woman's fault" and, in 1780, in Malone's Supplement (I. 184), had been attributed to "Amner," i.e., the Rev. Richard Amner, whose name Steevens had usurped for some rather off-color notes; the latter was upon Romeo's reference to "a rich jewel in an Ethiop's ear" (IX. 48.8). The errata list in the 1780 *Supplement* gives the former note to White, as well as that on "the ale-wife's new petticoat" in 2 *Henry IV* (I. 191). The fact remains, however, that White was not further identified until the 1793 *Shakespeare*, edited by Steevens, when his name was expanded to Holt White, with the first such appearance coming in a note on Warburton's Preface (I. 178.9). Steevens and White had probably met by 1793, for in a note on *As You Like It* the former writes, "as Mr. Holt White observes to me" (VI. 63.9), which words, incidentally, are omitted in the New Variorum edition of the play, thus creating the impression that the information was Steevens's. As Holt White merely quotes from "Barret's *Alvearie*, 1580," a well-known work, the matter is of no earthshaking significance, but the credit should be his. Since Steevens was a Fellow of the Royal Society, as was White, the two may have come together at one of the meetings of the Society. Holt White also knew Michael Lort at least as early as August 1775, and Lort knew or was known to most of London's learned.[7] What is more, Lort had contributed a few notes to the 1785 *Shakespeare* under the signature "L," expanded to "Lort" in later editions. Holt White had tried his hand as emendator as early as 1768, for in the Supplement to the *GM* for that year (p. 615) he suggested a change in one of the songs in the opening scene of *As You Like It*. The letter in which the emendation is made is anonymous, but in a letter to the same periodical in January 1784 signed T.H.W., Holt White refers to having made the suggestion in the *Gentleman's* "some years ago" (p. 21).

White's greatest contribution was to Steeven's edition in which there are just slightly over one hundred new notes by him. He had contributed, it is well to repeat, four notes to Malone's *Supplement*, six to the 1785 *Shakespeare*, and another two, one of which may not be his, to Malone's edition of 1790. One can only guess that the relative spate of notes in Steevens's edition resulted from some degree of intimacy between the two men. Possibly Holt White had been emboldened by his notes in Malone's *Supplement* to try his hand at more comments on Shakespeare, for he contributed notes on fourteen passages on Shakespeare's plays to the *GM* in November 1783 (pp. 933–35). Holt White's first note in the 1783 *GM* was on the famous song, "Where the bee sucks, there suck I," in *The Tempest;* he quoted parallels from Fairfax's *Tasso* and Virgil's *Aeneid*, without a word of introduction or explanation. When the note appeared in 1793, he had either revised it voluntarily or at Steevens's suggestion, for then it reads, "This thought is not thrown out at random. It composed a part of the magical system of these days." He then gives a fuller title of the translation and quotes the pertinent lines, followed by, "The idea was probably first suggested by the description of the venerable elm which Virgil planted at the entrance of the infernal shades," concluding with the quotation from the *Aeneid.* He adduced a parallel, reprinted in 1785, from Lyly's *Euphues* for a line in *The Merry Wives of Windsor,* "Then did the sun on dung-hill shine." In other notes he explained the phrase "turn girdle" in *Much Ado,* quoted a parallel from Chaucer's *Merchant's Tale* for a line in *As You Like It* (anticipated by Thomas Tyrwhitt in the 1778 *Shakespeare*), and had recourse to Lyly's *Euphues* again for a passage in *Twelfth Night.*[8] He quoted the French of DuBartas and the Latin of Linnaeus for the "tirra-lirra" of the lark in Autolycus's song, went still again to Lyly's *Euphues* for the defilement of those who touch pitch (in 1 *Henry IV*), explained the meaning of "the elements be kind" in *Antony and Cleopatra,* and paralleled the "hollow hell" of *Othello* with lines from the first Book of *Paradise Lost.*[9] The one note reprinted in 1790 was on the "rich jewel in an Ethiop's ear" in *Romeo and Juliet,* for which he again quoted from Lyly's *Euphues* the line the "pearle in a Marian's eare."

A little less than two years later Holt White again sent some remarks on Shakespeare's plays to the *GM;* they were printed in the April number for 1785 (pp. 277–78). Dr. Johnson, in the course of his commentary on *A Midsummer Night's Dream,* had pointed to the similarities in the accounts of Puck in the play and in Drayton's *Nymphidia,* and had admitted that "whether Drayton or Shakespeare wrote first, I cannot discover." Holt White pointed out that "if Drayton wrote the *Nymphidia* after the *Midsummer Night's Dream* had been acted, he could with very little propriety say," quoting,

> Then since no muse hath bin so bold,
> Or of the *later* or the ould,
> Those elvish secrets to unfold
>   Which lye from others reading;
> My active muse to light shall bring
> The court of that proud fayry king . . .

which, while it does nothing to disprove the priority of Shakespeare's play, does convict Drayton of impropriety (1785, III. 28.9). Eight of the remarks went into the 1793 edition, three unchanged and a fourth only slightly changed. Two of these are on *Love's Labour's Lost*, one in explanation of "white, as whale his bone," Holt White writing that "*the white whale his bone,* which is now superseded by ivory, was the tooth of the *horse-whale,* morse, or walrus, as appears by King Alfred's preface to his translation of Orosius." For his second note, on the staring Owl's "to whit! to whoo!," Holt White went to Lyly's *Mother Bombie* for a parallel.[10] His quotation of two lines from the sixth book of Lucretius as a parallel to Macbeth's "Will all great Neptune's ocean wash this blood / Clean from my hand?" also appeared unchanged in 1793 (VII. 421.8). He had explained "childing" in *A Midsummer Night's Dream* an "an old term in botany, when a small flower grows out of a large one" and had concluded, in the *GM,* by stating that "florists have a childing rose, a childing daisy, and a childing scabious." He omitted the "childing rose" for the note in 1793, evidently having caught himself in an error (V. 49.5).

The remaining four notes that got into the 1793 edition show that Holt White was alert to improve on his notes if he could. Slender says of Anne Page in *The Merry Wives of Windsor* that she "speaks small like a woman" and Holt White was ready with apposite parallels from *The Flower and the Leaf* and from Tasso. In 1793 he added, "When female characters were filled by boys, to *speak small like a woman* must have been a valuable qualification. So, in Marston's *What you will:* 'I was solicited to graunt him leave to play the lady in comedies presented by children; but I knew his voice was too *small,* and his stature too low. Sing a treble, Holofernes;—a very *small* voice I'le assure you'" (III. 309.4). In a second note, in explication of the epithet "shard-born" in the "shard-born beetle" in *Macbeth,* he quoted Dryden's *The Hind and the Panther,* "Such souls as *shards* produce, such beetle things, / As only buzz to heaven with evening wings." The 1793 edition included notes by Warburton, Steevens, Tollett, Ritson, and Malone, with Holt White's last. There he wrote,

Mr. Steevens's interpretation ["the beetle borne along the air by its *shards* or *scaly wings*"] is no doubt the most suitable to the context. The succeeding passages, however, make in favour of Mr. Tollet's explanation ["the shard-born beetle is the beetle born in dung"]. In a *Briefe Discourse of the Spanish state,* 1590, p. 3 there is "How that nation rising like the *beetle* from the *cowshern* hurtleth against al things." [He quotes Dryden again.] "The Beetle and the Chafer are distinct insects." (VII. 466.9)

In the same play, the Doctor's "my mind she has mated," recalled lines from "Scory to Drayton," "Yet with these broken reliques, *mated mind*, / And what a justly-grieved thought can say." In 1793 he expands the terse reference to "Scory, in the commendatory verses prefixed to Drayton's *Heroicall Epistles*, makes use of this phrase, and exactly in the same sense" (VII. 549.9), either at Steevens's suggestion or because he later realized that not everybody would know what was meant by "Scory to Drayton," something he seems to have assumed in 1785. He went to Lyly's *Mother Bombie* again for a parallel to "Philip ! Sparrow" in *King John*; in 1793 he added, "From the sound of the sparrow's chirping, Catullus in his *Elegy on Lesbia's Sparrow*, has formed a verb.

> 'Sed circumfiliens modo huc, modo illuc,
> Ad solam dominam usque *pipilabat*' " (VIII. 24.2).

Twenty-six months later Holt White again addressed Mr. Urban: "If I have not already overloaded you with remarks on Shakespeare, please insert the following." The "following" were seven somewhat longer comments which were inserted in the GM for June 1787 (pp. 478–80). The first and longest was an analogue to the Induction to *The Taming of the Shrew*, an analogue from "*A Discourse of the Felicitie of Man, by Sir Richard Barckley, Knt.* 1598, p. 24."[11] Steevens reprinted a note on "strike the vessels" in *Antony and Cleopatra* in which Holt White mistakenly took "vessels" to be "kettle-drums," which "were beaten when the health of a person of eminence was drank . . . They are called *kettles* in *Hamlet*.

> Give me the cups;
> And let the *kettle* to the trumpet speak." (XII. 518.2)

He was right on "kettle," wrong on "vessels." Steevens also included Holt White's quotation of a line from Menander "*Fragm*. p. 22 Amstel. 12 mo. 1719," which obviated Warburton's emendation of Hamlet's "sea of troubles." Holt White had provided both a Latin and an English translation of the Greek verse in 1793 he, or Steevens, omitted the English translation of the Greek verse, presumably on the assumption that the Latin would suffice (XV. 157.7). Like Johnson and others, Holt White at

empted an explanation of the wager at the end of *Hamlet*. Osric,
this water-fly," it may be remembered, says, "The king, sir, hath
ay'd, that in a dozen passes between yourself and him [Laertes],
e shall not exceed you three hits; he hath laid, on twelve for
ine." By 1793 there had been so many long and conflicting
ttempts to explain the wager that Steevens gave up in amused
isgust and wrote,

> As three or four complete pages would scarcely hold the remarks
> already printed, together with those which have lately been commu-
> nicated to me in MSS. on this very unimportant passage, I shall avoid
> both partiality and tediousness, by the omission of them all.—I
> therefore leave the conditions of this wager to be adjusted by the
> members of Brookes's, or the Jockey-Club at Newmarket, who on such
> subject may prove the most enlightened commentators, and most
> successfully bestir themselves in the cold unpoetick dabble of cal-
> culation. (XV. 336.4)

Nevertheless, Holt White's terse explanation is worth quoting,
specially since it anticipates notes quoted in the New Variorum
dition (p. 433), although the note itself is ignored. He wrote that
Laertes, being the most expert fencer, was to give Hamlet *nine*
its out of *twelve* passes." He added, in supremely tactful fash-
on: "Johnson's note seems more difficult to be understood than
he passage itself. But this learned annotator, employed in un-
avelling such trivial entanglements, is Hercules spinning: Et
nanu, clavam modò quâ gerebat, / Fila deduxit." The lines are
rom Seneca's *Phaedra* (sometimes called *Hippolytus*), 323–24.
ohnson was dead, but if he were alive, he would have been
lelighted with Holt White's tactful compliment, for Johnson on
ne occasion corrected John Wilkes's censure of quotation as
edantry: "No, Sir, it is a good thing; there is a community of
nind in it. Classical quotation is the *parole* of literary men all
ver the world" (*Life*, IV. 102).
    Holt White queried of Kent's "Stand, rogue, stand, you neat
lave" in *King Lear*: "Does 'neat slave' mean any thing more than
owherd?" and most subsequent editors agree in ignoring the
uestion, although the New Variorum edition lists the same
uggestion on the part of a later editor (p. 118). The lark, un-
velcome "herald of the dawn" in *Romeo and Juliet*, brought to
nind "the mounting lark, daie's herald" of "*Browne's Britannia's
Pastorals, book* 1. *s.* 3." and "the herald lark" of Milton's *Paradise
Regained*, but both parallels have also been ignored by later
ditors. In the last of these notes in the 1787 *GM* Holt White puts

the date of composition of Middleton's *The Witch*, a play that Steevens and Malone and others thought a source for some of the scenes in *Macbeth*, at some time after 1597 because of a reference to a statute passed in that year. He went on to suggest, however, that "it is probable from the familiar mention of tobacco, to which Shakespeare hath no allusion, that this performance did not appear till several years after the accession of James. Middleton, in his dedication to this play, says it was '*ignorantly ill-fated*,' which seems to be a mild and tender way of owning that it was damned by an ignorant audience." Modern scholarly opinion puts the time of first performance as 1609?–1616?, with 1615 as the favored date, so that Holt White's putting its performance "several years after the accession of James" was fairly accurate, if indefinite.

If T.H.W. had written nothing else but these three series of notes on Shakespeare's plays, one could have come to some fairly obvious conclusions about him. He was evidently an erudite person, displaying knowledge of Greek, Latin, French, and Anglo-Saxon, quoting, in the first three languages, Theocritus, Menander, Virgil, Persius, Lucretius, Aulus Gellius, and DuBartas. His knowledge of Anglo-Saxon is explicit from his reference to King Alfred's Saxon translation of Orosius. His reading also included Fairfax's translation of Tasso, Chaucer, Milton, Drayton, William Browne, John Heywood, Beaumont and Fletcher, Thomas Middleton, and Hakyluyt's *Voyages*. John Lyly would seem to have been a favorite with him; at least he quotes *Euphues* four times, *Mother Bombie* twice, and *Alexander and Campaspe* once. He quotes Linnaeus and is knowledgeable in matters botanical. Other corners of his learning include certain customs of Shakespeare's time, wrestling, and the religion of the Saracens. Somehow or other he had had access to Middleton's *The Witch*, privately printed for Reed in 1778 to the number of one hundred copies. It is, hence, not surprising that a number of his notes were impressed into service, mainly by Steevens. And it may have been these notes in the *GM* that prompted Steevens to discover the identity of T.H.W. and, possibly, to seek him out.

Holt White, it is necessary to repeat, contributed a little over one hundred new notes to Steevens's *Shakespeare*, so that his part in the edition, at least quantitatively and probably qualitatively, was second only to Samuel Henley's and Steevens's. And it was to Steevens's edition, for the most part, that later editors who cite or quote Holt White went.[12] As with other eighteenth-century commentators, a number of his notes have been quoted wholly or in part, while the far greater number have been forgotten, sometimes with reason, at other times for no discernible good reason. For example, I have consulted the New Arden edition for those plays which have not appeared in the New Variorum series, and while the New Arden edition makes no pretense at inclusiveness in its commentary I have come upon but one mention of his name. In 1793 he had quoted as "a maxim in our law," without identifying the source, "Dormiunt aliquando leges, moriuntur nunquam" (IV. 238.3). The editor of the New Arden *Measure for Measure* notes that "White cited a maxim attributed to Coke" and quotes the maxim. "White" is not identified anywhere in the edition, nor is the source of the note. What is possibly more disturbing is that the New Arden editor completely ignores another of Holt White's notes, one on a passage some fourteen lines before that which elicited the quotation from Coke. Disturbing, because Holt White's interpretation anticipates the lengthier, seemingly original interpretation of the editor. Isabella says to Angelo, "O, think on that, / And mercy then will breathe within your lips, / Like a man new made." Holt White paraphrased these lines as follows: "*And you, Angelo, will breathe new life into Claudio, as the Creator animated Adam*, by 'breathing into his nostrils the breath of life'" (IV. 237.2). Part of the note in the New Arden edition reads, "As Adam was given a soul when the Creator breathed life into his nostrils, so the new Adam is redeemed from the first Adam's sin by the breath of the divine mercy in Christ, which moves on his lips when he speaks mercifully to his fellow men" (p. 43).

Other examples of what I take to be injustice to or ignorance of Holt White's notes on the part of editors of the New Arden are not wanting. Thus, in *Henry V*, the Chorus to Act IV speaks of "A largess universal, like the sun, / His [Henry's] liberal eye doth give to every one," for which Holt White found parallels in Quintilian and in Pope's *Rape of the Lock* (IX. 401.2). The New Arden gives T. W. Baldwin, in his *William Shakspere's small Latine and lesse Greeke*, credit for the parallel from Quintilian, although Baldwin quite properly cites Holt White's note. Similarly, a later editor, S. W. Singer, is given credit for the parallel from Spenser's *Fairy Queen* for "the lily, / That once was mistress of the field" in *Henry VIII* (p. 98), when it was Holt White who had first remarked it (XI. 107.5). Talbot, in *1 Henry VI*, says that

A witch, by fear, not force, like Hannibal,
Drives back our troops, and conquers as she lists:

So bees with smoke, and doves with noisome stench,
Are from their hives, and houses, driven away.

Holt White wrote, "See Hannibal's stratagem to escape by fixing
bundles of lighted twigs on the horns of oxen, recorded in *Livy*,
Lib. XXII. c. xvi" (IX. 544.5). The New Arden editor's note begins,
"Livy, xxii. xvi.–xvii." without, of course, any mention of Holt
White.[13] Holt White was first correctly to explicate Pericles's
"heaven forbid / That kings should let their ears hear their faults
hid" (XIII. 417.4) In the same play Lysimachus says that Marina's
sweet harmony "would allure, / And make a battery through his
deafen'd parts" and Holt White produced a most apposite parallel from *Antony and Cleopatra*, "Make battery to our ears with
the loud musick" (XIII. 576.4), which has also been ignored.

Two more of Holt White's notes that might have deserved some
attention at the hands of the New Arden editors merit full quotation. The first of these is on Richard II's statement that "The
breath of worldly men cannot depose / The deputy elected by the
Lord." The New Arden editor refers one back to the note on I. ii.
38–41, i.e., the lines that describe the king as "God's substitute, /
His deputy anointed in his sight," the note ending with citations
from the *Homilies*, and specifically from that against Rebellion
(p. 19). Here is Holt White's note, a rejoinder to one by Johnson:

> Far be it from me to palliate the conduct of the wretched James; but
> the truth is that the inherent rights of the people had been ill under-
> stood, or rather were not acknowledged, by his predecessors. The
> doctrine of the divine right of kings, and of the passive obedience of
> subjects, have never been carried further in any country than in this
> island, while the house of Tudor sate on the throne. Of this fact, the
> Homilies, composed during the reign of young Edward, and ap-
> pointed in the Thirty-nine Articles to be read in churches, furnish
> striking and abundant proof. Take, as an instance, the following
> extract from the Homily *Against Disobedience and wilful Rebellion*:
> "As the name of the king is very often attributed and given unto God
> in Holy scriptures, so doth God himself in the same scriptures some-
> time vouchsafe to communicate his name with earthly *princes*, term-
> ing *them Gods*." *1st part*. And in the 4th *part*, we are directed to "call
> to remembrance the heavy wrath and dreadful indignation of Al-
> might God against subjects as do *only but inwardly* grudge, mutter,
> and murmur against their governors, though their inward treason, so
> privily hatched in their breasts come not to an open declaration of
> their doings" (VII. 273.3).

The similarities are obvious, and the note is a fine example of what Holt White could do when moved by deep conviction. The remaining note is on *Pericles, King of Tyre* and suggests an analogue for a number of important events of the play. Pericles says to Marina "such a one / My daughter might have been" and Holt White is reminded of Plautus's *Rudens*.

> ——*such a one*
> *My daughter might have been:* So, Demones, in the *Rudens* of Plautus, exclaims on beholding his long-lost child:
>
> > "O filia
> > "Mea! cum ego hanc video, mearum me absens miseriarum
> >   commones,
> > "Trima quae periit mihi: *jam tanta esset, si vivit,*
> > scio."
>
> It is observable that some of the leading incidents in this play strongly remind us of the *Rudens*. There Arcturus, like Gower, προλογιζει.—In the Latin comedy, fishermen, as in *Pericles,* are brought on the stage, one of whom drags on shore in his net the wallet which principally produces the catastrophe; and the heroine of Plautus and Marina fall alike into the hands of a procurer. A circumstance on which much of the plot in both these dramatick pieces depends. (XIII. 584.2)

Plautus's play is not mentioned in the introduction to the New Arden edition and does not appear among the analogues to *Pericles* in Geoffrey Bullough's study of Shakespeare's sources.[14] What is more, J. C. Maxwell, editor of the New Cambridge edition of *Pericles*, notes that "affinities" between the *Rudens* and *Pericles* "were first noted by Malone" (p. xii., n. 2), thus depriving Holt White of credit for a very interesting and relatively ignored suggestion.

On the credit side of the ledger, and turning to the New Variorum volumes, it can be said that forty of Holt White's notes are quoted, wholly or in part, and four others are cited. Ten of the forty notes are quoted first, presumably meaning that he had not been anticipated in any of them and that they found favor with the New Variorum editors. A few notes are quoted in order that the editors might exercise their wit upon them or engage in a bit of quibbling. Thus, Holt White had quoted seven passages in five different authors, from Spenser to Thomas Gray, in exemplification of his statement that "*Bray* [in *King John*, "braying trumpets"] appears to have been particularly applied to express the harsh grating sound of the trumpet" (VIII. 92.3). The editor of the New Variorum *King John* writes, "Holt White, quite needlessly, I think, quotes seven passages from various writers in support of his statement [which he quotes]. It might, on the other hand, be said that such was but a transferred meaning, and that the word was particularly applied originally to the characteristic cry of the donkey" (p. 229). Of such are quibbles made. Antony's "Ho, ho, ho," in *Antony and Cleopatra*, is probably an expression of triumph or of derision, but it is also a command to stop, and so Holt White interpreted it in this passage. The note is another fine example of the fashion in which he could muster up a number of parallels from his wide reading.

> i.e. *stop,* or *desist.* Antony desires his followers to cease weeping. So, in *Chaucer, The Knightes Tale,* v. 1706. edit. 1775:

> > "This duk his courser with his sporres smote,
> > And at a stert he was betwix hem two,
> > And pulled out a swerd, and cried, *ho!*
> > No more, up peine of lesing of your hed."

> But Mr. Tyrwhittt in a note on ver. 2535, of the Canterbury tales doubts whether this interjection was used except to command a cessation of fighting. The succeeding quotations, however, will, while they illustrate an obscurity in Shakspeare, prove that *ho* was by no means so confined in its meaning. *Gawin Douglas* translates— "Helenum, farique vetat Saturnia Juno" (*Aeneid* L. 3. v. 380.) "The douchter of auld Santurn Juno Forbiddis Helenus to speik it, and crys *ho.*"

> In the Glossary to the folio edition of this Translation, *Edinb.* 1710, it is said that "*Ho* is an Interjection commanding to desist or leave off."

> It occurs again in *Langham's Letter concerning Queen Elizabeth's entertainment at Killingsworth Castle,* 1575, 12mo. p. 61, cited in *The Reliques of Antient Poetry.* "Heer was no *ho* in devout drinkyng."

> And in *The Myrrour of good manners compyled in latyn by Domynike Mancyn and translated into englyshe by Alexander Bercley prest, Imprynted by Rychard Pynson,* bl. 1. no date, fol Ambition is compared to

> > "The sacke insaciable,
> > The sacke without botome, which never can say *ho.*"

> > (XII. 594.3

When Holt White explains Octavius's "Defiance, traitors hurl w in your teeth" in *Julius Caesar* as, "Whence perhaps Miltor ıradise *Lost*, B.I. v. 669: 'Hurling *defiance* toward the vault of eaven.' Hurl is peculiarly expressive. The challenger in judicial ımbats was said to hurl down his gage, when he threw his glove ɔwn as a pledge that he would make good his charge against his lversary. So, in *King Richard II*: 'And interchangeably *hurl* ɔwn my gage/Upon this over-weening traitor's foot'" (XII. 76.8). The New Variorum editor condescendingly damns with int praise: "Good sentences and well pronounced; but is it ɔculiar to Shakespeare to choose the most 'expressive' word?" ı. 246).

Surely the grossest injustice done to Holt White is in the ɔatment accorded his note on "we have the receipt of fern-seed, e walk invisible" in *1 Henry IV*. The note, in 1793, reads,

> The ancients, who often paid more attention to received opinions than to the evidence of their senses, believed that *fern* bore *no seed*. Our ancestors imagined that this plant produced seed which was invisible. Hence, from an extraordinary mode of reasoning, founded on the fantastic doctrine of signatures, they concluded that they who possessed the secret of wearing this seed about them would become invisible. This superstition the good sense of the poet taught him to ridicule. It was also supposed to seed in the course of a single night, and is called in Browne's *Britannia's Pastorals*, 1613:
> The wond'rous one-night-seeding ferne.
> Absurd as these notions are, they were not wholly exploded in the time of Addison. He laughs at "a Doctor who was arrived at the knowledge of the green and red dragon, and *had discovered the female fern seed*." *Tatler*, No. 240. (VIII. 423.2)

ere is what Professor Hemingway does to it, ascribing it quite ·operly to "(ed. Steevens, 1793)." He omits the first sentence, words the second to read "Our ancestors believed that fern bore ed which was invisible," omits from the next sentence without ιy mark of ellipsis the words "founded on the fantastic doctrine signatures," changes "concluded" to "believed" and "they ho" to "those that," and omits (noting the omissions properly) e next two sentences and the quotation from Browne as well as at from Addison (pp. 100–101). A truly remarkable perform-ιce! Of incidental interest is the fact that the substance and deed the very words of this note made up part of Holt White's ticle on the common fern in the GM for January 1788 (pp. 19– l). Only the quotation from Browne was added in 1793.

While it is manifestly uneconomic in a variorum edition to ιote all notes in their entirety, students of Shakespeare will welcome all or some of the information omitted from a few of Holt White's notes in the New Variorum volumes. His parallel from *"Linnaei Fauna Suecica"* for "the lark, that tirra-lirra chaunts" in Autolycus's song, i.e., "Ecce suum *tirile tirile:* suum *tirile* tractat (1785, IV 376.5), gives scientific reinforcement to the passage from DuBartas which he had also quoted. In explanation of "it is a world to see" in *Much Ado about Nothing* he had quoted from John Barrett's *Alvearie, or Triple Dictionary of English, Latin, and French* (c. 1574) and from Horace, but his parallel from a rare book is omitted from the New Variorum edition. He wrote, "And in *The Myrrour of good maners compyled in latyn by Domynike Mancyn and translated into englyshe by Alexander Bercley prest. Imprynted by Richard Pynson,* bl. 1, no date, the line, *'Est operae pretium doctos* spectare colonos'—is rendered by *'A world it is to se* wyse tyllers of the grounde'" (IV. 494.7). So, too, was it for a parallel from William Browne's *Britannia's Pastorals* in exemplification of "trace" in "trace the forests wild" of *A Midsummer Night's Dream* (V. 32.3), Holt White having in the same note been the first to quote Milton's *Comus,* "May *trace* huge forests, and unharbour'd heaths" for this passage. He had remarked of Mercutio's "Nay, if thy wits run the wild-goose chase, I have done" that the reference was to a kind of horse-race, which he explained. He then referred the reader to *"Chambers's Dictionary* last edition under the article CHACE" and quoted Burton's *Anatomy of Melancholy* on this "barbarous sport." His last paragraph is omitted from the New Variorum edition, however. It reads, "This account explains the pleasantry kept up between Romeo and his gay companion. 'My wits fail, says Mercutio.'—Romeo exclaims briskly—'Switch and spurs, switch and spurs.'—to which Mercutio rejoins, 'Nay, if thy wits run the *wild-goose chace,'* etc." (XIV. 425.9). Since Holt White's is the first of only two notes included in the New Variorum *Romeo and Juliet* and since there is no note whatsoever on "switch and spurs," one would have thought that Holt White's last paragraph would have been retained. One last example. The "mobled" queen of the First Player's speech in *Hamlet* had sent the various editors and commentators on the lookout for other uses of the word. Richard Farmer had quoted the line, "The moor does mobble up herself" from James Shirley's *Gentleman of Venice,* and Holt White commented that the word was a "depravation of *muffled."* His next sentence, "It is thus corrupted in *Ogilby's Fables,* Second Part," is omitted from the New Variorum as is his last sentence, "In the West this word i still used in the same sense; and that is the meaning of *mobble* in Dr. Farmer's quotation" (XV. 144.8). All such information about Shakespeare's use of words peculiar to certain parts of England should find a place in a variorum commentary.

Another note clamors for admission into the variorum commentary. In the 1793 *Shakespeare*, act II, scene iii of *Romeo and Juliet* opens with Friar Lawrence's

> The grey-ey'd morn smiles on the frowning night,
> Checkering the eastern clouds with streaks of light;
> And flecked darkness like a drunkard reels
> From forth day's path-way, made by Titan's wheels.

Malone had favored a quarto reading, "From forth day's path, and Titan's fiery wheels," for the last of these four lines and had further remarked that "the modern editions read corruptly, after the second folio: From forth day's *path-way made* by Titan's wheels." Holt White pointed out, what obviously ought to command attention, that "these lines are thus quoted in *England's Parnassus, the choysest Flowers of our Modern Poets* etc. 1600:

> 'The grey-eyde morne smiles on the frowning night,
> Cheering the easterne cloudes with *streames* of light;
> And *darknesse flected*, like a drunkard reeles
> From forth daye's *path-way made by* Titan's wheels.'

So that the various readings in the last line do not originate in an arbitrary alteration by the editor of the second folio, as the ingenious commentator supposes" (XIV. 412.6).[15]

Most of Holt White's notes, it will have been seen, are given over to adducing parallels, with a far smaller number devoted to explication. Only once does he suggest an emendation, and that a most tentative one. As Pistol eats the leek at Gower's insistence in *Henry V*, he says "I eat, and eat, I swear," for which Holt White suggested "Perhaps, 'I eat, and *eating* swear'" (IX. 476.7). Some of his remarks were in correction of Johnson's notes, at one point catching "the learned commentator" quoting Homer from memory and thus compressing "a couplet into a single line" (VIII. 203.6). When Helena in *All's Well That Ends Well* says "Great floods have flown / From simple sources; and great seas have dried, / When miracles have by the greatest been denied" Johnson admitted that he could not "see the import or connection" of the last line quoted. And, he continued, "As the next line stands without a correspondent rhyme, I suspect that something has

been lost." The two lines preceding those quoted above read "S
holy writ in babes hath judgement shown, / When judges ha*
been babes," and Holt White based his own note on the who
passage:

> So holy writ, etc. alludes to Daniel's judging, when "a young youth
> the two Elders in the story of Susannah. Great floods, i.e. whe
> Moses smote the rock in Horeb, Exod. xvii.
> ——great seas have dry'd
> When miracles have by the greatest been deny'd.
> Dr. Johnson did not see the import or connection of this line.
> certainly refers to the children of Israel passing the Red Sea, whe
> miracles had been denied, or not hearkened to, by Pharaoh. (\
> 242.7)

The other occasions upon which he disagrees with Johnson
provides an explanation when Johnson could not are few.

Holt White, it is well to repeat, was "an elegant classic," as we
as "a good botanist, an Anglo-Saxon scholar, and interested
antiquities."[16] His botanical knowledge is displayed in his not
on "childing" (above, p. 91), "gossamer," and "orchard." H
stated that "the substance called Gossamer is formed of tl
collected webs of flying spiders, and during calm weather
Autumn sometimes falls in amazing quantities" (XIV. 230.:
OED corroborates, even to the seasonal reference. Act II, scene
of Julius Caesar takes place, according to the stage direction,
"Brutus's Orchard." Steevens had observed that "the mode
editors read garden, but orchard seems anciently to have had tl
same meaning" and Malone agreed that "these two words we
anciently synonymous." And Samuel Henley chimed in wi
"Orchard was anciently written hort-yard; hence its origin
meaning is obvious." But Holt White disagreed:

> By the following quotation, however, it will appear that these wor
> had in the days of Shakespeare acquired a distinct meaning. "It sh
> be good to have understanding of the ground where ye do plant eith
> orchard or garden with fruite." A Books of the Arte and maner ho
> to plant and graffe all sorts of trees, etc. 1574, 4to. And when Justi
> Shallow invites Falstaff to see his orchard, where they are to eat a lo
> year's pippin of his own graffing, he certainly uses the word in
> present acceptation. (XII. 271.6)

In the one scholarly note on this stage direction in the Ne
Variorum edition, G. L. Craik is quoted to the effect that "it

probable that the words 'Orchard' and *garden* were commonly understood in the early part of the seventeenth century [the probable date of the play is 1599] in the senses which they now bear; but there is nothing in their etymology to support the manner in which they have come to be distinguished" (p. 72). Holt White, first in the matter, had already demonstrated that the two words were distinguished at the very least a quarter of a century before the period assigned by Craik.

The germ of Holt White's note on "orchard" is to be found in the *GM* for May 1786 (pp. 365–67) in one of his series on the trees of Britain, this one being on the crab tree. He ends the article with this paragraph.

> If we had language that could at once express reproof and veneration, we would call on thee, illustrious shade, to say why thou puttest the following speech into the mouth of thy simple squire: "Nay, you shall see mine orchard, where, in an arbour, we will eat a last year's pippin of my own graffing." Thy comprehensive genius, *Shakespeare*, must have told thee, that cultivation is the great and peculiar business of man. + Thou hadst a right to expose the garrulity, the ostentation, and the folly of the object of thy ridicule, but his orchard should have been sacred.

His footnote reads, "+Many beasts, birds, and insects, build, and some sail, spin, and weave; but man is the only animal that plants by design." In his article on the beech tree in the *GM* for September 1784 (pp. 656–59), he had written of the difficulty of grafting, quoting a passage from Virgil's *Georgics*, and thereby setting off a minor controversy with a correspondent signing himself "P.B.C."

Although Holt White did not study law, it may be recalled that he quotes a legal maxim attributed to Coke (above, p. 95). No doubt as part of his antiquarian interests he picked up some bits and pieces of legal lore, including the account of the trial of Cardinal Wolsey by the Privy Council as reported in Coke's *Institutes*.[17] He was thus able to explicate two passages in *Henry VIII*, one on Wolsey's imprinting his Cardinal's hat on coins (XI. 28.3), and the other on the description of Wolsey as "fair spoken, and persuading," for in the charges against him "it was alleged that at the Privy Council 'he would have all the words to himself, and *consumed much time with a fair tale*'" (XI. 153.3). He knew some of the old statutes, for he could explain the verb to "jutty" in *Henry V* in these terms: "The force of the verb to *jutty*, when applied to a rock projecting into the sea [so in *Henry V*], is

not felt by those who are unaware that this word antiently signified a mole raised to withstand the encroachment of the tide. In
an act, 1 Edw. VI. c. 14, provision is made for 'the maintenance of
piers, jutties, walles, and bankes against the rages of the sea' " (IX
350.7). Finally, in a passage in *Cymbeline*, he thought he
discerned "a reference to the manner in which the tenant performed homage to his lord" and quoted "*Coke upon Littleton*,
85" in support of his statement, only to have his note later
ridiculed as well as characterized as "dry-as-dust."[18]

Holt White was much in the country and in various parts of
England as he reveals in his series on the trees of Britain in the
GM, and he had an eye for more than just natural phenomena. He
knew that "whiting-time" was "bleaching time; spring. The season when 'maidens bleach their summer smocks' " (III. 421.7).
Autolycus proclaims, "My traffick is sheets; when the kite
builds, look to lesser linen." Steevens quoted three parallel passages to show that this was a reference to stealing sheets from
hedges, and John Monck Mason explained that Autolycus's
"practice was to steal sheets and large pieces of linen, leaving the
smaller pieces for kites to build with." Holt White wrote, "This
passage, I find, is not generally understood. When the good
women, in solitary cottages near the woods where kites build,
miss one of their *lesser linen*, as it hangs to dry on the hedge in
spring, they conclude that the kite has been marauding for a
lining of her nest; and adventurous boys often find it employed
for that purpose" (VII. 110.3). The New Variorum edition quotes
Mason and Holt White, stating that the latter corroborates the
former (p. 167), while it seems to me that Holt White is implying
that Autolycus is merely comparing himself, vis-à-vis sheets, to
the kite, vis-à-vis lesser linen, an interpretation also put forth by
a later editor. Holt White's peregrinations may also have provided
him with the information in his note on Justice Shallow's "marry
good air," for he remarks that this is an allusion "to a witticism
frequent among rustics, who when talking of a healthy country
pleasantly observe: 'Yes, it is a good air, more run away than
die' " (IX. 224.6). In another note, this one on *Pericles*, he explains "to smooth" as "to stroke," quotes *Comus* for a parallel
use, and concludes that "they say in some counties *smooth*
instead of *stroke*, the cat" (XIII. 419.8). *OED* corroborates, quoting
the same passage in *Comus* as one illustration. When the
disguised Edgar, in *King Lear*, assumes a dialect in his confronta-
tion with Oswald he says "ise try whether your costard or my bat
be the harder." Steevens defined "bat" as a "club." Holt White

:new better: "Rather in this place a *staff*. In Sussex a walking-
tick is called a *bat*. *Bats* and *clubs* are distinguished in *Cor-*
olanus, Act I. sc. i. 'where go you with *bats* and *clubs*'" (XIV.
:47.3). Definition I. 1 in *OED* reads "Still *dial*. (Kent, Sussex,
:tc.) = staff, walking stick"; *Coriolanus* is quoted.

Something more of the quality of Holt White as a commentator
·n Shakespeare's works will be seen in a few more of his notes.
Jen Jonson's poem on Shakespeare was one of the "Poems on
;hakespeare" traditionally included in most eighteenth-century
·ditions. Jonson wrote "Of Shakespeare's mind, and manners,
·rightly shines / In his well-turned and true-filed lines; / In each
·f which, he seems to shake a lance." Holt White wrote,

Jonson is here translating the classick phrase *tornati et limati versus*.
Does not the poet in the next line by the expression *shake a lance*
intend to play on the name of *Shakspeare*? So, in *Two Bookes of*
Epigrammes and Epitaphs, by Thomas Bancroft, Lond. 1639. 4to.

> "To Shakespeare:
> Thou hast so used thy pen, (or *shooke thy speare*,)
> That poets startle, not thy wit come near."

Dryden in the Dedication of his Translation of Juvenal terms these
verses by Jonson an *insolent, sparing*, and *invidious panegyrick*. (II.
501)

n another note on these "Poems on Shakespeare" Holt White
·emarks that the four-line poem, "To Shakespeare," which be-
·ins, "Thy Muse's sugred dainties seem to us," was taken from
·ancroft's *Two Books* (II. 517). He went from works such as
·ancroft's to those but lately published, including his brother
·ilbert's *Natural History . . . of Selborne*, for he found there
·latter for the explanation of Friar John's seeking another member
·f his order to "associate" him on his errand to Romeo. "In *The*
·isitatio Notabilis de Seleburne, a curious record printed in *The*
Jatural History and Antiquities of Selborne, Wykeham enjoins
·e canons not to go abroad without leave from the Prior, who is
·rdered on such occasions to assign the brother a companion, *ne*
·uspicio sinistra vel scandelum oriatur. Append. p. 448" (XIV.
41.7).[19] In the *GM* for February 1789 (pp. 145–46) Holt White, in
·e second part of his review of Gilbert's *Natural History and*
·ntiquities of Selborne, selected this *Visitatio* for comment and
·e section on canons wandering without leave for quotation.
Holt White's parallel from *Comus* in Thomas Warton's edition

of Milton's early poetry, not the only such parallel from the
poem in that edition, and his direct reference to "Mr. Warton, i
his excellent edition of Milton's Juvenile Poems" followed b
quotation of three lines from *"in Quintum Novembris"* (XIV
155.6) lead inevitably to a note on the phrase "inland bred" in *A*
You Like It. Holt White had written some remarks, published i
the *GM* for March 1786 (pp. 211–13), on Warton's edition o
Milton's early poems.[20] Among these was one on "the uplan
hamlets" in *L'Allegro*. *"Upland,"* he explained, "means *rude c*
uncultivated, and is used in that sense to this day in Essex
Rustic festivities were antiently held at the borders of forests.
Hence, when he came to Orlando's claim to being "inland bred
Holt White could write that *"Inland* here, and elsewhere in thi
play, is the opposite to *outland*, or *upland*. Orlando means to sa
that he had not been *bred among clowns"* (VI. 63.8). While th
remark in the *GM* has been unnoticed by Miltonists, it is gratify
ing to report that the note on Shakespeare's play is quoted in th
New Variorum edition. Holt White's gloss, incidentally, is born
out by Caldecott in 1832 and by the *OED*.

Holt White of course knew his Bible. He was the second t
recognize Prince Hal's "wisdome cries out in the streets, and n
man regards it" as a conflation of Proverbs 1.20 and 24 (VI
379.6); Zachary Grey had recognized it earlier, but his note di
not get into editions of Shakespeare. And Holt White thought h
detected another biblical echo in *The Tempest* in Prospero's as
surance to Miranda that "not so much perdition as an hair,
Betid to any creature in the vessel," for he queried: "Ha
Shakspeare in his mind St. Paul's consolatory speech to the ship
company, where he assures them that though they were to suffe
shipwreck '*not an hair should fall from the head of any of them*:
Acts, xxvii. 34. Ariel afterwards says, '*Not a hair perish'd*'" (II
13.3). One will look in vain for any note on these lines in the Nev
Variorum edition. The disguised Duke in *Measure for Measur*
tells Escalus that "there is scarce truth enough alive, to mak
societies secure; but security enough, to make fellowships ac
cursed," and Holt White, the first to point to the pun, wrote the
"in excuse of this quibble, Shakspeare may plead higher au
thority.——'He that hateth *suretiship* is sure.' Prov. xi. 15" (IV
309.5).

One last note in 1793 is particularly worth quoting, not simpl
because Holt White took polite issue with Malone but becaus
the subject is of intrinsic interest over and above matters Shake

spearian. Steevens had reprinted Arthur Brooke's long poem *Romeus and Juliet,* and Malone, at a juncture where the poet mentions his "hearers," had written "From these words it should seem that this poem was formerly sung or recited to casual passengers in the streets" adding a reference to another similar line in the poem. Holt White was of a different opinion:

> In former days, when the faculty of reading was by no means so general as at present, it must have been no infrequent practice for those who did not possess this accomplishment to gratify their curiosity by listening while some better educated person read aloud. It is, I think, scarcely probable, that a poem of the length of the *Tragicall History* should be sung or recited in the streets: And Sir John Maundevile at the close of his work intreats "alle the *Rederes* and HERERES of his boke, zif it plese hem that thei wolde preyen to God," & p. 383, 8vo. edit. 1727. By *herers of his boke* he unquestionably meant *hearers* in the sense I have suggested. (XIV. 584. *)

Whatever the right or wrong of the matter, the quotation from Sir John Mandeville is a valuable bit of information.

Evidence of Holt White's continuing interest in Shakespeare exists in the form of two notes posthumously printed in the 1803 edition. He died in 1797; Steevens, in 1800; and Reed completed the edition after Steevens's death. Both notes are on *Othello,* the first is on the verb "trash" in Iago's "If this poor trash of Venice, whom I trash," which Steevens had explained to be "a hunter's phrase, and signifies . . . to fasten a weight on the neck of a dog, when his speed is superior to that of his companions." Holt White added, "That Mr. Steevens has given the true explanation of—to *trash,* is fixed by the succeeding authority from Harington, where it unquestionably means to *impede the progress:* prolongation of magistracy, *trashing the wheel of rotation,* destroys the life or natural motion of a commonwealth.' *Works,* p. 303, fol. 1747" (XIX. 327.9). Othello exclaims to Desdemona, when I love thee not. / Chaos is come again." Steevens gave a parallel from *Venus and Adonis;* Malone, one from "Muretus, a poet of the 16th century." Holt White provided a third: "There is the same thought in Buchanan: 'Cesset amor, pariter cessabunt pedera rerum, / In chaos antiquum cuncta elementa ruent.' Vol. . 400, 1725, 4to" (XIX. 366.2).

Holt White deserves a place, however small, in the history of English scholarship, largely because of his contribution to

Shakespeare studies, partly because of his remarks on Milton's early poems, and partly, too, for his other learned contributions to the GM and to the *Philosophical Transactions of the Royal Society*. And it will not go unremarked that in the small corpus of his notes on Shakespeare he was able to correct some of the errors of the major editors of Shakespeare—Johnson, Steevens, and Malone.

5

Samuel Henley, Translator of *Vathek*

In mid-1786 there appeared *An Arabian Tale, From an Un-published Manuscript: With Notes Critical and Explantory;* so ran the title-page. The half-title proclaimed the book to be *The History of the Caliph Vathek With Notes,* and the editor opted for anonymity. It is well known, of course, that the book was the Reverend Mr. Samuel Henley's translation from the French original of William Beckford and that Beckford had forbidden Henley to publish it. Henley wrote long, learned, and often quite unnecessary notes in explication of the text, and about a half year after the publication of *Vathek* (the convenient title) a correspondent to the GM who signed himself "S.W." criticized one of these notes. Henley had devoted some five and a half pages to the words "a vast wood of palm-trees," quoting Virgil's "Primus Idumaeas referam tibi, Mantua, palmas" from the third *Georgic*. S.W. wrote, "These verses are quoted and commented upon in a late publication, under the name of *Vathek*, p. 269, which, it would seem, has been composed as a text, for the purpose of giving to the publick the information contained in the notes." The letter appeared in the January 1787 number of the *GM* (pp. 55–56); Henley's reply was prompt, appearing in the next month (p. 120). And when Henry James Pye, poet laureate, took it upon himself to correct the various commentators on Shakespeare in his *Coments on the Commentators on Shakespeare*, published in 1807, Henley came in for a lot of attention. When Henley remarked, of Launcelot Gobbo's asking his father's blessing in *The Merchant of Venice*, that "in this conversation between Launcelot and his blind father, there are frequent references to the deception pracsed on the blindness of Isaac, and the blessing obtained in consequence of it," Pye confessed that he could not find those references (p. 69). Pye's confession served as prelude to a more wide-ranging condemnation of Henley's propensity for seeing scriptural references in Shakespeare, for in 1821 James Boswell, the younger, who had completed Malone's edition of Shakespeare, wrote in his Advertisement to that edition, "In a very few instances I have ventured to take the liberty of expunging a note where Shakespeare has, I think, most perversely and injuriously been charged with an irreverent allusion to Scripture. When Proteus, in *Two Gentlemen of Verona*, says to Speed, among many quibbles upon the word sheep, 'Nay, in that you are astray; 'twere best pound you!' what but the very cacoethes of commenting could lead any one to suppose, with Dr. Henley, that the poet had in view the general confession of sins in the liturgy?" (I.viii.). Stephen Weston, the "S.W." of the letter in the *GM*, classical scholar and a contributor to the 1785 Johnson-Steevens *Shakespeare*, and James Boswell, the younger, editor of the Boswell-Malone *Shakespeare*, were in agreement—the Rev. Dr. Samuel Henley wrote too many unnecessary notes.

No definitive study of Henley exists. For present purposes it is enough to say that he was born in 1744, attended a Dissenting Academy, became connected with the University of Cambridge in 1768 and 1769, was a member of the faculty of the College of William and Mary in Virginia from 1770 to 1775, was elected a Fellow of the Society of Antiquaries in 1778, met Beckford in late 1781, published the *Vathek* translation in 1786, did some miscellaneous writing, and died in 1815. What is important for this study is the fact that there are some one hundred notes by him in Malone's *Supplement* to the 1778 *Shakespeare*. Malone's two-volume *Supplement* was published in 1780, two years after Henley had been admitted into the Society of Antiquaries and only five years after he had returned from Virginia. Henley knew Michael Lort as early as his Cambridge years, corresponded with Bishop Percy and Daines Barrington while in Virginia, and was nominated for the Society of Antiquaries by Lort, Richard Farmer, and Benjamin Heath. He was the intimate friend of Michael Tyson, antiquary and artist of Corpus Christi College Cambridge,[1] and he was the brother-in-law of John Henderson the actor. Henderson had married a daughter of Thomas Figgins Esq. of Chippenham, Wiltshire in 1779; Henley married a sister of Henderson's wife in 1780. He dined in the company of Isaac Reed a few times between 1780 and 1790, although in his four appearances in Reed's Diary he never coincided with Malone, Farmer, or Steevens, being three of the four times in the company of Henderson. Steevens had been a Fellow of the Society of Antiquaries since 1767; Malone became a Fellow much later, in 1793. Henley, it is obvious, was well connected in the Cambridge-London intellectual life of the late eighteenth century by 1780, the year of publication of Malone's *Supplement*.

At some time before 15 September 1777 Henley sent Steevens a drawing that the latter acknowledged in the following very informative letter.

Hampstead Heath
Sept. 15, 1777

Sir,

I return you my best and earliest thanks for your favour, which I received this morning from Mr. Hamilton.[2] The drawing came most opportunely, as I am printing off one of the prefaces, at the end of which I had quoted a chapter from a satirical pamphlet called the *Gull's Hornbook*, written by Decker, a contemporary with Shakespeare. We learn from it "How a Gallant should behave himself in a Playhouse"; and indeed so satisfactory a peep behind the curtain of one of our antient theatres I had despaired to meet with. To this chapter your drawing will be appositely subjoined. I have already delivered it to an artist famous for cutting in wood (as there was not time for engraving) and in a few days will not fail to return you the original.

We have avoided printing any copies of Shakespeare on large paper, as it would have been impossible to have made a beautiful book of the present edition, on account of the unequal distribution of notes and text. The booksellers have some thought of reprinting it hereafter in quarto, and with very fine engraving. Should this scheme take place, the commentary (of which at present there is too great a load) shall be abridged and thrown to the end of each volume.

I am, Sir, with many thanks for your favour, your most obliged & obedient humble sert.
Geo. Steevens

I know not when our present edition, which will not be ready before Christmas, is to be published. I am obliged to hasten it on account of the expected death of a near relation, which when it happens cannot fail to encumber me with a very tedious & troublesome executorship.

teevens obviously wasted no time having a woodcut made of ae drawing, for three days later he wrote to Henley again, this me confining himself to a single sentence: "Mr. Steevens takes is opportunity to repeat his thanks to Mr. Henley for the use of e enclosed drawing, and has sent him a proof or two of the ooden cut that has been made from it." The drawing in question appears in the first volume of the 1778 *Shakespeare* (p. 85) llowing the extract from Dekker's *Gull's Hornbook*, and shows he Globe on the Bancke Side where Shakespeare acted. From e long Antwerp View of London in the Pepysian Library." eevens acknowledged that "with the drawing from which this t was made I was favoured by the Reverend Mr. Henley, of

Harrow on the Hill." Henley was then an assistant-master at Harrow School, and it is perhaps because of his continuing to spend much of his time at Harrow, even after receiving a living elsewhere, that he remained outside the immediate Steevens-Malone circle.

The next public notice of Henley's interest in Shakespeare came in the GM for January 1780 (pp. 21–22). "Mr. Urban," "S.H." wrote, "I am happy to hear that Mr. Steevens and Mr. Malone, to whom the public is already so much indebted for their notes on Shakespeare, are continuing their illustrations of this incomparable author. On what plan their supplemental observations are to be published, I am not informed; but if any of the following remarks, or such others as I have incidentally made, should appear to be worthy of their notice, they are very much at their service." Despite his wide acquaintance in London, this is further evidence that Henley did not know Steevens or Malone personally. On February 10, either immediately after the GM for January appeared or possibly even before, Malone wrote to Henley from his home in Queen Anne Street East.

> Sir,
>   I had the favour of your letter by yesterday's post. If you can revise the papers which you are so obliging as to promise me, by the first of next month, it will be as early as I could make use of them; having yet a few sheets of each of my volumes to print; but I should be glad if it should suit your convenience to have them by that time. When you transmit the notes to me, I request you will inform me whether I am at liberty to assign your name to them.

Henley obviously gave permission for his name to be assigned to his notes; equally obviously he had "incidentally" made a number of remarks on Shakespeare far in excess of the six on *Measure for Measure* and the one on *Much Ado about Nothing* which he had sent to the GM. For Malone not only printed verbatim the seven remarks and the footnote that accompanied the last but also included nearly a hundred more notes by Henley.

Fifty-seven of Henley's notes in Malone's *Supplement* were omitted from the next edition of Shakespeare, that edited by Reed in 1785. If Henley's pride was hurt, the blow to it must have been softened by Reed's acceptance of thirty-three new notes. And either Henley was too busy to contribute substantially to Malone's edition in 1790 or Malone was less cordial, for there are only eight new notes by Henley, and three of these were printed in the Appendix to the last volume of that edition. Steevens's own edition of Shakespeare was published in 1793; Henley contributed almost two hundred new notes to it, a startling number in view of Steevens's occasional sharp comments on Henley's disagreements with his own notes. Thus, Steevens could write of him "But perhaps the critick (with a flippancy in which he has sometimes indulged himself at my expense) will reply, like Pistol, 'Why then lament therefore;' or observe, like Hamlet, that 'a knavish speech sleeps in a foolish ear'" (VI. 197.3). Perhaps the following exchange will serve best to show how Steevens and Henley went at it hammer and tongs. Antony cries out to the messenger from Rome, "O, then we bring forth weeds, / When our quick winds lie still, and our ills told us, / Is as our earing." Warburton emended to "quick minds," Sir William Blackstone suspected that "quick winds is, or is a corruption of, some provincial word, signifying either arable lands, or the instruments of husbandry used in the tilling of them," and Steevens, approving of Blackstone's conjecture, wrote a seemingly well-informed note on "wind-rows," which word he managed to ring in somehow. Part of Henley's note reads, "Mr. Steevens's description of wind-rows will gain him, I fear, but little reputation with the husbandman; nor, were it more accurate, does it appear to be in point, unless it can be shown that quick winds and wind-rows are synonymous; and, further, that his interpretation will suit with the context." He concluded by stating that "when the quick winds lie still, that is, in a mild winter, those weeds which 'the tyrannous breathings of the north' would have cut off, will continue to grow and feed, to the no small detriment of the crop to follow." Steevens, in whose edition this appeared, naturally had the last word.

> Whether my definition of winds or wind-rows be exact or erroneous, in justice to myself I must inform Mr. Henley that I received it from an Essex farmer; observing at the same time, that in different counties the same terms are differently applied. Mr. Henley is not apt to suspect there is any thing which, at a single glance, he does not perfectly understand, and therefore his remarks are ushered in with as little diffidence as can well be expressed. For one piece of knowledge, however, (in common with the rest of the world) I shall think myself still further obliged to him. Will he be kind enough to tell us what sort of winds they are which cut off the weeds and spare the flowers, destroy the noxious but leave the salutary plants without an injury? The winter of 1788–9 was as hard a one as has been hitherto

remembered; but I could not discover by my own attention, or fro
the report of others, that the garden or the field had one weed the le
for its severity. Let me do justice, however, to the general turn of M
Henley's note, which is very ingenious, and perhaps is right. (X
424.5)

One must at the very least applaud Steevens's decision to incluc
Henley's note.

Steevens died in January 1800; in August of that year Henle
wrote a letter to Bishop Percy which John Nichols reprinted i
his *Illustrations of Literature*. "My Lord," Henley wrote, and
have condensed his letter,

> I am much mortified that I have been prevented by unavoidab
> business from waiting upon your Lordship, and communicating
> person what I now transmit by letter. This, however, I trust will be
> time.
> "The passages I referred to, in which Mr. Steevens, from pique
> me, altered the last edition of his Shakespeare, are, (Tempest, Act
> Sc. 1):—
> " 'The *peonied* and lillied brims,' for *pioned* and *twilled*.
> "Macbeth, Act 3, Sc. 4:— 'if trembling I *inhabit*,' changed again
> the nonsense '*inhibit*.'
> "There are other things, had I his edition by me, which I cou
> point out, but the only one in general besides that I remember is tl
> putting poor Amner's name to his own obscene notes." (VIII. 334–3

Here, seven years after the 1793 *Shakespeare* and less than a yea
after Steevens's death, is further evidence of the acrimoniou
relationship between the two men, Henley obviously not inte
ested in speaking only good of the dead.

Back, however, to Henley's notes in Malone's *Supplement*. A
one who had fairly recently come back from a five-year sojourn i
America, Henley must have felt himself something of an expe
on *The Tempest*. His first note, not thereafter reprinted in tl
editions under study here, was of a general and introducto
nature.

> Whatever might have suggested to Shakspeare the fable of this dram
> it is obvious to remark that he frequently refers in it to the la
> discoveries made in America, and the adventures thither, which
> many engaged in from the hopes of inordinate gain. The absu
> stories brought from thence by those who had been thither, co
> cerning the country, its natives, and praeternatural inhabitants, ga
> ample scope to the poet for displaying a system of magick ar

daemonology, happily adapted to the popular belief of his time; and also for ridiculing that boundless credulity and avarice, which then so generally prevailed.[3]

He stated categorically that "*Setebos*, the god of Caliban's dam, was an American devil, worshipped by the giants of Patagonia" (p. 683) and saw a reference "to the productions lately imported from America" in "the dead Indian" and "this is no fish but an islander." He concluded that these "point out, in the person of Caliban, of what kind the inhabitants of that country were pretended to be" (p. 684). But, as has been seen, Henley most offended in insisting on a scriptural source for passages in the plays. There were eleven such notes among the one hundred; two have been thought to have some merit. Jessica, Shylock's daughter, says "I shall be saved by my husband," and Henley wrote "From St. Paul: 'The unbelieving wife is sanctified by the husband.' " And when Shylock cries out, "My deeds upon my head," Henley declared the outcry "an imprecation adopted from that of the Jews to Pilate: 'His blood be on us, and our children.' "[4]

Not many of Henley's notes in Malone's *Supplement* found favor with the editors of the New Variorum volumes or those of the New Arden series. An interesting conjecture on Camillo's "shook hands, as over a vast: and embrac'd, as it were, from the ends of opposed winds" in *The Winter's Tale* is summarized and partly quoted. The full note reads,

Shakspeare has, more than once, taken his imagery from the prints, with which the books of his time were ornamented. If my memory do not deceive me, he had his eye on a wood cut in Holinshed, while writing the incantation of the weird sisters in *Macbeth*. There is also an allusion to a print of one of the Henries holding a sword adorned with crowns. In this passage he refers to a device common in the title-pages of old books, of two hands extended from opposite clouds, and joined as in token of friendship. (p. 702)

Henley's allusion to "one of the Henries" may be to Henry V, for in the Chorus of act II of Shakespeare's play there is reference made to such a sword, but the monarch in question is probably Edward III.[5] Oddly enough, the New Variorum attributes to "Anonymous" Henley's note on Macbeth's "Besides, this Duncan Hath borne his faculties so meek," a note which captures a bit of stage history, for Henley wrote that "as Mr. [John] Henderson speaks this speech these lines should be thus pointed: '*Besides* this; Duncan, etc.' " (p. 705). Henley protested to Bishop Percy that in 1793 Steevens had taken liberties with some of his notes, among them Macbeth's "If trembling I inhabit." The New Variorum quotes Henley's note on this passage, but in a later version than that in Malone's *Supplement* and hence omits Henley's rather mawkish name-dropping. He wrote that "the best *living commentator* on Shakspeare had acutely conjectured that the poet might have written—*if trembling* I EXHIBIT (i.e. *if I discover fear*), but acquiesced in the interpretation I have given" (p. 706). David Garrick had died in 1779, and I believe Henley was referring to his brother-in-law, John Henderson, as the best "*living commentator*" on Shakespeare.

A few of Henley's notes in Malone's *Supplement* deserve more attention than they have received. Alonso, in *The Tempest*, says "there is in this business, more than nature / Was ever conduct of," and Henley, remembering his stay in Cambridge, wrote: "*Conduct* is yet used in the same sense: the person at Cambridge who reads prayers in King's and in Trinity College chapels, is still so styled" (p. 685). He was the first to remark on this meaning of the word. And he was also first to point out that "peer out, peer out" in *Two Gentlemen of Verona* was a reference "to the practice of children, when they call on a snail to push forth his horns: Peer out, peer out, peer out of your hole, / Or else I beat you black as a coal" (p.688). Twice he adduced parallels from *The Two Noble Kinsmen*. One (p. 704) is "white as the fann'd snow, / That's bolted by the northern blasts" of *The Winter's Tale*, the parallel passage being "white *as wind-fann'd snow*." The other parallel spoken by a Doctor, "I think she has a perturbed mind, which cannot minister to," is to Macbeth's anguished question, "Canst thou not minister to a mind diseas'd?" (p. 708). Both notes are of more than cursory interest, since the shares of Shakespeare and Fletcher in *The Two Noble Kinsmen* are, in Professor Kittredge's words, "beyond the scope of sane criticism." It is another indication of the neglect of this body of notes that the editor of the New Variorum *Macbeth* gives Verity credit for the parallel from *The Two Noble Kinsmen*.

The matter of the authorship of *The Two Noble Kinsmen* is worth a slight digression. George Steevens, in Malone's *Supplement*, advanced the theory that the play was entirely by Fletcher and adduced thirty-eight parallels between it and fifteen plays of the accepted Shakespeare canon. He listed the parallel to Macbeth's "Canst thou not minister to a mind diseas'd," which Henley had also pointed out independently. Steevens's argument was part of his long end-note on *Pericles* in the second volume

e *Supplement,* while all Henley's notes were in an appendix at
e end of the second volume. Given the lateness of Henley's
ntributions to the *Supplement* and the absence of any evince to indicate that he had seen any part of the two volumes,
e must assume his ignorance of Steevens's list of parallels.
hat is more, Steevens does not list the *Winter's Tale* parallel
ted by Henley nor two others by him. Henley thought of
"aidenhearted, a husband I have *pointed*" in *The Two Noble*
nsmen as a parallel to Macbeth, "Old Siward, with ten thou-
nd war like men, / All ready at a *point*" (p. 706) and of "quit me
these cold gyves" in the former play as a parallel to "cancel
ese *cold bonds*" in *Cymbeline* (p. 711). Possibly Steevens knew
Henley's contributions and thought his parallels worthless,
t it is more probable, since two of Henley's parallels are as
ose as many in his list, that he was unaware of them. In any
ent, Steevens's argument is given respectful attention by one of
e most recent scholars to reopen the question of authorship;
nley is never mentioned.[6] It is most interesting to note that
nley's parallels from *The Two Noble Kinsmen* are drawn from
.i., IV.iii, and two from V.i. Two of these scenes are commonly
ributed to Shakespeare, while the third (IV.iii) is doubtful but
o usually given to him.[7]

Henley explained a reference to "magot-pies" in *Macbeth* as
lows:

The magpie is called in the west to this hour, a *magatipie,* and the
import of the augury is determined by the number of these birds that
are seen together: "One for sorrow: Two for mirth: Three for a wedding: Four for death." It is very observable that in the unfrequented
villages of Devonshire, not only a greater part of the customs to which
Shakspeare alludes, but also most of his colloquial phrases and
expressions, are still in common use. (p. 706)

nley was born in Abbots Kerswell, Devonshire, and presum-
ly wrote with some authority.[8] He quoted a close parallel to the
al-by-fire passage at the end of *The Merry Wives of Windsor*
m Fletcher's *The Faithful Shepherdess* (p. 689);[9] the New
den editor gives credit to H. C. Hart, the editor of the first
den edition, for this parallel. Henley believed that "perhaps
ere is no character through all Shakspeare, drawn with more
irit, and just discrimination, than Shylock's. His language,
usion, and ideas, are every where so appropriate to a Jew, that
ylock might be exhibited as an examplar of that peculiar

people" (p. 699). One play that Henley had much in mind was George Chapman's *Bussy d'Ambois*, invoking it for a note on *The Merry Wives of Windsor* (p. 689) and for one on *The Merchant of Venice* (p. 699). And he was evidently struck with resemblances between *Macbeth* and Chapman's play, seeing a parallel to Lady MacBeth's soliloquy, "Come, you spirits / That tend on mortal thoughts" in Chapman's play (pp. 704–5). And for Lennox's question to Macbeth in the banquet scene, "What is't that moves your highness?," he was able to produce another parallel from *Bussy d'Ambois*, prefacing it with the remark that "there are many instances of resemblance between the two dramas of *Macbeth* and *Bussy d'Ambois*, particularly in this scene, and it is but justice to acknowledge, that Chapman's tragedy appears to be the elder" (pp. 705–6). Perhaps these resemblances do exist, but there is no mention, among other works, of Chapman in Henry N. Paul's thorough study of *Macbeth*.[10]

Although Reed omitted fifty-seven of Henley's notes in the 1785 *Shakespeare*, he also printed thirty-three new ones. Henley's contributions to Malone's *Supplement* had been limited to relatively few plays, but in 1785 he repaired some of these omissions by remarks on *A Midsummer Night's Dream*, *All's Well That Ends Well*, *King John*, *Richard II*, *1* and *2 Henry IV* (eight notes on the latter), *Henry V*, *Antony and Cleopatra*, and *King Lear*. As might be expected, some of the interests discernible in the 1780 notes form the bases for the 1785 notes. The King of France says to Bertram in *All's Well*, "I am not a day of season, For thou may'st see a sun-shine and a hail / In me at once," and this reminds Henley of his stay in Virginia, for he writes, of "a day of season," "That is of *uninterrupted rain*. The word is used in the same sense in Virginia,[11] in which government, and especially on the eastern shore of it, where the descendants of the first settlers have been less mixed with later emigrants, many expressions of Shakspeare's time are still current" (IV. 140.3 Coupled with knowledge of things American is Henley's knowledge of his native Devonshire and the west of England. Davy offers a "dish of leather-coats" in *2 Henry IV*; Henley explains that "the apple commonly denominated russetine in Devonshire is called the *buffcoat*" (V. 632.9). Reference to "that brake" in *A Midsummer Night's Dream* results in a note to the effect that "brake, in the west of England, is used to express a large extent of ground over-grown with furze, and appears both here and in the next scene to convey the same idea" (III. 64.3). Difference of opinion still exists on the precise sense of "brake" in these passages. Sergeant Phang, in *2 Henry IV*, hopes fervently to "fis

Falstaff just once, if he come but within his "vice." Henley noted that "the *fist* is vulgarly called the *vice* in the West of England" (V. 499.1).

Henley's contributions to the 1785 *Shakespeare* have received more attention from the editors of the New Variorum volumes than his notes in Malone's *Supplement*. The following notes are quoted wholly or in part in the New Variorum edition. "Paved fountain" in *A Midsummer Night's Dream* is thus explained: "The epithet seems here intended to mean no more than that the beds of these fountains were covered with peebles [sic] in opposition to those of the rushy brooks which are oozy" (III. 34.5). King Philip of France asks Cardinal Pandulpho in *King John*, "And shall these hands so lately purg'd of blood, / So newly join'd in love, so strong in both, / Unyoke this seizure, and this kind regreet?" and Johnson believed the meaning to be "*love so strong in both* parties." But Henley's explanation, "Rather, in *hatred* and in *love*; in deeds of *blood* or *amity*" (V. 67.5), was favored by the New Variorum editor over Johnson's and other interpretations (p. 214). The Earl of Westmorland tells Henry IV that the Earl of Worcester is "malevolent to you in all aspects," and it remained for Henley to remark this as "an astrological allusion. Worcester is here represented as a malignant star that influenced the conduct of Hotspur" (V. 275.8). Morton, in *2 Henry IV*, echoes Worcester's warning to Hotspur in *1 Henry IV*, and Henley caught the echo, but his contemporaries thought so little of the note that they did not reprint it.[12] Falstaff's tirade against master Dombledon the tailor for not accepting Bardolph as assurance of payment begins, "Let him be damn'd like a glutton! may his tongue be hotter!" Henley saw this as "an allusion to the fate of the rich man [Luke xvi. 24]who had fared sumptuously every day, when he requested a drop of water to cool his tongue being tormented with the flames" (V. 482.2). Much has been made, and properly so, of Falstaff's knowledge of scripture; Henley's notes helped to establish the fact of that knowledge. His emendation of Lord Bardolph's "if this present quality of war, / Indeed the instant action" to "Induc'd the instant action" in *2 Henry IV* (V. 495.4), "although never actually adopted, has met with the most favor," according to the New Variorum editor (p. 94).

The first sentence of Henley's note on "the gilded puddle" from which Antony is said to have drunk is the only note on those words in the New Variorum. Henley wrote that "there is frequently observable on the surface of stagnant pools that have remained long undisturbed, a reddish gold coloured slime: to

this appearance the poet there refers" (VIII. 160.1), adding
conjecture on Lady Macbeth's "I'll gild the faces of his groom
withal," which it is no disservice to him to ignore. Another not
on King Lear, is quoted, however, of which Henley need not hav
been ashamed. Cordelia describes Lear as this "child-change
father." Henley explained that "Lear is become insane, and this
the change referred to. Insanity is not the property of secon
childhood, but dotage. Consonant to this explanation is wh
Cordelia almost immediately adds:

> O my dear father! restoration hang
> Thy medicine on my lips; and let this kiss
> Repair those violent harms, that my two sisters
> Have in thy reverence made!"
>
> (IX. 575.

One of Henley's notes that should have been quoted in the Ne
Variorum 1 Henry IV, especially as there is no note on the word
is that on Hotspur's "three times did they drink," part of h
description of the combat between Mortimer and Glendower:

> It is the property of wounds to excite the most impatient thirst, tl
> poet therefore hath with exquisite propriety introduced this circur
> stance, which may serve to place in its proper light the dying kin
> ness of Sir Philip Sydney; who, though suffering the extremity
> thirst from the agony of his own wounds, yet, notwithstanding, ga
> up his own draught of water to a wounded soldier. (V. 299.9)

Another serious omission is the failure of the editor of the Ne
Variorum Winter's Tale to remark Henley's note on Leonte:
declaration that "calumny will sear / Virtue itself," again e
pecially since there is no note on those lines therein. Henle
wrote, "That is, will stigmatize or brand it as infamous. So, :
All's Well that Ends Well: 'My maiden's name sear'd / Othe
wise'" (IV. 332.6). OED gives one definition of "to sear" as "1
brand, to stigmatize" and quotes the lines from All's Well, almo
as though its source had been Henley's note.[13]

It will be recalled that Henley wrote of "the exquisite pr
priety" with which Shakespeare introduced the circumstance
Mortimer and Glendower being forced to drink three times du
ing their combat. He saw much, too, to admire in the Countess
Rousillon's question to Helena, "What's the matter, / That th
distemper'd messenger of wet, / The many-colour'd Iris, rour
thine eye?" for he wrote of the passage that "there is somethii

exquisitely beautiful in this representation of that suffusion of colours which glimmers around the sight when the eye-lashes are wet with tears. The poet hath described the same appearance in his *Rape of Lucrece:*

> And round about her tear distained eye
> Blue circles stream'd like rain-bows in the sky."

(IV. 35.3)

Henley expressed his appreciation of Shakespeare's artistry in one other note in 1785. The passage is part of the scene in which Cleopatra asks for details of Octavia's appearance, including the command that she be told the color of her hair.

> This is one of Shakspeare's masterly touches. Cleopatra, after bidding Charmian to enquire of the messenger concerning the beauty, age, and temperament of Octavia, immediately adds, *let him not leave out the colour of her hair;* as from thence she might be able to judge for herself, of her rival's propensity to those pleasures upon which her passion for Antony was founded. (VIII. 199.5)

One other note, a fine example of explication, deserves full quotation. It is Henley's explanation of Richard II's

> For now hath time made me his numb'ring clock:
> My thoughts are minutes; and, with sighs they jar
> Their watches to mine eyes, the outward watch,
> Whereto my fingers, like a dial's point,
> In pointing still, in cleansing them from tears.
> Now sir, the sound, that tells what hour it is,
> Are clamorous groans, that strike upon my heart,
> Which is the bell: So sighs, tears, and groans,
> Show minutes, times, and hours.

Johnson had given various readings from the quartos and first folio, but had thrown up his hands in helplessness. Henley wrote,

> There appears to be no reason for supposing with Dr. Johnson, that this passage is corrupt. It should be recollected, that there are three ways in which a clock notices the progress of time, viz. by the libration of the pendulum, the index on the dial, and the striking of the hour. To these, the king, in his comparison, severally alludes; his sighs corresponding to the jarring of the pendulum, which, at the same time that it watches or numbers the seconds, marks also their

progress in minutes on the dial or outward watch, to which the king compares his eyes, and their want of figures, is supplied by a succession of tears, or (to use an expression of Milton) *minute drops:* his finger, by as regularly wiping these away, performs the office of the dial's point: his clamorous groans, are the sounds that tell the hour.

In Henry IV. P. II. Tears are used in a similar manner:

> "But Harry lives, that shall convert those *tears,*
> By number, into *hours* of happiness." (V. 257.3)

Edmond Malone printed eight new notes by Henley in his 1790 *Shakespeare*, chary of giving too much space to others and also practicing a somewhat greater degree of selectivity than he had in his *Supplement* a decade earlier. In the event, as far as Henley's few notes are concerned, he selected well, for three of the notes and a later revision of a fourth are quoted in the New Variorum series. Cordelia tells her sisters that "Who covers faults, at least shame them derides, / Well may you prosper," and Henley, ever alert for scriptural parallels, recognized this as an allusion to Proverbs xxviii. 13, "He that *covereth* his sins, shall not *prosper*" (VII. 504.8). Ophelia, in her distribution of flowers, offers a daisy, and Henley quoted Robert Green's *Quip for an upstart Courtier* for the significance of this flower, i.e., "Next them grew the DISSEMBLING DAISIE, to warne such light-of-love wenches not to trust every faire promise that such amorous bachelors make them" (IX.371.2),[14] a note that has preëminence over two others in the New Variorum edition. Part of his subsequently revised note on Cassio as "A fellow almost damn'd in a fair wife," a famous crux in *Othello*, is quoted (IX. 442.6), as well as the whole of his note on Cassio's "my hopes, not surfeited to death, / Stand in bold cure." For the latter note he had recourse to the Bible again: "I believe that Solomon upon this occasion will be found the best interpreter: *Hope deferred maketh the heart sick*'" (IX. 495.5), another of the Proverbs (xiii. 12).

Henley continued to find scriptural parallels or allusions, two of his notes in the Appendix to the tenth volume of Malone's edition further exhibiting his fondness for this activity. The first of these is on Angelo's "Shall we desire to raze the sanctuary, / and pitch our evils there" in *Measure for Measure*. Both Steevens and Malone produced passages to show that "evils" meant "excrement," but Henley was moved to remark that "no language could more forcefully express the aggravated profligacy of Angelo's passion, which the purity of Isabella served but the more to inflame," adding that "the desecration of edifices devoted to religion, by converting them to the most abject purposes of nature, was an eastern method of expressing contempt. See 2 Kings, X. 27" (p. 563). The second of these notes is on Helena's "When miracles by the greatest have been deny'd" in *All's Well*. Henley, whose note I do not quote in full, saw this as a reference to the Elders of Israel who, despite the miracles performed on their behalf, "refused that compliance they ought to have yielded. See the book of Exodus, and particularly ch. xvii. 5, 6, etc." (p. 595). Possibly as a result of Henley's note Malone added, "See also Psalm lxxviii. 13, etc. and Psalm cvi., St. Matthew's Gospel, xi. 21, and St. Luke's Gospel, vii. 30," for this once, at least, beating Henley at his own game. In his third note, in the Appendix, Henley explained that the King of France's statement that he had "both sovereign power and father's voice" over the young bachelors he presents for Helena's choice meant that "they were his *wards*, as well as his subjects" (p. 595). The last of his notes in 1790 was on "hey no nonny." Steevens had quoted two songs with the same refrain, and Henley commented,

> It is observable that the two songs to which Mr. Steevens refers for the burden of *Hey no nonny*, are both sung by girls distracted from disappointed love. The meaning of the burden may be inferred from what follows: Drayton's *Shepherd's Garland*, 1593, 4to.

> > 'Who have ever heard thy pipe and pleasing vaine,
> > And both but heare this scurrill minstralcy,
> > These *noninos* of filthie ribauldry,
> > That doth not muse."

> Again, in White's *Wit of a Woman*:

> > "—these *dauncers sometimes do teach them trickes above trenchmore, yea and sometimes such lavoltas, that they mount so high, that you may see their hey nony, nony, nony, no."* (VIII. 592.6)

Obviously the Reverend Mr. Samuel Henley was conversant with areas of literature far removed from the scriptural. The reference to White's *Wit of a Woman* is to an anonymous comedy of 1604, printed for Edward White.

Despite their differences of opinion on the interpretation of a number of passages in Shakespeare, Henley and Steevens either met and discussed the plays or corresponded about them, for in at least twelve of Steevens's notes in the 1793 *Shakespeare* he states that Mr. Henley observes, supposes, explains, or says thus and so. It is clear, too, that Steevens was allowing Henley to see his, Steevens's, reactions to his notes and giving him opportunity to reply to them. The relationship seems to have been that of an uneasy armed truce with occasional border skirmishes. Henley, it may be recalled, complained to Bishop Percy in 1800 that Steevens altered the "pioned and twilled brims" of The Tempest to "peonied and lillied brims" (see above, p. 114). Steevens wrote a long note justifying his reading of "lillied" ("peonied" was Sir Thomas Hanmer's emendation), and Henley wrote one twice as long in defense of the old reading. Steevens thereupon countered with a rejoinder longer than his original note, the first sentence of which reads, "Mr. Henley's note contends for small proprieties, and abounds with minute observations," and which concludes, "Unconvinced therefore by his [Henley's] strictures, I shall not exclude a border of flowers to make room for the graces of the spade, or what Mr. Pope, in his Dunciad, has styled—'the majesty of mud'" (III. 118.7). Almost the entire exchange can be read in the New Variorum Tempest (p. 196) where Alexander Dyce is quoted as pronouncing Henley "the most provoking of all the editors on Shakespeare" but also where Horace Furness calls Henley's note "the best" he ever wrote. It should also be pointed out that there was the occasional begrudging civility on Steevens's part. John Monck Mason had taken issue with Steevens's note on "the green'ey'd monster" in Othello, and Henley had come to Steevens's support, whereupon the latter added, "I think myself particularly indebted to Mr. Henley for the support he has given to my sentiments concerning this difficult passage; and shall place more confidence in them since they have been found to deserve his approbation, a circumstance in which I have not always proved so fortunate" (XV. 520.6). Even Steevens's compliments were barbed.

With the 1793 Shakespeare notes Henley had contributed at least one note on every play in the Shakespeare canon except Twelfth Night and Pericles. He continued to see Scriptural parallels and sources in Shakespeare's plays and he continued to explain various words and phrases by recourse to the language of Devonshire and the West of England. Some of his other attempts to see Scripture in the plays have found some favor; others, pretty farfetched, have wisely been ignored. An example of the latter is his note on the phrase "the wide vessel of the universe" in the Chorus to act IV of Henry V. "Shakespeare in another play," he wrote, "styles night the blanket of the dark: it is probable that the affinity between *blanket* and *sheet* suggested to him the further relation between *sheet* and *vessel*, which occurs in the *Acts*, ch. x. v. ii.: 'and saw heaven opened, and a certain *vessel* descending unto him, as if it had been a *great* SHEET, *knit at the four corners, and let down unto the earth*'" (IX. 397.8). This is Henley at his worst. But perhaps enough has been made of this aspect of his commentary, although the record should be set straight on one other note. Lord Bardolph, in *2 Henry IV*, has a long speech involving an elaborate comparison, beginning "When we mean to build, / We first survey the plot, then draw the model," which, it was pointed out in *Notes and Queries* in 1853 (quoted in the New Variorum edition, p. 95), is very close to Luke xiv. 28–30. In 1793 Henley wrote, "whoever compares the rest of this speech with St. Luke xiv. 28 etc. will find the former to have been wrought out of the latter" (IX. 44.5).[15]

Not only did Henley locate certain of Shakespeare's words and phrases in his (Henley's) native Devonshire, but he also located others in Cheshire and in Suffolk, having had a living in Rendlesham in Suffolk. "No phrase," he wrote, "is so common in the eastern countries of this kingdom, and particularly in Suffolk, as *good tightly*, for *briskly and effectually*," and "*For the nonce* is an expression in daily use amongst the common people in Suffolk, to signify *on purpose; for the turn*."[16] His explanation of "with good life" in *The Tempest* that "to do any thing with *good life*, is still a provincial expression in the West of England, and signifies, to do it *with the full bent and energy of mind*" (III. 111.5) is quoted in the New Variorum edition. The disguised Duke in *Measure for Measure* states that "the strong statutes / Stand like the forfeits in a barber's shop, / As much in mock as mark," a reference to a list of penalties for patrons who idly handled the barber's surgical tools. Henley called upon personal experience to corroborate Warburton's explanation: "These forfeits were as much in *mock* as *mark*, both because the barber had no authority of himself to enforce them, and also as they were of a ludicrous nature. I perfectly remember to have seen them in Devonshire (printed like Charles's Rules,) though I cannot recollect their contents" (IV. 373.3). He knew that Dr. Samuel Musgrave, who explained that "asinego" in *Troilus and Cressida* was Portuguese for a *little ass*," was of Devonshire, writing that "Dr. Musgrave might have added, that, in his native county [Musgrave was born in Washfield, Devonshire], it is the vulgar name for an *ass* at present" (XI. 276.3). Edmund's "queazy question" in *King Lear* reminded Henley that "*queazy* is still used in Devonshire, to express that sickness of stomach which the slightest disgust is apt to provoke" (XIV. 81.5). And Hamlet's disgust at an "enseamed bed" similarly reminded him that "in the West of England, the *inside fat* of a goose, when dissolved by heat, is called its *seam*; and Shakspeare has used the word in the same sense in his *Troilus and Cressida:* 'shall the proud lord, / That bastes his arrogance with his own *seam*" (XV. 231.9). Many years earlier London-born Lewis Theobald had remarked that "*seam* is properly the fat or grease of a hog. It is used in *Troilus and Cressida*," referring to the same passage quoted by Henley.[17]

Henley explained that the reference to "bruising irons" in *Richard III* was an allusion to "the ancient mace" (X. 674.4) where the New Variorum is content with a parallel from Psalm ii. 9 "thou shalt bruise them with an iron rod." Again, perhaps Steevens's acid note, "I do not perceive how this explanation . . . will accord with Timon's train of reasoning; yet the antiquary may perhaps derive satisfaction from that which affords no assistance to the commentator," has diverted attention from Henley's conjecture, for it is no more than that, about Timon's "Be whores still" and "be no turncoats." He stated that "by an old statute, those women who lived in a state of prostitution, were, among other articles concerning their dress, enjoined to wear their garments, with the *wrong-side outward*, on pain of forfeiting them," adding the tentative "perhaps there is in this passage a reference to this" (XI. 599.8). Steevens sneered but offered no explanation of his own. More than one commentator paralleled Brutus's "take thought, and die for Caesar" to Enobarbus's "Think and die" in *Antony and Cleopatra*. Henley quite properly quoted *St. Matthew,* "Take no thought for the morrow" in his note on the passage in *Julius Caesar* (XII. 286.7), but his note is ignored, although the New Variorum editor cites his own note, quoting *St. Matthew,* on Enobarbus's words.

Two of Henley's notes on *Richard II* also deserve a place in the commentary on that play. Bushy speaks to the Queen:

> Each substance of a grief hath twenty shadows,
> Which show like grief itself, but are not so:
> For sorrow's eye, glazed with blinding tears,
> Divides one thing entire to many objects;
> Like perspectives, which, rightly gaz'd upon,
> Show nothing but confusion; ey'd awry,
> Distinguish form——

The editor of the New Arden *Richard II* states that Bushy seems to be thinking of one kind of perspective, i.e., the "multiplying glass cut into a number of facets each giving a separate image," a definition taken from F. L. Lucas's edition of the *Works of John Webster*. But Henley had noted this years before:

> The *perspectives* here mentioned, were not pictures, but round chrystal glasses, the convex surface of which was cut into faces, like those of the rose-diamond; the concave left uniformly smooth. These chrystals—which were sometimes mounted on tortoise-shell box lids, and sometimes fixed into ivory cases—if placed as here represented, would exhibit the different appearances described by the poet.
>
> The word *shadows* is here used, in opposition to substance, for reflected images, and not as the dark forms of bodies, occasioned by their interception of the light that falls upon them. (VIII. 247.9)

The explanation of "perspective" is much more detailed and technical than that in the *OED*; that of "shadows" anticipates the *OED*, "A reflected image" (5a).

When Dr. Johnson was confronted with the word "coffin" in the last act of *Titus Andronicus*, he correctly defined it as "the term of art for the cavity of a raised pye," but he failed to see a possible quibble on the word in Lear's Fool's example of the cockney that put the eels in "the paste alive." Johnson's note on the Fool's words reads simply, "hinting that the eel and Lear are in the same danger," whereas Henley asserted that "this reference is not sufficiently explained.—The *paste, or crust of a pie,* in Shakspeare's time was called a coffin" (XIV. 122.6), a definition corroborated by the *OED*, with illustrations from *Titus Andronicus* and *King Lear*. Finally, Henley's explanation of the following lines in *Measure for Measure* seems eminently plausible but is ignored. The Duke utters a choruslike speech at the end of act IV which contains the lines "Twice treble shame on Angelo, / To weed my vice and let his grow!" Malone had written that "*my,* does not . . . relate to the Duke in particular, who had not been guilty of any vice, but to any indefinite person. . . . The speaker, for the sake of argument, puts himself in the case of an offending person," an interpretation which, while not attributed to Malone, is favored by the editor of the New Arden edition. The editor writes that "[Harold] Jenkins points out that the Duke is at this point in the monologue speaking chorically as an 'everyman.' 'My vice' here signifies that of other persons in contrast to Angelo's own" (p. 94). Henley's note follows Malone's in 1793 and takes direct issue with it. "The Duke is plainly speaking in his own person," he wrote, "What he here terms 'my vice,' may be explained from his conversation in Act I. sc. iv. with Friar Thomas, and especially the fol!owing line: '——'twas my fault to give the people scope.' The *Vice of Angelo* requires no explanation" (IV. 312.9). The Duke's "fault" had been to allow his "strict statutes, and most biting laws" to sleep "for these fourteen years," a neglect which might, given a speaker other than the Duke himself in the first passage, have also been described as a "vice." Henley's explanation need not be accepted; it ought not be ignored.[18]

Two notes on *Othello* are given a place in the New Variorum edition but in severely abbreviated form. Iago advises Roderigo, among other things, to "defeat" his "favour" with an usurped beard" and the New Variorum editor, understandably jealous of space, quotes only the first sentence of the following note:

> *Favour* here means that combination of features which gives the face its distinguishing character. *Defeat*, from *defaire*, in French, signifies to unmake, decompose, or give a different appearance to, either by taking away something, or adding. Thus, in *Don Quixote*, Cardenio *defeated* his *favour* by cutting off his beard, and the Barber his, by putting one on. The beard which Mr. Ashton *usurped* when he escaped from the Tower, gave so different an appearance to his face, that he passed through his guards without the least suspicion. In *The Winter's Tale*, Autolycus had recourse to an expedient like Cardenio's, (as appears from the *pocketing up his pedlar's excrement*,) to prevent his being known in the garb of the prince. (XV. 446.5)

Cassio's description of Desdemona as "One that excels the quirks of blazoning pens, / And in the essential vesture of creation, / Does bear all excellency" is the reading of the quartos; the First Folio has "Do's tyre the ingeniver," a reading that has puzzled the commentators. John Monck Mason had stated that "ingeniver" was an incorrect spelling of "engineer" and that while Ben Jonson had "ingine, inginer, and inginous" these words were not "the language of Shakspeare." Henley wrote,

> Whoever shall reject uncommon expressions in the writings of Shakspeare, because they differ either from the exact rules of orthography, or from the unsettled mode of spelling them by other writers, will be found to deprive him no less of his beauties, than that the ornithologist would the peacock, who should cut out every eye of his train because it was either not circular, or else varied from some imaginary standard.—*Ingenieur* is no doubt of the same import with

ingener or *ingeneer*, though perhaps differently written by Shakspeare in reference to *ingenious*, and to distinguish it from *ingeneer*, which he has elsewhere used in a *military* sense. Mr. M. Mason's objection, that it is not the language of Shakspeare, is more than begging the question; and to affirm that Jonson is singular in the use of *ingine*, *inginer*, and *inginous*, is as little to the purpose. For we not only have those expressions in other writers, but others from the same root, as *ingene*, *engene*, &c. in Holinshed, and Sir T. More; and Daniel uses *ingeniate*:

> "Th' adulterate beauty of a falsed cheek
> Did Nature (for this good) *ingeniate*,
> To shed in thee the glory of her best." (XV. 458.6)

The New Variorum editor quotes only the second sentence and "Daniel uses *ingeniate*" with two lines of the quoted verses. How very much is lost thereby.[19]

Jacques's well-known seven ages of man speech reminded Henley of an "old print entitled, *The Stage of Man's Life*, divided into seven ages" which he had seen "more than once." He suggested that "as emblematical representations of this sort were formerly stuck up, both for ornament and instruction, in the generality of houses, it is more probable that Shakspeare took his hint from thence, than from Hippocrates or Proclus" (VI. 66.5), two possible sources cited by Malone. Henley's abilities as explicator are seen to best advantage in his note on Iago's "friends all but not, even now, / In quarter." Johnson had offered "in their quarters; at their lodgings," and Joseph Ritson, disagreeing with him, had written, "rather at *peace, quiet*. They had been on that very spot (the court or platform, it is presumed before the castle) ever since Othello left them, which can scarcely be called being in *their quarters*, or *at their lodgings*." Henley cleared up the matter.

It required one example, if no more, to evince that in *quarter* ever signified *quiet, at peace*. But a little attention would have shown, that the *them*, whom he speaks of Othello's having left, was only Cassio; who, being joined by Iago, where Othello (but not on the *platform*) had just left him, is dissuaded from setting the watch immediately; entreated to partake of a stoop of wine, in company with a brace of Cyprus gallants, then waiting without; and prevailed upon, though reluctantly, to invite them in. In this apartment the carousal happens, and wine is repeatedly called for, till at last Cassio, finding its too powerful effects, goes out to set the watch. At the proposal of Montano, himself and Iago follow Cassio towards the platform, and the latter sets on Roderigo to insult him. The scuffle ensues; an alarm is given, and Othello comes forth to inquire the cause. When, therefore, Iago answers:

> I do not know:—friends all but now, even now
> In quarter—

it is evident the quarter referred to, was that apartment of the castle assigned to the officers on guard, where Othello, after giving Cassio his orders, had, a little before, left him; and where Iago, with his companions, immediately found him.[20]

Other notes might also be quoted, but still others, those which are not recorded in any way in the New Variorum or New Arden series, must be given precedence.

Henley was aware, as some commentators seem not to have been, that Shakespeare was both a dramatist and a poet. Thus, he could say of one of the Poet's speeches in the opening scene of *Timon of Athens* that "this jumble of incongruous images, seems to have been designed, and put into the mouth of the Poetaster, that the reader might appreciate his talents: his language therefore should not be considered in the abstract" (XI. 466.2). When the disguised Kent gives Oswald, Goneril's Steward, a verbal lashing full of bawdy descriptive phrases, Henley sees another example of Shakespeare's knowledge of human nature, for he states that "Kent is not only boisterous in his manners, but abusive in his language. His excessive ribaldry proceeds from an over solicitude to prevent being discovered: like St. Peter's swearing from a similar motive" (XIV. 92.7). In Malone's *Supplement* in 1780 Henley had written of the "sharded beetle" in *Cymbeline* that it was the beetle sheltered under a shell of cow-dung (II.711 In 1793 he wrote a new note, one designed to explain wh Shakespeare contrasted the "sharded beetle" with the "full wing'd eagle" of the next line: "The epithet *full-wing'd* applied t the eagle, sufficiently marks the contrast of the poet's imagery for whilst the bird can soar towards the sun beyond the reach c the human eye, the insect can but rise above the surface of th earth, and that at the close of day" (XIII. 111.4). And then agai on the consonance between Shakespeare's characters and the mode of speech, this time on Parolles in *All's Well*, "the obscurit of the passage arises only from the fantastical language of character like Parolles, whose affectation of wit urges his ima ination from one allusion to another, without allowing time fc his judgment to determine their congruity" (VI. 236.2).

Thomas Jefferson bought some of Henley's books which he had left in Virginia, and while students of American history may be interested in all the titles, some fifty in all, present interest focuses on the presence in the list of eight works by Linneaus as well as "Clayton Flora Virginica."[21] Not only is Henley's botanical knowledge seen in his note on the famous crux in The Tempest, "thy banks with pioned and twilled brims" (quoted above, p. 114), but it is evident in a few others. Iago tells Roderigo to fill his purse with money for "the food that to him is as luscious as locusts, shall be to him as bitter as coloquintida." Steevens thought that the locusts referred to were the insects of that name, but an anonymous correspondent informed him that it was the fruit of the locust tree, "a long black pod, that contains the seeds, among which there is a very sweet luscious juice of much the same consistency as fresh honey." Henley was able to add that the "viscous substance which the pod of the locust contains, is, perhaps, of all others, the most luscious. From its likeness to honey, in consistency and flavour, the locust is called the honey-tree also. Its seeds, enclosed in a long pod, lie buried in the juice" (XV. 447.7). Arviragus, in Cymbeline, says "let the stinking elder, grief, untwine / His perishing root, with the increasing vine," and Johnson and Sir John Hawkins both suggested emendations, while Malone defended the text. But it was Henley who stated roundly that there was "no need for alteration" and explained that "the elder is a plant whose roots are much shorter lived than the vine's, and as those of the vine swell and outgrow them, they must of necessity loosen their hold" (XIII. 154.2). And there is, too, the exchange between him and Steevens on Antony's "we bring forth weeds, / When our quick winds lie still" (see above, pp. 113–14).

One biographer of William Beckford wrote of "the sinister and quarrelsome Samuel Henley, who wormed his way into Beckford's confidence and then betrayed him [by the unauthorized publication of Henley's translation of Vathek from the French], impinging periodically on Beckford's existence like a tiresome mosquito."[22] There is no good evidence for such an extreme statement, and perhaps Henley's naive note on Aaron's "Go pack with him" in Titus Andronicus may serve both as conclusion and as a belated answer to the words quoted above. "To PACK a jury," he wrote, "is an expression still used; though the practice, I trust, obsolete" (XIII. 334.4).

6

Francis Douce, Keeper of MSS in the British Museum

If the account of Francis Douce (1757–1834) by A. H. Bullen in the *DNB* is right, he had published, at age seventeen and still in school, an anonymous essay on the Dance of Death, evidence not only of precociousness but of an almost life-long interest in the subject, for one year before his death he re-edited the Dance of Death, "exhibited in elegant engravings on wood" (Bullen). The more prosaic truth probably lies in the British Museum's catalog of printed books where *The Dance of Death Edited with Preface and Descriptions by F.D.* is tentatively dated 1794. Douce, who did not attend University, studied for the bar for a while and had rooms in Gray's Inn which he gave up in 1799 when he married. Although he was disappointed with his share of his father's estate, he was left enough money and land to allow him to pursue his literary and antiquarian tastes. He was for a time keeper of manuscripts in the British Museum and, with R. Nares and S. Shaw, revised the catalog of Harleian MSS in 1808–12 and, with Sir Henry Ellis, cataloged the Lansdowne MSS in 1819. The writer of the long obituary notice of Douce in the GM for August 1834 states that Douce's "independent spirit could not brook the pragmatical interference of one of the Trustees [of the British Museum], who was but ill-calculated to judge of his peculiar fitness for the office he had undertaken, and he resigned his situation" (p. 213).[1] The same writer numbers among Douce very many friends, for he seems to have known everybody: Richard Farmer, Sir John Hawkins, Edmond Malone (with whom he "to the last lived in habits or friendly intercourse"), and George Steevens, "and, in short, all who cultivated the study of Antiquity either in Literature or in Art" (pp. 213, 214). Douce was made Fellow of the Society of Antiquaries in 1779.

Of special relevance is the account of the relationship between

Douce and Steevens, for my primary concern is, of course, with Douce's contribution to Shakespeare studies.

With George Steevens he was for some years intimate, but that eccentric genius ceased to visit him soon after his marriage, for it was one of his peculiarities to cut all his acquaintance when they became Benedicts. . . . Upon his first meeting with Mr. Douce, "the Puck of Commentators" led the conversation to the subject of Shakespeare, and told Mr. Douce that he was projecting a new edition saying, "I doubt not you have some observations you can give me, for I lay every one under contribution." Mr. Douce acknowledged that he had made some remarks on his favourite author, but modestly added they were not worth Mr. Steevens's notice. At length, however, he consented to communicate them, and Steevens called on him the next morning, and received them from him. From this period for three or four years he paid Mr. Douce a visit every morning at his chambers at 9 o'clock, staying till 10. Mr. Douce was used to speak of his intercourse with Steevens with great pleasure; he was delighted with his gentlemanly manners, his wit, and command of language, which gave great zest to his conversation. With another Commentator on Shakespeare, the eccentric and unfortunate Ritson, Mr. Douce was also upon intimate terms, and was one of the very few persons visited by him. (p. 214)

It is a remarkable tribute to Douce that he could be on "intimate terms" with two men as remarkably difficult to get along with as Steevens and Ritson.

Since Steevens and Douce first met "about the time of the hoax played off by Steevens upon Mr. Gough," i.e., late 1789 (DNB), Douce had less than three years in which to contribute the one hundred and thirty-six notes that appear over his name in Steevens's fifteen-volume 1793 Shakespeare. (There are also eight of Steevens's notes in which he acknowledges Douce's help.) Douce must have had some observations to hand over to Steevens the morning after their meeting, with the rest probably being added during Steevens's subsequent morning visits. Fortunately, eight of Douce's letters to Steevens are extant and one can trace a small part of their relationship through them.[2] The first letter is dated 2 August 1791, and is of no importance here, other than that it records Douce's acquaintance with Richard Farmer. On 25 November 1791, among other matters, Douce, who almost always refers to himself in the third person and writes in a very formal style, concludes his letter by writing, "Mr. D. cannot add to the enclosed Note on the Candle-holder which he conceives to be quite sufficient."[3] While there is no letter from Douce thanking Steevens for a present of the 1793 *Shakespeare*, one feels sure such a present was made. In any event, about two months after the publication of the 1793 edition Douce sent Steevens, on 27 June 1793, a copy of his edition of *The Dance of Death*. Shortly thereafter, and almost surely evidence that Steevens had no sooner finished the 1793 *Shakespeare* than he began immediately to collect materials for a subsequent edition, Douce wrote, in July 1793, "Mr. Douce presents his compliments to M[r] Steevens and in answer to his query concerning the fool's bauble refers him to the prints in the Ship of Fools, and to those in Erasmus's praise of folly after Holbein which will furnish him with a few specimens." It is rather curious that Douce should have cited *The Ship of Fools*, for in his note on the Clown's reference to his bauble in *All's Well that Ends Well* Steevens had written that "in the STULTIFERA NAVIS, 1497, are several representations of this instrument" (VI. 342.6). And it is also curious that Steevens, desiring and getting more information on the fool's bauble, for Douce not only gave him still other sources but also sent him duplicates of three prints, should not use any of the new information for a more complete note for the edition he was planning and that Reed completed in 1803. But Douce included some of the information in his dissertation on the fools and clowns in Shakespeare in his *Illustrations of Shakspeare and of Ancient Manners*, 1807. On 31 August and 3 September 1793 Douce wrote about some MS Latin plays belonging to Dr. Lort and in the earlier letter raised a question about an edition of *Pericles* printed by Pavier. In the next year Steevens had evidently asked Douce about prints of Eulenspiegel, for on 7 May 1794, the latter begged leave "to inform him that there is a print of Ulinspiegle by Hondius after Luc Van Leyden" and added that a manuscript diary that had recently passed through his hands contained an entry dated 12 June 1593, which recorded the purchase of a copy of Shakespeare's *Venus and Adonis*.[4] The last letter is undated, but since it was accompanied by a drawing of a candlestick of which Steevens was to have a woodcut made, it was written presumably before the 1793 *Shakespeare* was published, as there is a cut of a candlestick acknowledged to be in the possession of Douce.

There are no new notes by Douce in the 1803 *Shakespeare* edited by Reed. Steevens had died, and Douce was working on his own two volumes of *Illustrations of Shakspeare and of Ancient Manners*, 1807, with dissertations on Shakespeare's clowns and fools, on the morris dance, and on the *Gesta Romanorum*. The genesis of these dissertations, it will be seen, is to be found in notes to the 1793 *Shakespeare*. While it is curious that Reed records no meeting with Douce in his diary, the two, having so many friends and acquaintances in common, must have known each other, but the fact remains that Reed seems not to have solicited Douce's help for the 1803 edition and Douce seems not to have offered it. Indeed, Douce evidently had nothing to do with any edition other than that of 1793.

In the Preface to his *Illustrations* Douce wrote that "the late Mr. Steevens . . . presented to public view such of the author's [Douce's] remarks as were solely put together for the private use and consideration of that able critic" and that now he could withdraw some and render others "less exceptionable" (p. vi). He went on to acknowledge that "one design of these volumes has been to augment the knowledge of our popular customs and antiquities, in which respect alone the writings of Shakspeare have suggested better hints, and furnished ampler materials than those of any one besides" (p. ix). Indeed, Alexander Dyce once wrote that "except for those explanatory of customs, dress, etc. the notes of Douce are nearly worthless" and on another occasion he remarked of one of Douce's comments that "the absurdity of Douce's remarks is beyond belief."[5] Douce was firmly against conjectural emendation and expressed the wish "that the text of an author, and more especially that of our greatest dramatic writer, could be altered as seldom as possible by conjectural emendation, or only where it is manifestly erroneous from typographical causes" (p. xiii). Only one of his own hundred and thirty-six notes in the 1793 *Shakespeare* is an emendation, one that had already been made by Capell and has gained wide acceptance (IX. 354.2). It entailed printing a few lines of prose as verse, clear evidence that in the matter of conjectural emendation Douce practiced what he preached.

Since virtually whatever scholarly attention focused on Douce's Shakespearian efforts has been on the *Illustrations*, to the gross neglect of his notes in 1793, it may be well to analyze the use he made of the earlier notes in the later work. And perhaps, too, as one preliminary indication of such neglect, or possible confusion, witness Horace Howard Furness's error in the new Variorum *Much Ado*. Benedict says "hang me in a bottle like cat, and shoot at me," an allusion to a rather brutal sport. Douce wrote, "This practice is still kept up," at which point Furness added "[anno 1807]" and quoted the rest, or most of the rest, of

the note. The fact, albeit trifling, is that the note is *not* in the 1807
Illustrations but in a note in 1793 (IV. 412.8). In any event, Douce
chose to use only twenty-nine of the one hundred thirty-six notes
for his *Illustrations*, so that a large body of his criticism is
available only in the 1793 *Shakespeare*. And the twenty-nine
notes he did use are very much altered, usually by extensive
additions in which he adduces parallels and quotes or cites
authorities. For example, in Steevens's 1793 end-note on the
various places in which analogues to the plot of *The Merchant of
Venice* are noted, he attributes a two-sentence observation on one
analogue to Douce. In the *Illustrations* Douce devotes over
twenty pages (I. 272–92) to the same subject, giving only a line to
his 1793 observation. He canceled, or recanted on, six notes from
1793. Thus, he wrote of a note on *Measure for Measure* in the
Illustrations, "None of the explanations of this speech are satisfactory, but least of all such part of a note by the author of these
remarks, as refers to the *picklock*, which has been better ac-
counted for by Mr. Ritson" (I. 136). A reference to "twangling
Jack" in *The Taming of the Shrew* had brought about a very polite
difference of opinion between Douce and Malone; in 1807 Douce
prefaced his new note with the statement that "it is the author's
desire to withdraw a former note on this passage, which, as well
as a few others of a confidential nature, was not intended for
publication" (I. 331), a blanket statement which may or may not
account for the omission of more than one hundred notes. The
dissertations on the fools and clowns in the plays, mentioned on
the title-page of the *Illustrations*, owe something to the notes on
Death and the Fool in 1793 (V. 316.5 and XIII. 498.2), which
should be compared, specifically, with the new versions.[6] In
1793 Steevens, in his note on "to please the fool and death" in
Pericles (XIII. 498.2), related a pertinent anecdote told him by
"Mr. Douce, to whom our readers are indebted for several happy
illustrations of Shakspeare," thereby possibly providing Douce
with the title of his book as well as giving evidence of Douce's
long preoccupation with the subject, for Duce was "very young
when he observed that which furnished the matter for the anecdote.

Many of Douce's illustrations come from works that Steevens,
according to Douce's Preface, had "somewhere called 'books not
mean to be formally quoted'" and from what Douce himself
described as "what is often absurdly denominated *black letter*
learning" (p. x), and hence they, with so many of the 1793 notes,
are rarely quoted in modern editions. But, as has already been

suggested, the *Illustrations* are well known, the notes in 1793 relatively little known as well as much neglected. The New Variorum *Twelfth Night*, to begin documentation of the neglect of Douce's 1793 notes, states of the "sweet sound" of the eighth line of that play, that Knight was "the first editor to recall the Shakespearian word to the grey and venerable authority of the Folio from the emendation 'sweet south [wind].'" Here is Douce's note: "I see no reason for disturbing the text of the old copy, which reads—*Sound*. The wind, from whatever quarter, would produce a sound in breathing on the violets, or else the simile is false. Besides, *sound* is a better relative to the antecedent, *strain*" (IV. 6.4). Viola says of Olivia, "methought, her eyes had lost her tongue," and Douce corrected Johnson's note by writing, "It rather means that the very fixed and eager view she took of Viola, perverted the use of her tongue, and made her talk distractedly. The construction of the verb—*lost*, is also much in Shakspeare's manner" (IV. 47.9). The note is unnoticed in the New Variorum, which does, however, reprint a note by Halliwell-Phillips much like Douce's: "The plain meaning seems to be that her eyes were so occupied in looking at Viola, her talk was distracted" (p. 103). "Tilly-valley lady" in the same play has given the commentators pause, the New Variorum editor quoting the *Century Dictionary* on the obscurity of its origin (p. 120). The *OED* is even blunter, proclaiming its origin "unknown." No attention has been paid to Douce's etymology: "*Tilly-valley* is a hunting phrase borrowed from the French. In the *Venerie de Jacques Fouilloux*, 1585, 4to. fo. 12 the following cry is mentioned: 'Ty a hillaut & vallecy'; and is set to music in pp. 49 and 50" (IV. 60.4). Here is a major oversight.

Douce contributed fifteen notes on *Much Ado about Nothing*, the largest number for any play, with *The Merry Wives of Windsor* and *Twelfth Night* next, with eleven each. Mention has already been made of the New Variorum editor's error as to the year of one of the notes on *Much Ado* and of Dyce's condemnation of Douce's notes. Douce's note on "bird bolt" or "burbolt" (IV. 399.2) is quoted and labeled "absurd," but the editor is unable to provide a satisfactory explication of the passage himself (p. 13). Another puzzling reference in *Much Ado* is the Messenger's remark, "the gentleman is not in your books," which Richard Farmer, whose note is quoted, said "originally meant to be in the list of his *retainers*" and which Douce, whose note is not quoted, was able to corroborate, "There is a MS. of Lord Burleigh's, in the Marquis of Lansdowne's library, wherein, among many other household concerns, he has entered the names of all his servants, etc." (IV. 402.9). (Some twenty-five years later, it may be recalled, Douce and Sir Henry Ellis published a catalog of the Lansdowne MSS.) Douce's note lends more weight to Farmer's explanation. His is the only note (IV. 496.3) on "inward impediment," which he recognized as from "our Marriage Ceremony" (p. 192). And his note on "foining fence" (IV. 525.9) is given precedence, as it should be, over later definitions (p. 246). But when Claudio says "what though care kill'd a cat" and Douce recognized it as a "proverbial expression" and cited *Ray's Proverbs* (IV. 528.6), the New Variorum editor preferred to paraphrase only one note, Reed's parallel from Ben Jonson's *Every Man in His Humour* (p. 252), without remarking that Reed's note, which begins "This proverb is recognized by," is in corroboration of Douce's.[7] From the New Variorum note one would not know that the expression was proverbial and that Douce was the first to point this out.

Other examples of similar neglect exist. Thus, in *A Midsummer Night's Dream*, Bottom exclaims, "The eye of man hath not heard, the ear of man hath not seen; man's hand is not able to taste, his tongue to conceive, nor his heart to report, what my dream was." Douce's note reads, "He is here blundering upon the scriptural passage of 'Eye hath not seen, nor ear heard, neither have entered into the heart of man the things,' etc. 1 Cor. ii. 9" (V. 136.4). All one gets in the New Variorum is Halliwell-Phillipps's note on "mistaking words" being common even before Shakespeare, with his further statement that "this kind of humour was so very common, it is by no means necessary to consider, with some [whom?], that Shakespeare intended Bottom to parody Scripture [which part of Scripture?]" (p. 195). I find this most unsatisfactory. And it is strange that Rosaline's allusion to a "fool" and his "fate" in *Love's Labour's Lost* should go unannotated in the New Variorum despite the wealth of comment, very largely Douce's, lavished on these figures and their connection with the Dance of Death.

Although the New Variorum volumes quote a number of Douce's notes, they are often severely shortened, so that if one wishes to get the full force of many of these notes, he must go to the 1793 *Shakespeare*. Celia, in *As You Like It*, tells Touchstone that he will "be whipp'd for taxation, one of these days." Douce wrote, "This was the discipline usually inflicted upon fools. Brantome informs us that Legat, fool to Elizabeth of France having offended her with some indelicate speech, 'fut bien fouetté à la cuisine pour ces paroles.' A representation of this ceremony may be seen in a cut prefixed to B. II. ch. c. of the German Petrarch already mentioned in Vol. V. p. 44" (VI. 18.2), of which the New Variorum editor quotes only the first sentence. Falstaff, in 2 Henry IV, inquires of Mistress Doll's health and is answered by the Hostess that Doll is "sick of a calm." Falstaff's rejoinder is, "So is all her sect; an they be once in a calm, they are sick." Johnson could not understand why "sect" was "printed in all the copies," since he believed that "sex" was meant; Steevens believed that "sect" was right and that Falstaff meant "all of her profession," but he concluded that the two words were "anciently synonymous"; Malone, recalling a note by Farmer, also concluded that "sect was licentiously used by our author, and his contemporaries, for sex"; Douce was the first to explicate: "I believe sect is used here in its usual sense, and not for sex. Falstaff means to say, that all courtezans, when their trade is at a stand, are apt to be sick" (IX. 77.2). The New Variorum editor quotes only the second sentence of Douce's note, expresses his own opinion that the passage is "surely a reference to the proverbial shrewishness of all women," but then adds, of the words, "sick of a calm" that "Falstaff's quibble is obvious, but whether this means 'in a calm frame of mind' or 'out of work' depends upon the meaning of sect; see preceding note" (p. 168). All of which is a strange state of affairs. Professor Shaaber, the New Variorum editor, admits as one possibility Douce's explanation of "sick of a calm" but evidently disagrees with his explanation of "sect," which he does not quote, although that latter explanation is necessary for his own note on "sick of a calm." How much simpler and more logical to have quoted both sentences![8]

If one turns to the New Variorum King Lear, IV. vi. 86, he will find only one note, attributed to Douce, under "press-money," part of one of the mad king's speechs. The note reads simply "The money paid to soldiers when they were retained in the king's service" (p. 276). Should one wonder why Lear refers to such a practice at this juncture in this speech, no answer would be forthcoming. But if he had access to the 1793 Shakespeare he would find the answer in a fine note.

It is evident from the whole of this speech, that Lear fancies him in a battle: But, There's your press-money has not been properly explained. It means the money which was paid to soldiers when they were retained in the King's service; and it appears from some antient statutes, and particularly 7 Henry VII. c. I. and 3 Henry VIII. c. 5. that it was felony in any soldier to withdraw himself from the King's

service after receipt of this money, without special leave. On the
contrary, he was obliged at all times to hold himself in readiness. The
term is from the French "prest," ready. It is written prest in several
places in King Henry VIIth's Book of household expenses still preserved in the Exchequer. This may serve also to explain the following
passage in Act. V. sc. ii. "And turn our imprest lances in our eyes;"
and to correct Mr. Whalley's note in Hamlet, Act. I. sc. i.—"Why such
impress of shipwrights?" (XIV. 233.4)

OED gives "Earnest money paid to a sailor or soldier on his
enlistment" as the third, and applicable, definition of "press-
money," but pronounces the derivation from French "prest" a
fanciful derivation of some seventeenth-century etymologists.
Whatever the etymological derivation, the note deserves recognition.

Steevens, to go on to another area of neglect of Douce's notes,
emended to read "ring [not "rang"] time" in the line, "In the
spring time, the only pretty ring time," from the song in As You
Like It, "It was a lover and his lass," explaining that "ring time"
was the aptest season for marriage." Douce's note would seem to
put the matter beyond reasonable doubt: "In confirmation of Mr.
Steevens's reading, it appears from the old calendars that the
spring was the season of marriage" (VI. 156.2). Leontes, in The
Winter's Tale, speaks of "the blank / And level" of his brain, and
Johnson commented that that these were terms of archery. Douce
disagreed, saying they were "terms of gunnery, not of archery"
(VII. 65.4). The New Variorum editor quotes Douce's note and
adds, "It is hazardous to make a positive assertion with regards to
Shakespeare's language. Compare 'a well-experienced archer hits
the mark His eye doth level at.'—Pericles, I. i. 164" (p. 97).
"Level" in the line in Pericles is a verb; in The Winter's Tale, a
noun. OED upholds Douce and quotes Hamlet, "As level as the
cannon to his blank." It was hazardous for Furness to take issue
with Douce on matters dealing with archery, for the writer of
Douce's obituary notice in the GM (August 1834) tells us that "he
had also in early life been a Toxophilite and an Angler" (p. 216).
Further evidence of his familiarity with archery will appear
below. Leontes commands Antigonus to "Swear by this sword;"
the only note on this in the New Variorum is by Halliwell-
Phillipps. The first sentence reads, "It was anciently the custom
to swear by the cross on the handle of a sword, or by the sacred
name of Jesus, which was sometimes engraved on the top of the
blade or on the pommel of the sword" (p. 111), prompting the

uspicion that he helped himself to Steevens's note *verbatim*, "It vas anciently the custom to swear by the cross on the handle of a word," and to the substance of part of Douce's note, "I remember ɔ have seen the name of Jesus engraved upon the pummel of the word of a Crusader in the Church at Winchelsea" (VII. 75.4). teevens had directed the reader to a note on *Hamlet*, I.v.; there e himself quotes a parallel passage from a manuscript; the same assage from the MS is quoted by Halliwell-Phillipps!

Lady Macbeth's "pall thee in the dunnest smoke of hell" was xplained by Warburton as "wrap thyself in a *pall*," but Douce bserved to Steevens that the verb, "in the present instance . . . ɑay simply mean—to *wrap*, to *invest*" (VIII. 376.6). The New 'ariorum edition quotes Warburton's note and then this from S. V. Singer in 1853, "From the Latin pallio, to wrap, to invest, to over or hide as with a mantle or cloak" (p. 80). This note and that y Halliwell-Phillipps quoted above give one pause: Did these .ineteenth-century editors and critics look upon the work of ɪeir predecessors as a reservoir of information they could use ʋithout acknowledgment? Pistol, in *Henry V*, says that "hold-fast ; the only dog," which Douce correctly identified as "a prov- rbial saying,—'Brag is a good dog, but *holdfast* is a better'" (IX. 36.4). In the absence of a New Variorum *Henry V*, I turned to the Jew Arden edition where I found the identical proverb quoted ut without any reference to Douce. Probably more surprising is ɪe New Arden note on "the horsemen sit like fixed can- lesticks," for although Steevens quotes an explanatory parallel ·om Webster's *The White Devil*, the New Arden note lamely oncludes, "Apparently candle-sticks were made in this form" (p. 09). Had the editor looked at the 1793 edition, he would have een a representation of such a candlestick, "now in the posses- ɪon of Francis Douce, Esq." (IX. 424.9). And had he then gone on ɔ Douce's *Illustrations*, he would have found additional matter ɔr his edification (I. 502–3). "Apparently," indeed!

It is gratifying that Douce has been given somewhat his due in ɔme notes in the New Variorum series. Excluding the notes lready discussed, his are the only notes on three more passages. ne, Calchas's description of Antenor in *Troilus and Cressida* as such a wrest in their affairs" (XI. 338.5), is especially interest- ɪg. Douce defined "wrest" as "an instrument for tuning the harp y *drawing up* the strings." Unfortunately, the entire note is so ʋoefully shortened in the New Variorum that Douce's quotation ·om "Wynne's *History of the Gwedir family*," his citation of linsheu's Dictionary, and his concluding sentence, "The form of

the *wrest* may be seen in some of the illuminated service books
wherein David is represented playing on his harp; in the Secon
Part of *Mersenna's Harmonics,* p. 69; and in the *Syntagmata* c
Praetorius, Vol. II. Fig. xix," are all omitted.[9] Five more c
Douce's notes are quoted first in the New Variorum editions
Those on "the Tartar's bow" in *Love's Labour's Lost* (V. 96.5), o
"the old carlot" in *As You Like It* (VI. 122.4), on the "fond many
in *2 Henry VI* (IX. 46.4), and on "pluck'd all gaze his way" ii
Coriolanus (XII. 27.4). All these are short explications or glosse
The note on "carlot" is interesting, for Douce wrote, "i.e. *peasan*
from *carl* or *churl;* probably a word of Shakspeare's coinage," an
the *OED* gives the same derivation and quotes only the exampl
from *As You Like It.* The fifth note is on the mad Ophelia
reference to the owl's being a baker's daughter, and Douce re
called "a common story among the vulgar in Gloucestershire
about the baker's daughter who complained at the size of th
dough set to bake for our Saviour and was transformed into a
owl. "This story," Douce concluded, "is often related to childrer
in order to deter them from such illiberal behaviour to poc
people" (XV. 261.7).[10]

It remains now to give a more comprehensive view of Douce
notes. One can point out that sixty-two of the notes give definit
evidence in the form of titles, often abbreviated, of Douce's erud
tion and the diversity of his preoccupations. A number of hi
notes exist because of the inaccuracies of previous editors an
critics. Indeed, in the Preface to his *Illustrations* he was to writ
of Johnson "that he was certainly unskilled in the knowledge c
obsolete customs and expressions. His explantory notes therefor
are, generally speaking, the most controvertible of any" (pp. vii
viii). And hence it is not surprising that he took direct issue wit
Johnson a number of times in 1793, never in any disrespectfu
tone. One example will suffice. Dromio of Syracuse says "he wh
sets up his rest to do more exploits with his mace, than a morri
pike," and Johnson had noted, in part, that "a *morris-pike* was
pike used in a *morris* or a military dance." Douce wrote, "Ther
is, I believe, no authority for Dr. Johnson's assertion that th
Morris-Pike was used in the Morris-dance. Swords were som
times used upon that occasion. It certainly means the Moi
rish-pike, which was very common in the 16th century. Se
Grose's [his friend, Francis Grose's] Hist. of the English Arm
Vol. I., p. 135" (VII. 281.6).

In the same paragraph of the Preface to the *Illustrations* i
which he spoke of Johnson's lack of knowledge of "obsole

customs and expressions" Douce praised "the indefatigable exertions of Messrs. Steevens, Malone, Tyrwhitt, and Mason," yet he did not let his admiration for their efforts inhibit him when he thought them in error. Tyrwhitt had commented of Helen's "move the still-piecing [sic] air, / That sings with piercing" in *All's Well* that he saw no reason to doubt "still piercing" but suggested "rove" for "move," explaining the word as *"fly at random through.* The allusion is to shooting at rovers in archery, which was shooting without any particular aim." Douce, who, it will be remembered, was a keen archer in his youth, objected that "Mr. Tyrwhitt's reading destroys the designed antithesis between *move* and *still;* nor is he correct in his definition of roving, which is not shooting without a *particular aim,* but at *marks of uncertain lengths"* (VI. 286.5). The first definition of the verb "to rove" in the *OED* is "to shoot with arrows at a mark set at pleasure or at random, and not of any fixed distance." Prince Hal says that he will procure Falstaff "a charge of foot; and, I know, his death will be a march of twelve-score." John Monck Mason was sure that "twelve-score" meant "feet" not "yards," as interpreted by Johnson, Steevens, and Malone, and suspected a quibble between his "feet" and a "charge of foot." Douce was more emphatic than the others in his disagreement: "Twelve-*score* always means so many *yards* and not *feet.* There is not the smallest reason to suppose that Shakespeare meant any quibble" (VIII. 485.5).[11] Interestingly enough, Justice Shallow says that old Double, an archer of his town, "would have clapp'd i' the clout at twelve score and carry'd you a forehand shaft fourteen and fourteen and a half." Malone noted, "i.e., of yards. So, in Drayton's *Polyolbion,* 1612: 'At markes full fortie score they us'd to prick and rove.'" Douce remarked that "this mode of expression certainly in this instance, and I believe in general, means *yards;* but the line from Drayton makes this opinion doubtful, or shows the extreme inaccuracy of the poet, for no man was ever capable of shooting an arrow forty score *yards"* (IX. 127.3). *OED* defines the "twelve (twenty-four) score prick" as "a 'prick' or target placed 240 (or 480) paces distant, the regular distance at which shooting at the prick was practised," thus confirming Douce's explanation. But what Douce, in all his seriousness, failed to remark was that Drayton was describing the fabulous feats of archery of Robin Hood and his band (*Polyolbion,* xxvi. 315 ff.). Malone further commented, on the "forehand shaft a fourteen and fourteen and a half," that the "utmost distance that the archers of ancient times reached, is supposed to have been about three hundred yards.

Old Double therefore certainly drew a good bow," to which Douce added that "Shakspeare probably knew what he was about when he spoke of archery, which in his time was practised by every one. He is describing Double as a very excellent archer, and there is no inconsistency in making such a one shoot fourteen score and a half; but it must be allowed that none but a most extraordinary archer would be able to *hit a mark* at twelve score. Some allowance however should be made when the speaker is considered" (IX. 217.4). Professor Shaaber, editor of the New Variorum *2 Henry IV,* notes that "though it has been much commented on, the import of this passage still remains uncertain," and after quoting or citing various notes on the passage, but not Douce's, concludes that "whatever contradictions there may be here can be explained, I think, by supposing that while twelve score yards was a common mark to shoot at, it was by no means common to clap it in the clout at such a distance" (pp. 241 and 242), precisely Douce's conclusion. Beatrice says of Benedick that he "challenged Cupid at the flight," and George Tollet had attempted to ascertain the length of a "flight-shot" by quoting a passage from Leland's *Itinerary,* 1769, but Douce observed to Steevens that "the length of the shot depended on the strength and skill of the archer," and that nothing could "with certainty be determined by the passage quoted from Leland" (IV. 398.9).

Douce was also forced to disagree with his good friend Steevens. Falstaff, in *2 Henry IV,* had referred to riding "the mare,' which Steevens took to be an allusion to the gallows, adducing parallels from a play of 1587 (IX. 52.9). Later Falstaff says of Poins that he "rides the wild mare with the boys and jumps upon joint stools," and Malone wrote that the allusion was probably to the "two-legged mare," i.e., the gallows, of Steevens's earlier note. Douce revealed a dry strain of humor in himself, writing that "if Poins had ever ridden the mare alluded to by Mr. Steevens, she would have given him such a fall as would effectually prevent him from mounting her a second time. We must therefore suppose it was a less dangerous beast [a whore], that would not have disabled him from afterwards jumping upon joint stools, etc." (IX. 99.6). Another disagreement with Steevens was on Coriolanus's "woolvish gown." Steevens had quoted "A Merye Jest of a Man called *Howleglas*" as authority for a ploughman's gown being called a "wolfe," so that "Shakspeare might have meant *Coriolanus* to compare the *dress of a Roman candidate to the coarse frock of a ploughman,* who exposed himself to solicit the votes of his fellow rusticks," a tribute, incidentally, to Steevens ingenuity. Douce queried whether the ploughman's "wolf" was "called so in this country? it must be remembered that *Howleglas* is literally translated from the *French* where the word 'loup' certainly occurs, but I believe it has not the same signification in that language. The French copy also may be *literally* rendered from the *German*" (XII. 99.3).

Douce lived to the last in "habits of friendly intercourse" with Malone but that did not preclude differences of opinion. Viola's memorable description of her fictitious sister who "pined in thought; / And, with a green and yellow melancholy, / She sat like patience on a monument, / Smiling at grief," prompted Malone to define "thought" as "melancholy." Douce objected: "Mr. Malone says, *thought* means *melancholy*. But why wrest from this word its plain and useful acceptation, and make Shakspeare guilty of tautology? for in the very next line he uses 'Melancholy'" (IV. 75.6). And when Sir Richard Vernon, in 1 *Henry IV*, spoke of seeing "young Harry—with his beaver on" Malone, learning from Dr. Michael Lort, whose note is quoted to that effect, that "*Bever* and *visiere* were two different parts of the helmet. The former part let down to enable the wearer to *drink*, the latter was raised up to enable him to see," accused Shakespeare of having "confounded" the two, "for, in *Hamlet*, Horatio says, that he saw the old king's face, because 'he wore his *beaver up*.'" Douce, who later devoted some four pages of text and one of various representations of the helmet and its parts (*Illustrations*, I. 438–43) corrected both Lort and Malone: "The poet is certainly not guilty of the confusion laid to his charge with respect to the passage in *Hamlet*; for the beaver was as often made to *lift up* as to *let down*" (VIII. 546.9).[12]

Douce's glosses are the least interesting of his efforts; fortunately, however, they are much shorter than those of many of his contemporaries. But the occasional gloss borders on explication, and so the "Provost" who appears in the opening stage-direction of act II of *Measure for Measure* "is not a *military officer*, but a kind of sheriff or gaoler, so called in foreign countries" (IV. 215.7). Compare the sixth definition in the *OED*: "An officer charged with the apprehension, custody, and punishment of offenders. *Obs.*" Shakespeare's *Measure for Measure* is one of the examples quoted. Some of the slightly fuller and more interesting of Douce's explications are of phrases or passages that had given earlier editors trouble. Isabella tells her brother that "The sense of death is most in apprehension; / And the poor beetle that we tread upon, / In corporal sufferance finds pang as great / As when a giant dies." Johnson had interpreted this to mean "*that death is no more than every being must suffer, though the dread of it is peculiar to man; or perhaps, that* we are inconsistent with ourselves, when we so much dread that which we carelessly inflict on other creatures, that feel the pain as acutely as we" (IV. 281.5). The New Arden *Measure for Measure* quotes only Douce's note: "The meaning is—fear is the principal sensation in death, which has no pain; and the giant when he dies feels no greater pain than the beetle.——This passage, however, from its arrangement, is liable to an opposite construction, but which would totally destroy the illustration of the sentiment." In *2 Henry IV* the Earl of Northumberland refers to "a sullen bell, / Remember'd knolling a departing friend." Steevens thought this a reference to "the *passing* bell, i.e. the bell that solicited prayers for the soul *passing* into another world." Since the New Variorum edition quotes Steevens's note and not Douce's, there is additional reason to quote the latter here. Douce was "inclined to think that this bell might have been originally used to drive away demons who were watching to take possession of the soul of the deceased. In the cuts of some of the old service books which contain the *Vigiliae mortuorum*, several devils are waiting for this purpose in the chamber of the dying man, to whom the priest is administering extreme unction" (IX. 15.9). The Clown in *All's Well*, in a spate of comparisons, says that his answer is as fit as "Tib's rush for Tom's forefinger" to serve all occasions. Sir John Hawkins contributed a long learned note to prove this was a reference to the practice of marrying with a rush ring; Joseph Ritson supposed it a covert sexual allusion; and Malone, quoting four lines from John Cleveland's poem "on an *Hermaphrodite*," supported him. Douce wrote that "at the game of Gleek, the ace was called *Tib*, and the knave *Tom*; and this is the proper explanation of the lines cited from Clieveland [*sic*]. The practice of marrying with a *rush ring* mentioned by Sir John Hawkins is very questionable, and it might be difficult to find any authority in support of his opinion" (VI. 249.6). *OED* corroborates Douce's explanation of Cleveland's lines, also quoting them in exemplification of the two words. Douce, who had done Hawkins an injustice as a result of not having seen his "*entire* note, which had originally appeared in the edition of 1778, but was injudiciously suppressed in that of 1785" (*Illustrations*, I. 316), made his apologies but also elaborated on his note in his *Illustrations*, quoting further parallels (I 315–19). His statement, "*Tib* and *Tom* were names for any low or vulgar persons, and they are usually mentioned together in the same manner as *Jack* and *Gill*, etc.," is echoed by the *OED*, which also makes the Jack and Jill comparison.

Some indication has been given above of Douce's interest in and knowledge of archery, hunting, gunnery, and fencing. To the first may be added his note on Bassanio's recollection of how in his youth when he had lost an arrow he shot "his fellow of the self-same flight / The self-same way" and observed where the second arrow fell, a practice Steevens found an allusion to in a pamphlet by Dekker. Douce was able to add from his vast store of erudition that "this method of finding a lost arrow is prescribed by P. Crescentius in his Treatise *de Agricultura,*[13] Lib. X. cap xxviii. and is also mentioned in *Howel's Letters,* Vol. I, p. 183, edit, 1665. 12mo." (V. 405.7). He tentatively suggested that Hamlet's "They fool me to the top of my bent" was "perhaps a term in archery, i.e. as far as the bow will admit of being bent without breaking" (XV. 208.5). To Douce's note on "tilly-valley" as a corruption of a French hunting cry may be added his comment on Prospero's "whom / To trash for over-topping." He thought the phrase meant "to correct for too much haughtiness or overbearing" and said that it was "used by sportsmen in the North when they correct a dog for misbehaviour in pursuing the game." He quoted the parallel use of "to trash" in *Othello* and acknowledged he had not seen Warton's note on the *Othello* passage which corroborated his own explanation (III. 15.9).

Douce's reading or personal interests extended beyond sports, of course. As has been seen, he knew the game of Gleek. He was not entirely unaware of the niceties of Elizabethan feminine attire, so that when Steevens explained "muffler" in *The Merry Wives of Windsor* as "some part of dress that covered the face" Douce could be more precise, noting that it was "a part of female attire, which only covered the lower half of the face" (III. 448.2). He knew, to his cost, as his was to be an unhappy marriage, the words of the marriage ceremony (IV. 496.3). Possibly the few notes that demonstrate knowledge of the law are a vestige of the period when he studied for the bar and had rooms in Gray's Inn. He saw an allusion to "itinerant sword-dancers" in Claudio's "I will bid thee draw, as we to the minstrels" in *Much Ado* and explained, "in what low estimation *minstrels* were held in the reign of Elizabeth, may be seen from Stat. Eliz. 39. C. iv. and the term was probably used to denote any sort of vagabonds who amused the people at particular seasons" (IV. 528.5). He differed with Johnson on Costard's "You cannot beg us," in *Love's Labour's Lost,* for Johnson wrote, "That is, we are not fools; our next relations cannot beg the wardship of our persons and fortunes," and Douce believed that "it is the wardship of *Lunaticks* not *Ideots* that devolves upon the next relation. Shakspeare, perhaps, as well as Dr. Johnson, was not aware of the distinction" (V. 345.4). Ritson corrected Douce to the effect that it was not the next relation *alone* who could have the wardship of an idiot and quoted a story to prove his point. In his later Illustrations (I. 240–43) Douce expanded Ritson's story from the "original source," a collection of tales . . . preserved among the Harleian MSS. in the British Museum, No. 6395," another time when his work on these MSS served him well. In a long note on "Sir" as a title for priests he cited Dyer's and Godbolt's *Reports*, i.e., Sir James Dyer's *Reports in the Reign of King Henry VIII, Edward VI, and Queen Mary and Elizabeth*, 1585 and John Godbolt's *Reports of certain Cases, arising in the several Courts of Register at Westminster*, 1652 (III. 509 and 511). He, of course, knew Sir Edward Coke, quoting him in the long end-note on *The Merry Wives of Windsor* on "Sir" as a title for the minor clergy (III. 510), and he cites "Justinian's Code Lib. III. Tit. 43" as one place where reference was made to "the use of the quintain" (VI. 179).

Something of Douce's interest in old prints has already been noticed, and any scholar who has worked extensively in the Bodleian Library will almost inevitably have come upon the Douce collection of printed books, prints and drawings, illuminated manuscripts, other books and manuscripts, coins and medals.[14] In corroboration of George Tollet's note on the "nine-men's morris" in *A Midsummer Night's Dream*, Douce wrote that "the *jeu de merelles* was also a table-game. A representation of two Monkies engaged at this amusement, may be seen in a German edition of Petrarch de remedio utriusque fortunae, B. I. ch. 26. The cuts to this book were done in 1520."[15] A Reference to "men of hair" in *The Winter's Tale* elicited an anecdote from French history from Johnson and a note and a full-page copy of an illuminated page from Froissart from Douce. In the note he wrote that "the following copy of an illumination in a fine Ms. of Froissart's Chronicle preserved in the British Museum, will serve to illustrate Dr. Johnson's note, and to convey some idea, not only of the manner in which these *hairy men* were habited, but also of the rude simplicity of an ancient Ballroom and Masquerade. See the story at large in Froissart, B. IV. chap. lii. edit. 1559" (VII 145.8). The copy shows five men dressed in skins, wearing long nosed masks, performing various antics to the amusement and consternation of four ladies and three or four gentlemen. An when Talbot invokes "antick death" Douce was reminded of another book with "cuts." "It is not improbable," he wrote, "that Shakspeare borrowed this idea from one of the cuts to that most exquisite work called *Imagines Mortis,* commonly ascribed to the pencil of Holbein but without any authority. See the 7th print" (IX. 634.6). In a reference to "fool" and "feather" in *Henry VIII* Douce saw "an allusion to the feathers which were formerly worn by fools in their caps. See a print on this subject from a painting of Jordaens,[16] engraved by Voert, and again, in the ballad of *News and No News*" (XI. 45.9). Douce was probably wrong, but it is his interest in prints that is the present concern, not his accuracy. He also knew where one could see a cut cf a "sweating tub," i.e., in an edition of the works of Ambrose Paraeus (XI. 593.5).[17]

Before some slight further analysis of the wide range of Douce's reading and erudition, a few more notes should be quoted. He was an observant man with a good memory. He remembered, for example, that he had seen the name of Jesus engraved on the pommel of a sword of a Crusader in the Church at Winchelsea (VII. 75.4). He had evidently examined MSS preserved in the Exchequer, remembering a single word in certain household accounts of Henry VII (XIV. 233.4). Falstaff's reference to "red-lattice" in *The Merry Wives of Windsor* had been explained by Steevens, bolstered up by Malone, as "the external denotements of the ale-house," to which Douce added, "This designation of an ale-house is not altogether lost, though the original meaning of the word is, the sign being converted into a green *lettuce;* of which an instance occurs in Brownlow Street, Holborn" (III. 374.5). And when Slender, in the same play, says that Pistol robbed him, among other coins, of two "Edward shovel-boards," the annotators (Steevens, Farmer, Mason, and Reed) all wrote notes to explain that shillings minted under Edward VI were used at the game of shove-board. Douce brought the practice up to Thomas Shadwell's time, quoting from two of his plays, and concluding by adding, "It [the game] is still played; and I lately heard a man ask another to go into an alehouse in the Broad Sanctuary, Westminster, to play at it" (III. 318.4). In his long discussion of the "quintaine," mentioned in *As You Like It,* he noted that "at the village of Offham, near Town Malling in Kent, there is now standing a quintaine, resembling that copied from Stowe, opposite the dwelling-house of a family that is obliged under some tenure to support it, but I do not find any use has been ever made of it within the recollection of the inhabitants"

(VI. 179). Everything was evidently grist to his antiquarian, scholarly mill. But he also sometimes, albeit very rarely, betrayed another side of himself, and he could write, of Viola's description of an echo, "the babbling gossip of the air," that it was "a most beautiful expression for an *echo*" (IV. 41.2). He found the lines of Portia's "quality of mercy" speech "beautiful," suggesting, what has been unduly overlooked, that it was "probable that Shakspeare recollected the following verse in *Ecclesiasticus*, xxxv. 20: Mercy is seasonable in the time of affliction, as clouds of rain in the time of the drought" (V. 509.6).[18]

On 25 September 1807 Edmond Malone in London wrote a long gossipy letter to Bishop Percy in Ireland. Among other matters of interest were certain changes in the staff of the British Museum. "Mr. Douce," Malone wrote, "without any solicitation on his part, is appointed in [Nares's] room. Mr. Douce is a man of considerable knowledge; of great accuracy, very conversant with French literature,[19] and with ancient Manuscripts. He is therefore extremely well qualified for the office [as keeper of manuscripts]; his promotion to it therefore gives great satisfaction" (*Letters*, I. 237). By 1807, the year his *Illustrations* was published, Douce was a well-known figure in London, and it was only Percy's long absence from England that made it necessary for Malone to describe Douce's attainments to him. While it will, of course, be realized that only a small part of Douce's learning manifests itself in the notes in 1793, it is still well to mention a few of the works he quotes or cites, as well as some of his areas of interest. Douce's knowledge of Italian history is displayed in a note on *2 Henry IV* in which "fig me" is said to be of Italian origin, a statement which is reinforced by the story of the occasion upon which the incident giving rise to the expression took place.[20] He was personally acquainted with Joseph Strutt, author of *A Complete View of the Manners, Customs, Arms, Habits, etc. of the Inhabitants of England*, a book which he cites (IV. 228.7) and with Francis Grose, whose *History of the English Army from the Conquest to the Present Time*, 1789–91, which he also cites (VII. 281.6). These last two represent the kind of history, the history of *domestica facta*, in which Douce was most interested and most knowledgable. In his end-note on "quintaine" in *As You Like It* he writes,

It is hardly needful to add, that a knowledge of very many of our very ancient sports and domestic employments is not now to be attained Historians have contented themselves to record the vices of kings and princes, and the minutiae of battles and seiges; and, with very few exceptions, they have considered the discussion of private manners (a theme perhaps equally interesting to posterity,) as beneath their notice and of little or no importance. (VI. 179)

Much earlier I quoted Alexander Dyce's sneering remark that Douce's notes are "nearly worthless" except for those "explanatory of customs, dress, etc." I am not sure what the "etc." was meant to encompass, but without Douce and others like him there would be many lacunae in our understanding of Shakespeare's text. Perhaps it would be well, if possibly belatedly, to quote from a more appreciative source than Dyce. The Preface to the Catalogue of the printed books and manuscripts he bequeathed to the Bodleian Library contains this paragraph.

Mr. Douce, having been an early collector (from 1784), was enabled to avail himself of the dispersion by auction of many of the richest collections of rare books that have ever been brought to the hammer; such were those of Mr. Tutet, Henderson the actor, Major Pearson, Dr. Farmer, etc., from which he selected very many of his choicest gems. He also purchased largely from the collection of Mr. Herbert, the author of the new edition of the Typographical Antiquities of these kingdoms, and thus secured some of the more rare and valuable specimens of early English Typography. The history of the manners, customs, games, literary pursuits, and superstitions of the middle ages, seems to have engaged his peculiar attention: and connected with the latter subject a very curious series of works on witchcraft and magic will be found in his library; and it must be added that there is scarcely a volume of any interest in the whole collection which he has not enriched with some valuable note. (p. vi)

Douce, it will be remembered, became Keeper of Manuscripts in the British Museum in 1807, but long before this he was a regular visitor to the Reading Room of the Museum. There he came upon the unique MS of Ingulf's *Chronicle of Croy Abbey* and there, too, he studied other MSS. For in his notes he refers to or quotes from the old MS poem, *The Description of Women;* a letter from Sir John Hollis to Lord Burleigh and a "Ms. of Lord Burleigh's, in the Marquis of Lansdowne's library"; a "MS. *Book of Cookery.* Temp. Hen. 6"; and a MS in the Harleian collection, to which he gives the old Harleian catalogue number.[21] Steevens, in a note on "vixen" in *A Midsummer Night's Dream*, quotes from *The boke of hunting, that is cleped Mayster of Game*: an ancient MS in the collection of Francis Douce, Esqr. Grays Inn" (V. 109.4), evidence that by 1793 Douce already had a collection of manuscript material. Possibly the cookbook and the old poem were part of that collection. In another note Douce directed readers to "Plat's Delightes for ladies to adorne their persons, etc. 1611" and "The accomplisht Lady's Delight, 1675" for recipes for the pomanders being hawked, among other wares, by Autolycus in *The Winter's Tale*, adding that "they all differ" (VII. 161.8).[22] A recent (1975) bookseller's catalog that listed Douce's *Illustrations* contained the following comment: "As a critic, Douce leaves much to be desired, but the scholarship and archival research contained in these two volumes is impressive and valuable." Perhaps this is damning with faint praise, perhaps not.

Since Douce's notes in the 1793 *Shakespeare* have been so much neglected, it may not be amiss to quote his rejoinder to Henry James Pye's *Comments on the Commentators of Shakespeare*, a publication which led to an eleven-column letter in the GM for October 1807. In it, Douce, who signed the letter, defended himself and others from Pye's strictures. While the whole letter is worth reading, I shall quote only two short passages: the end of the second paragraph and the last two paragraphs.

> My sole purpose is to vindicate myself, to the best of my power, from the Laureat's attempt to show that I doubtless in very good and honourable company, am little short of a blockhead: and whenever any point between myself and my antagonist shall rest on mere matter of opinion, the publick shall be free to decide; where on matter of fact, appeal will be unnecessary. (p. 922)

> But notwithstanding the unfortunate difference in our opinions as to the preceding matters, I will not conceal that I have felt no inconsiderable degree of pleasure in perusing several of Mr. Pye's observations. In a few, where I had the happiness of thinking in common with him, he has got the start of me, but only in publication, as may perhaps hereafter appear.

> I have only to add, Mr. Urban, that if in the course of these strictures on Mr. Pye's Comments on the Commentators I have been betrayed into any expression that may be deemed inconsistent with that good humour and gentlemanly language which smooths the natural asperity of criticism, and even concilitates the esteem of the object of it, I must plead the example of honest Tom Coryat, who felt himself obliged to repel the aggression of a scold by retorting her own phraseology; and I beg leave to conclude with gently admonishing the Critic to attend to the advice of his and my late excellent and pleasant friend Captain Grose, "ever to hold in mind that one who has a head of glass should never engage in throwing stones." (p. 927)

Douce's apology was hardly necessary, for in the give-and-take of
scholarly controversy he was gentlemanliness itself. He answered all Pye's criticisms and his notes and took up the cudgels
or those who were no longer alive to defend themselves—Tyrwhitt, Farmer, and Steevens.

7

James Boswell, the Younger

Literary history does not contain many examples of the kind of relationship enjoyed by James Boswell, Dr. Johnson's biographer, and his son James (1778–1822) with Edmond Malone. The story of Malone's help with the elder Boswell's *Life* of Johnson is well known, but the almost reciprocal aid given Malone in his edition of Shakespeare by the younger Boswell is probably known only to a few Shakespeareans. Malone edited the third edition of Boswell's *Life* of Johnson; James Boswell, the younger, edited what may be called Malone's revised or second edition of Shakespeare, but what is usually referred to as the Boswell-Malone *Shakespeare* of 1821. About one year after publication of his 1790 *Shakespeare*, on 30 November 1791, Malone agreed to revise his edition for the publisher George Robinson. The edition was to be in fifteen volumes, quarto, and in the event that Malone did not live to finish the work the publisher was to have the volumes of the 1790 edition with Malone's corrections and additions.[1] Malone died in 1812 and entrusted the task of completing his *Shakespeare* to young Boswell. Published in twenty-one volumes, three of which are given over to prolegomena, one to the poems (not an invariable part of an edition of Shakespeare), and part of the last volume to various Addenda as well as a "Glossorial Index of Words, Phrases, Customs, and Persons, Explained or mentioned in the Notes," it was easily the most complete and valuable edition of Shakespeare yet to be published. To my knowledge there has been no attempt to analyze the full extent of Boswell's contribution to the 1821 *Shakespeare*. The *DNB* is content to state, inaccurately, that he contributed "various readings and notes of no great importance," but one modern scholar, concerned solely with the biographical accounts of Shakespeare, praises him for his presentation of Malone's scattered and fragmentary account of Shakespeare's life as well as of his own contribution to the vexed problem of the second-best bed Shakespeare willed to his wife. Boswell, as Samuel Schoenbaum relates it, "anticipates the prevailing modern view by supposing that Shakespeare provided for Anne in his lifetime, and that in those days such a bequest as the bed carried no reproach: he has found among Malone's Adversaria the will of Sir Thomas Lucy the younger, who in 1600 left his second son Richard his second-best horse, but no land, because this his father-in-law had already promised him."[2] Boswell's interpretation of the second-best bed proviso of Shakespeare's will and his careful editing of Malone's biographical account of Shakespeare are but a small part of his total contribution.

When Boswell died, shortly after the appearance of the Shakespeare edition, the writer of his obituary in the March 1822 GM stated that he had "possessed talents of a superior order, sound classical scholarship, and a most extensive and intimate knowledge of our early literature." He went on to relate the circumstances under which Malone entrusted the completion of his work to Boswell and listed the various contributions Boswell himself had made to the edition (p. 277). As one would expect in an obituary notice, Boswell's contributions were praised, and justly so, although only two were singled out: his defense of Malone against William Gifford's attack on him in his edition of the works of Ben Jonson, published in 1816, and the "considerable labour and attention" which he bestowed upon "the arrangement and completion" of the materials partly collected for an essay on the meter and phraseology of Shakespeare. Both contributions are major concerns in Boswell's forty-six page Advertisement in the first volume. But Boswell, as editor, did so very much more, albeit a good part of what he did might be termed busy work, those editorial chores that are necessary but certainly uninspired and uninspiring. Perhaps it will be best to analyze his major contributions seriatim much as they appear in the twenty-one volumes.

In his Advertisement, besides the two concerns already mentioned, the defense of Malone taking up twenty-two pages, Boswell devoted himself to laying down his editorial principles. The Advertisement was followed by a "Biographical Memoir" of Malone and the Essay on the Phraseology and Metre of Shakspeare and his Contemporaries. Boswell's part in the second volume consisted of a number of notes added to Malone's memoranda. Almost the whole of volume three was given over to Malone's "Historical Account of the English Stage" to which Boswell added a number of notes. His first note deserves full quotation. Malone's first two sentences state:

The drama before the time of Shakspeare was so little cultivated, or so ill understood, that to many it may appear unnecessary to carry our theatrical researches higher than that period. Dryden has truly observed, that he "found not, but created first the stage;" of which no one can doubt, who considers, that of all the plays issued from the press antecedent to the year 1592, about which time there is reason to believe he commenced a dramatick writer, the titles are scarcely known, except to antiquaries; nor is there one of them that will bear a second perusal. (p. 5)

Boswell very politely dissented.

I must be permitted to dissent from this sweeping censure passed upon all the predecessors of our great dramatick poet. The contempt with which they, and even his contemporaries in general, are usually mentioned by Mr. Steevens and Mr. Malone, may perhaps be thus explained: that having only referred to them with a view to discover what light they might throw upon the language and allusions of Shakspeare, their attention was constantly called to the inferiority of their productions to those of that matchless writer with whom they were brought into direct comparison. But since a taste for our ancient literature has sprung up to a greater degree than at any former period, they have met with a more candid judgment, and many have been found worthy of being valued for their own substantive merit, and not merely as subsidiary to the illustration of another. Ferrex and Porrex ought surely not to have been included in Mr. Malone's pre- scribed list: The plays of Marlowe give frequent evidence of no common genius, however little they may have been regulated by taste, which, had a more prolonged life made him acquainted with better models, gave promise of a high degree of excellence; and I cannot but think Nestor himself must have found his gravity relaxed by more than a second persual of Gammer Gurton's Needle. (pp. 5–6)

Modern opinion, certainly as far as Marlowe's plays are con- cerned, is solidly with Boswell. One other note is worth quoting, as it too has to do with Marlowe.

Tamar Cam is probably meant for Timur Cham, or Tamerlane. There is a play ascribed to Marlowe, in two parts, entitled Tam- burlaine the Great; but it does not correspond either in the names or incidents with the drama mentioned in the Plott. Mr. Malone con- jectured that Tamburlaine the Great was either written wholly or in part by Nashe, from the following passage in the Blacke Book, 4to. 1604: "The spindle-shanke spyder which shewed like great leachers with little legs, went stealing over his (Nashes) head, as if they had been conning of Tamburlaine." It is possible, however, that there might have been two plays on this subject, as we find, in p. 324, that there were two on that of Ferrex and Porrex. (p. 357)

Of interest is the fact that Marlowe's authorship of the two parts of *Tamberlane* seems still to have been in doubt. However, Boswell's conjecture was right, an anonymous *Tamar Cham* was acted in 1592 with a possible second part in 1596, but no texts have survived.

I have characterized as busy work certain editorial chores performed by Boswell. Some were necessary; others may not have been. Most plays were preceded by "Preliminary Remarks" by various editors and commentators, Boswell sometimes among them. At the end of the "Remarks" for those plays where the information about texts was incomplete, Boswell appended a textual note ranging from a single sentence (*Love's Labour's Lost*, for example) to most of a page (*Othello*). Of greater importance are such chores as bringing together at the end of 1 *Henry IV* all the notes on the Falstaff-Oldcastle problem in that play and in *Henry V* (XVI. 410–19), the shifting of the history plays from their chronological order of composition so that they might be exhibited, as Johnson had observed, in a regular connection, and the relegating to the back of *Twelfth Night* the many notes on Patience sitting on a monument smiling at grief." He wrote of the last chore that "for the sake of those readers who may think that this exquisite passage stands in no need of explanation, I have saved them from the interruption which would have been occasioned by the long notes written upon it, and have thrown them to the end of the play" (XI. 411.9). In addition, at various junctures, some of which will figure in later discussion, he wrote notes based upon information in works published after 1790, the date of Malone's first edition. These include Francis Douce's *Illustrations of Shakespeare*, 2 vols., 1807; Todd's edition of Spenser, 5 vols., 1805; Henry William Weber's *Metrical Romances of the Thirteenth, Fourteenth, and Fifteenth Centuries*, 3 vols., 1810; and his edition of Beaumont and Fletcher, 14 vols., 1812.

Boswell's editorial stance was one which favored the old readings, evidenced by many notes quoting them and by his rejection of a number of emendations, as well as his reluctance to indulge in conjecture himself. What few conjectures he did allow himself were tentatively and hesitantly put forward and were on punctuation, speech headings, and the addition of a word to a line. Thus, in *The Comedy of Errors* in the line "For ever hous'd, where it gets possession," where the meter was in question, he suggested, "if we were to read housed, the difficulty would be got over by a very slight alteration."[3] At one juncture, he championed adherence to old spelling, noting of "Syracusians" in the opening scene of *The Comedy of Errors*, "Thus the first folio. The modern editors have altered it to the Syracusans, but it will be sufficient indication of the old spelling to state, that it has the sanction of Bentley, in his Dissertation on Phalaris" (IV. 153.1). Some forty or more of Boswell's notes have to do with matters metrical; in many of these he refers back to his "Essay on the Metre and Phraseology of Shakspeare and His Contemporaries." He was especially severe on Steevens's rearrangement of some lines in Banquo's description of Macbeth's castle and caught him having his cake and eating it in another note in the same play.[4] Where most editors, including Steevens and Malone, had found the Third Witch's line, "There to meet with Macbeth," defective and had tinkered with it, Boswell wrote, in a typical note, "I have endeavoured to show in the Essay on Shakspeare's versification that this line is not defective, and that neither Mr. Steevens's supplemental *whom*, nor Mr. Malone's dissyllabical pronunciation of *there*, is required" (XI. 12.4). Two more of his notes on versification are particularly interesting. Johnson had once thought that in Macbeths "My genius is rebuk'd; as, it is said, / Mark Antony's was by Caesar. He chid the sisters," the words "as, it is said, / Mark Antony's was by Caesar," were an interpolation of a player. Benjamin Heath in his anonymous *Revisal of Shakespeare's Text*, 1765, had claimed that the meter was not faulty. Johnson wrote, "Every boy or girl finds the metre imperfect, but the pedant comes to its defence with a tribachys or an anapaest, and sets it right at once, by applying to one language the rules of another. If we may be allowed to change feet, like the old comick writers, it will not be easy to write a line not metrical. To hint this once is sufficient." Boswell wrote:

To produce the example of the old Greek or Latin comick writer would, it is true, be applying to one language the rules of another; but if it can be shown that versification equally licentious may be found in Shakspeare himself elsewhere, and was consistent with the practice of his contemporaries, for which I refer the reader to the Essay on Shakspeare's Versification, it may not perhaps prove the line to be metrical, but it will certainly furnish a strong presumption that the poet wrote it, and did not consider it as faulty. Mr. Steevens's sugges tion, that the praenomen *Mark* might be omitted, would leave the verse quite as harsh as he found it. (XI, 141.4)

Possibly indicative of the modern advances in textual sophistication is the absence of any comment in the New Variorum *Macbeth* on the possible metrical faultiness of these lines.[5]
One service Boswell performed was his attempt to adjudicate between Malone and William Gifford, the latter having taken strident issue with a number of Malone's notes on Shakespeare in his edition of Ben Jonson's works published in 1816, four years after Malone's death. It will be recalled that Boswell devoted the last twenty-two pages of his Advertisement to this question, but he also found it necessary on some twenty occasions to examine Gifford's animadversions on Malone's notes as well as to cite or quote Gifford's interpretations of words in phrases used by both Jonson and Shakespeare. Boswell tried, and I believe succeeded, in his efforts to be objective, giving Gifford his just due, and only in one note did he reflect more in sorrow than in anger at Gifford's intemperate language. Gloucester has been blinded and one of Cornwall's servants says that he will "fetch some flax, and whites of eggs, / To apply to his bleeding face." Steevens stated that Jonson had ridiculed this passage in *The Case is Alter'd*, 1609, and Malone wrote, "The Case is Alter'd was written before the end of the year 1559; but Ben Jonson might have inserted this sneer at our author, between the time of King Lear's appearance, and the publication of his own play in 1609." Boswell added, "I was not at liberty to omit this [Malone's] note, but Mr Gifford has shown this charge against Jonson to be entirely groundless. I wish he had not expressed his dissent in such strong language" (X. 188.4).[6] Boswell had thought it necessary, in his biographical memoir of Malone, to recount the history of Malone's relationship with Steevens (I.lvi–lxi), quite understandably taking Malone's part in the controversy that had surrounded the two. Equally understandable is his close scrutiny of Steeven's notes, with the consequent result in a number of disagreements with some of those notes. Steevens had been very severe on Lorenzo's speech on the power of music in the fifth act of *The Merchant of Venice*, quoting Lord Chesterfield's letters in corroboration of his jaundiced view of music. Boswell wrote, "The lovers of music may submit to have the opinion of Lord Chesterfield quoted against them, while they have that of Shakspeare in their favour" (V. 141.8). Steevens would have "marriage" a trisyllable in the line, "In the estate of honourable marriage," in *Much Ado about*

Nothing, but Boswell would not: "Why should it be a trisyllable here? Mr. Steevens, after cutting and clipping several hundred lines in order to avoid a verse of twelve syllables, would here introduce a 'needless alexandrine.' "[7]

Steevens said that a word "which is wanting in the old copies, is transplanted (for the sake of metre) from a redundant speech in the following page"; Boswell was equally laconic, merely remarking that "to transplant a word from one page to another, is surely the very cacoethis of emendation."[8] Further, Steevens had tampered with some lines in *Pericles*, with the result, as Boswell pointed out, that he had "thus mammocked the first four lines of this chorus" (XXI. 129.9).

Two more of Steevens's notes with Boswell's comments appended must be quoted in their entirety. The first is on the last speech in Act III of *Macbeth*, a speech Steevens printed as "My prayers with him!"

The old copy, frigidly, and in defiance of measure, reads—

> "*I'll send* my prayers with him"
>
> I am aware, that for this, and similar rejections, I shall be censured by those who are disinclined to venture out of the track of the old stage-waggon, though it may occasionally conduct them into a slough. It may soon, therefore, be discoverd, that numerous beauties are resident in the discarded words—*I'll send*; and that as frequently as the vulgarism—*on*, has been displaced to make room for—*of*, a diamond has been exchanged for a pebble.—For my own sake, however, let me add, that, throughout the present tragedy, no such liberties have been exercised, without the previous approbation of Dr. Farmer, who fully concurs with me in supposing the irregularities of Shakespeare's text to be oftener occasioned by interpolations, than by omissions. (XI. 188.1)

Boswell waxed sarcastic:

> Mr. Steevens has proposed three alterations of the text in twenty-one lines and has given the rein to his critical boldness in this play, more, perhaps, than in any other. The *old stage-waggon* may offend the refinement of those who may accuse Shakspeare "*Plaustris vexisse poemata:*" but his genuine admirers will prefer the vehicle which he himself has chosen to the modern curricle which Mr. Steevens would provide for him.

The other notes take their point of departure from Warburton's assertion, in a note on *All's Well*, that Shakespeare "is extremely delicate in this respect [the use of "stinking metaphors"]; who, throughout his large writings, if you except a passage in Hamlet, has scarce a metaphor that can offend the most squeamish reader." Steevens disagreed.

> Dr. Warburton's recollection must have been weak, or his zeal for his author extravagant, otherwise he could not have ventured to countenance him on the score of delicacy; his offensive metaphors and allusions being undoubtedly more frequent than those of all his dramatick predecessors or contemporaries. (X. 468.7)

And Boswell disagreed with Steevens, taking occasion also to sum up others of Steevens's shortcomings as a man and as a critic.

> In the earlier editions of Shakspeare by Mr. Steevens, he was content to pass over Warburton's remark in silent acquiescence. But his propensity to satire so far increased in later years, that even the great poet, whose works he had been so long employed in illustrating, could not escape his lash. Of this the reader may have observed abundant proofs in his bitter comments upon the character of Hamlet, and his contemptuous depreciation of Shakspeare's poems. The charge which he has brought forward in the present instance, is unfortunately of such a nature, that it will scarcely admit of more than a general contradiction, without incurring the very censure which is applied to the poet; but, as to our author's "dramatick predecessors," some judgment may be formed of their superior delicacy, by Mr. Steeven's own note on The Taming of A Shrew, vol. v. p. 370. Without referring to dramas that are not accessible to every reader, the plays of Beaumont and Fletcher throughout will serve to show with what justice his contemporaries are placed above him, either for purity of thought or language. The first scene of Jonson's Alchemist, and his masque of The Metamorphosed Gipsies, *performed at Court*, will also be more than sufficient to show how little foundation there is for Mr. Steevens's assertion.[9]

But Boswell did not allow his feelings entirely to color his judgment, and he could defend Steevens when the latter was misunderstood and hence condemned (VII. 348.6).

Boswell brought a good deal of downright common sense to his editorial labors, a necessary corrective to some of the efforts to explain the obvious, or fairly obvious, on the part of earlier editors. Grumio, in *The Taming of the Shrew*, says that Petruchio will so "disfigure" Katherina "that she shall have no more eyes to see withal than a cat," which Steevens did not understand and which Johnson explained as, "It may mean, that he shall swell up her eyes with blows, till she shall seem to peep with a contracted pupil, like a cat in the light." Boswell simply noted that "nothing is more common in ludicrous or playful discourse than to use a comparison where no resemblance is intended. When Johnson said of himself, that at one time he read like a Turk, he certainly did not mean to be understood, that the Turks were a remarkably studious people" (V. 402.8). Boswell's comments on some of the language in *Twelfth Night* should have found a place in the New Variorum edition. The editors and commentators had made much ado about Sir Toby's "Castiliano vulgo," his "passy measures pavin," and the Clown's "I did impeticos thy gratility." Boswell wrote: "An attempt to *define the meaning* of many of this merry knight's phrases would, I suspect, be a very hopeless task" (XI. 351.3); "It is surely rather ludicrous to see four sober commentators gravely endeavouring to ascertain the correct meaning of what Sir Toby says when he is drunk" (XI. 492.5); and "I cannot think it [the Clown's dialogue] was meant to be understood. The greater part of this scene is *gracious fooling*" (XI. 388.6). Steevens saw an allusion to "Clytus refusing the Persian robes offered him by Alexander" in the mad Lear's reference to "Persian attire." Boswell burst that bubble by writing that he could "see no ground for suspecting any classical allusion in Lear's ravings in this passage, any more than where he terms Edgar a *Theban*" (X. 178.6). Parolles, in *All's Well*, speaks of a "kicksy-wicksy"; Zachary Grey noted that Taylor, the water-poet, had a poem entitled "A kicksy-winsy, or a Lerry come-twang" and Boswell suggested that "one nonsensical phrase is as good as another; the old copy has *kickie wickie*" (X. 390.7).

In a few places Boswell objected to what in his Advertisement he had labeled "reprehensible" annotations that he felt obliged to retain but to whose number he did not add. Whalley had read a bawdy meaning into the words "did it" in Posthumus's "did it with / A pudency so rosy," and Douce, characterizing Whalley's note as "useless" and making Shakespeare "vulgar and obscene," said it could "well be dispensed with in any future edition. Boswell agreed wholeheartedly: "I have not hesitated to adopt Mr. Douce's suggestion. Mr. Whalleys's imaginations must have been 'as foul as Vulcan's stithy;' when he attempted to discover in this beautiful passage the language of a brothel" (XIII. 90.9). Late in the same play, when Imogen tells Pisanio, "Thou art all the comfort / The gods will diet me with," Boswell has this note: "Mr Steevens has a note on this passage, which is, if possible, mor disgustingly absurd than that of Mr. Whalley's, mentioned p. 90. He says Imogen is alluding to the spare regimen prescribed in some diseases. This interpretation is at once gross and nonsensical. If any doubt could be entertained as to so common a metaphor, it might be easily supported. One instance shall suffice. When Iago (vol. ix. p. 135) talks of *dieting his revenge*, he certainly does not mean putting it on *a spare regimen*" (XIII. 127.1). Edgar's "ha no nonny" in *King Lear* had been invested with a bawdy meaning by Samuel Henley who noted that it occurred as the refrain line in two songs sung by "girls distracted from disappointed love." Boswell would have none of this, remarking that the refrain "although sometimes used by those who thought an indecent meaning might not be so offensive, when nonsensically expressed, was nothing more than a common burthen of a song, like *fal lal* or *derry down*. Amiens, in *As You Like It*, was certainly not a girl distracted from disappointed love, and he employs it without any such meaning as is here ascribed to it" (X. 156–7). One more example. Hotspur says that to "be still" is a "woman's fault," which Thomas Holt White had rather modestly explained as follows: "The whole tenor of Hotspur's conversation in this scene shows, that the stillness which he here imputes to women as a fault, was something very different from silence; and that an idea was couched under these words, which may be better understood than explained.——He is still in the Welsh lady's bedchamber." Boswell wasted no words: "Without attempting to penetrate Mr. White's occult meaning, it may be questioned whether there is any ground for supposing that this scene takes place in the Welsh lady's bedchamber" (XVI. 319.4). The note, erroneously ascribed to Holt White, was actually by "Amner," i.e., Steevens, but whoever wrote the note, the fact is that the locale of the scene is unspecified in the old editions, Pope being the first to set it in "the Archdeacon of Bangor's House of Wales," something the mischievous Steevens knew full well.

One learns much about Boswell from his notes. He had a mind of his own, as has already been seen and as can further be seen in a note on *Coriolanus* where he writes, "I should not consider myself as dealing fairly by the reader; if I had not laid before him Mr. Malone's emendation and the reasons he has assigned for it; although I can by no means acquiesce in either the one or the other" (XIV. 189.9). When Falstaff, in *2 Henry IV*, asks what the doctor had said to his water Steevens explained the allusion to urinalysis and told an anecdote about "English credulity" on this score. Boswell remarked that "the time has not yet come, when this is to be thought incredible. The same impudent quackery is carried on at this day" (XVII. 22.7), evidence of his disgust with contemporary pseudomedicine. Despite his avowed intention to try to be impartial, one fancies he detects a note of quiet satisfaction when he can tell off Joseph Ritson, Malone's old enemy who had predeceased him by about nine years. A reference to Wittenberg in *Hamlet* caused Ritson to suggest that Shakespeare "may have derived his knowledge of this famous university from The Life of Iacke Wilton, 1594, or the Hystory of Doctor Faustus . . .," to which Boswell added, "or from Marlowe's Doctor Faustus, or a multitude of other publications of that period" (VII. 200.2). Anne, Duchess of Gloster, in *Richard III*, cries out, "O, would to God, that the inclusive verge / Of golden metal, that must round my brow, / Were red-hot steel, to sear me to the brain!" Ritson wrote a learned note in which he quoted *Goulart's Admirable and Memorable Histories*, 1607," explained Goldsmith's line, "Luke's iron crown, and Damien's bed of steel," and quoted Holinshed on the Earl of Athol's being "crowned with a hot iron before his death." He ended his note with "See Holinshed." Boswell caustically added, "See also Boswell's Life of Johnson; from which Mr. Ritson's note is taken almost verbatim" (XIX. 153.6).[10] And there is also Ritson's note on the ballad of King Lear,

> This ballad, which by no means deserves a place in any edition of Shakspeare, is evidently a most servile pursuit,—not, indeed, of our author's play, which the writer does not appear to have read, but of Holinshed's Chronicle, where, as in Geoffrey of Monmouth, the King of France is called Aganippus. I suppose, however, that the performance and celebrity of the play might have set the ballad-maker at work, and furnished him with the circumstance of Lear's madness, of which there is no hint either in the historian or the old play. The omission of any other striking incident may be fairly imputed to his want of either genius or information. All he had to do was to spin out a sort of narrative in a sort of verse, to be sung about the streets, and make advantage of the publick curiosity. I much doubt whether any common ballad can be produced anterior to a play upon the same subject, unless in the case of some very recent event.

with Boswell's comment:

> It is not easy to guess at Mr. Ritson's meaning in this strange note. The ballad-maker, it seems, servilely copied Holinshed's Chronicle

and yet introduced a circumstance not mentioned by the Historian, but furnished by Shakspeare's play, which it is said he does not appear to have read. The rest of his observations are equally confused.[11]

Considering the language employed by Ritson in his criticism of others, Boswell's forbearance is admirable.

One gleans a few other facts about Boswell from one or two other notes. He must have attended the debates in the House of Commons, for when Malone stated that "Biron," or "Berowne," of Love's Labour's Lost was pronounced "Biroon" in Shakspeare's time, he could add that "this was the mode in which all French words of this termination were pronounced in English. Mr. Fox always in the House of Commons said Touloon when speaking of Toulon" (IV. 380.5). He was aware of contemporary fashions, for preparatory to reprinting the spate of commentary on the tailor who "had falsely thrust [his slippers] on contrary feet" (King John), he wrote that "the following notes afford a curious specimen of the difficulties which may arise from the fluctuations of fashion. What has called forth the antiquarian knowledge of so many learned commentators is again become the common practice at this day" (XV. 325.4). One would expect Boswell to be a collector of books, and in his Advertisement he bemoaned the cost to him of the first Folio that had belonged to Kemble the actor. He had acquired, probably from his father, the copy of Warburton's Shakspeare "which Dr. Johnson made use of in selecting quotations for his Dictionary" (XIII. 91.1) and had compared Warburton's text, with its emendations and misreadings, against the old editions, so that he could state that a number of errors in the quotations from Shakespeare in the Dictionary were traceable to this source, not to Johnsons's carelessness. He was "possessed of a volume containing Legh's Accedens of Armory, and Boswell's Works of Armorie, bound up together, which is ascertained to have been formerly the property of Randle Holme (I suppose the antiquary)"(XV. 238.8). When Thomas Warton noted that there was "an old piece entitled, Old Meg of Herefordshire for a Mayd-Marian . . ., Lond. 1609," Boswell was ready with the information that a "reprint of it was published by Mr. Triphook in 1816" (XVI. 346.6), further evidence that he was a courant in the world of books.

An editor of Shakespeare would be expected to be well read, especially in earlier English literature, dramatic as well as non-dramatic. In the course of his commentary Boswell had occasion to quote or cite twenty-two plays of the Beaumont and Fletcher canon, no doubt from Weber's edition of 1812, which he names in one note (XI. 396.1). He, of course, knew Ben Jonson in Gifford's edition and the same editor's edition of the plays of Massinger.[12] He also had recourse, largely for parallel passages, to some thirty-five other early plays. He had read and quoted from a Spanish translation of *Hamlet*, published in 1798 (VII. 322.2). That he was an attentive follower of contemporary acting is evident in a note on *The Tempest*, Prospero's "Fall all thy bones with aches, make thee roar," for he writes, " The word *aches* is evidently a dissyllable. This would not have required a note but for the ignorant clamour that was raised against Mr. Kemble, because he understood Shakspeare better than the newspaper criticks who censured him, and did not at once violate the measure, and act contrary to the uniform practice of the poet, his contemporaries, and those who preceded and followed him till about the middle of the last century, by pronouncing it as a monosyllable" (XV. 57.3).

While some of the notes already quoted may fall into the category of literary criticism, there are a few which can more properly be so termed. Perhaps, indeed almost surely, Boswell had the advantage over Johnson, a very infrequent playgoer, when the latter wrote, at Isabella's discovery that her brother ws still alive, "It is somewhat strange that Isabel is not made to express either gratitude, wonder, or joy, at the sight of he brother." Boswell provided the necessary corrective "Shakspeare, it should be recollected, wrote for the stage, or which Isabel might express her feelings by action" (IX. 205.9). He was among those who thought Shakespeare had little classica knowledge, remarking of one of Caesar's bombastic speeches tha there could not be "stronger proof of Shakspeare's deficiency i classical knowledge, than the boastful language he has put in th mouth of the most accomplished man of all antiquity, who wa not more admirable for his achievements, than for the dignifie simplicity with which he has recorded them" (XII. 64.5). Joh Monck Mason saw Coriolanus as a modest man, one who coul not endure to hear "his nothings monster'd," but Boswell, mor acutely, pointed out that "the pride of Coriolanus is his stronge characteristic" (XIV. 188.8). Warburton had long ago observe that Shakespeare had borrowed Prospero's speech. "Ye elves hills, brooks, standing lakes, and groves," from one of Medea's Ovid, and Richard Farmer had shown that the borrowing w from Golding's translation rather than from the Latin, although is now known that Shakespeare consulted Ovid in Latin. Malo carried Farmer's suggestion further by reprinting the passage in Golding's version and italicizing the verbal borrowings, but it remained for Boswell to take the matter out of the realm of scholarship into that of literary criticism by remarking that "it would be an injustice to our great poet, if the reader were not to take notice that Ovid has not supplied him with any thing resembling the exquisite fairy imagery with which he has enriched this speech" (XV. 159.9). The editor of the New Variorum *Tempest* quotes Warburton, Farmer, and Malone—but not Boswell.

Horace Walpole enrolled himself in the number of critics of Shakespeare with the following remarks on *The Winter's Tale* which occur in his *Historic Doubts on the Life and Reign of King Richard the Third*, 1768, and which appeared in most editions of Shakespeare thereafter.

> The Winter's Tale may be ranked among the historic plays of Shakspeare, though not one of his numerous criticks and commentators have discovered the drift of it. It was certainly intended (in compliment to Queen Elizabeth,) as an indirect apology for her mother, Anne Boleyn. The address of the poet appears no where to more advantage. The subject was too delicate to be exhibited on the stage without a veil; and it was too recent, and touched the Queen too nearly, for the bard to have ventured so home an allusion on any other ground than compliment. The unreasonable jealousy of Leontes, and his violent conduct in consequence, form a true portrait of Henry the Eighth, who generally made the law the engine of his boisterous passions. Not only the general plan of the story is most applicable, but several passages are so marked, that they touch the real history nearer than the fable. Hermione on her trial says:
>
> > "———for honour,
> > 'Tis a derivative from me to mine,
> > And only that I stand for."

This seems to be taken from the very letter of Anne Boleyn to the King before her execution, where she pleads for the infant Princess his daughter. Mamillius, the young Prince, an unnecesary character, dies in his infancy; but it confirms the allusion, as Queen Anne, before Elizabeth, bore a still-born son. But the most striking passage, and which had nothing to do in the tragedy, but as it pictured Elizabeth, is, where Paulina, describing the new-born Princess, and her likeness to her father, says:" *She has the very trick of his frown.*" There is one sentence indeed so applicable, both to Elizabeth and her father, that I should suspect the poet inserted it after her death. Paulina, speaking of the child, tells the King:

> ————'Tis yours;
> And might we lay the old proverb to your charge,
> So like you tis the worse.————

The Winter's tale was therefore in reality a second part of Henry the Eighth. (XIV. 234)

Boswell was skeptical.

> I confess I am very sceptical as to these supposed allusions by Shakspeare to the history of his own time. If the plots of his plays had been of his own invention, he might possibly have framed them with a view of that kind; but this was unquestionably not the case with the play before us; and if any one had intended a courtly defence of Queen Elizabeth's mother, it must have been Greene, and not Shakspeare. Garinter, the Mamilius of our poet, dies under the same circumstances, in the novel; nor is it, as Mr. Walpole seemed to suppose, an unnecessary incident, because it fulfils the declaration of the oracle, "that if the child which was lost could not be found, the king would die without an heir." To say that a child resembles her father is surely not so uncommon a remark as to make it evident that it had reference to a particular individual; nor is there any thing very courtly or complimentary in Paulina's angry allusion to the old proverb. (XIV. 234–5)

References to Greene and to Garinter are to Robert Green's *Pandosto, The Triumph of Time*, 1588, reprinted in 1607 as *Dorastu and Fawnia*, the subtitle of the original edition, and to a character in that "novel." Boswell's reservations, although not based upon the date of composition of the play, are well taken, for the generally accepted date is about 1611, some years after the death of Queen Elizabeth.

It has been seen that the editor of the New Variorum *Tempest* quoted Warburton, Farmer, and Malone, but omitted Boswell's remarks, in one of Prospero's speeches. Others of Boswell's notes have been slighted. Thus, in the matter of Holofernes in *Love's Labour's Lost* being a satiric portrait of John Florio he was on the side of the angels, i.e., Florio did not sit for the portrait of Shakespeare's pedant, but one will not find his eminently sensible note in the New Variorum edition. He wrote:

> That Florio was not meant by Holofernes may be farther [he bolstering Malone's arguments] shown by a general examination that writer's general style, which is characterized by a fondness for the most homely phrases that our language can supply. But after a

may not Shakspeare have intended a general satire upon the pedantry which was prevalent in his time. See before, p. 362, the quotation [Steevens's] from "Lingua," or for the practice of an earlier period, see Wilson's Arte of Rhetorique, 1553, folio 86, where he has given us a ludicrous specimen of an "ynkehorne letter." (IV. 483)

. small body of scholarly writing exists on the question of hakespeare's use of Wilson's *Arte of Rhetorique*, but I do not elieve Boswell's suggestion has been mentioned. Instead, the ew Variorum editor (p. 119) gives Halliwell-Phillipps credit for iggesting Wilson's book as a possible source or antecedent for on Armado's letter. This may seem venial, but Furness's utter isregard of Boswell's note on the line "This man hath bewitch'd ie bosom of my child" in *A Midsummer Night's Dream* is a more rious matter. Compare Furness's note:

The Textual Notes show the editorial struggles to evade what has been deemed the defective metre of this line. It is needful to retain "man" as an antithesis to "man" in line 32; and the change of "bewitch'd" into *witch'd* has only THEOBALD for authority. To my ear the line is rendered smooth by reducing "hath" to "'th;" "This man 'th bewitch'd," etc.—just as in the next line "thou'st given her rhymes" better accords with due emphasis than "thou hast giv'n her rhymes." (p. 9)

urness is buttressing his lisping 'th emendation by another of is own making in the next line. Compare Boswell:

As reading, "This *man* hath bewitch'd," is found in all the old copies, and as the two quartos were printed in the same year, abounding in variations, and probably sent forth by persons who were wishing to outrun each other at the press, it is surely improbable that they should chance upon the same error. A redundant syllable, at the commencement of a verse, perpetually occurs in our old dramatists. See the Essay upon Shakspeare's Versification. (V. 177.7)

et the reader decide, even in the light of Boswell's ignorance of ie true nature of the two quartos.
Certain of Boswell's notes on *Hamlet* and Macbeth, arbitrarily select two of the more heavily annotated tragedies, should also ave been included in the New Variorum editions. His note on "a ast, that wants discourse of reason" is severely cut, so that his xplication of the passage is completely omitted. He wrote, with arburton's note in mind,

Brutes certainly have not what Warburton in his dashing language
terms reason, but they have faculties which philosophers in all ages
have been puzzled to define. They have memory; and they have that
degree of judgment which enables them to distinguish between two
objects directly before them; as a dog knows his master from a
stranger. Hamlet means to say that even their imperfect faculties,
without an abstract knowledge of good or evil, would have made
them capable of feeling such a loss as his mother had sustained, and
of seeing the difference between his father·and his uncle.[13]

Much controversy has arisen over whether Gertrude knew that
her husband had been murdered by Claudius, the whole matter
being relegated to an Appendix in the New Variorum. Nowhere is
Boswell's very pertinent question mentioned. Deprecating the
length of the notes on the subject, he contented himself "with
asking if it can be supposed that Shakspeare intended so important a point to be left in doubt; or that Hamlet, in this interview,
would directly reproach his mother with her marriage alone, if
she had added to it guilt so much more enormous as the murder
of her husband?" (VII. 385.7). Rather, Furness elects to sneer at
Boswell's suggestion that "rose" in Hamlet's "takes off the rose /
From the fair forehead of an innocent love" in the same scene
means "the ornament, the grace of an innocent love" (VII. 388.8).

Boswell fares somewhat better in the commentary on Macbeth,
but there are still areas of neglect. Duncan asks a soldier,
"Dismay'd not this / Our captains, Macbeth and Banquo," and
receives a monosyllabic "Yes" in answer. Steevens confidently
asserted that "the reader cannot fail to observe, that some word,
necessary to complete the verse, has been omitted in the old
copy." Boswell recalled that Francis Douce in his Illustrations of
Shakspeare had conjectured that "captains" was pronounced
"capitaine," and added that it so appeared "frequently in
Spenser" (XI. 21.3). Furness quotes W. S. Walker, in an 1860
work, "was captain ever pronounced as a trisylable—capitain—
in that age, except by such as, like Spenser, affected old forms?"
and then quotes another authority for such a pronunciation in
Beaumont and Fletcher and in Shirley (p. 22). Douce and Boswell
are forgotten. Furness quotes "Anonymous (qu. Litchfield?)" or
the Doctor's "his Majesty went into the field," part of which
comment depends on reference to Ross's statement that he 'saw
the tyrant's power afoot" (p. 302). There was no need to introduce
Anonymous and to guess at his identity, for Boswell had long
before pointed out Ross's words as part of his explanation of the
line (XI. 238.5). The commentators were assiduous in their a

mpts to find parallels or sources for Malcolm's order that his
ldiers camouflage themselves with the boughs of trees, Collier
lducing a ballad by Deloney (1607) and others citing or quoting
amples in Arabic literature, in Saxo Grammaticus, and in Scot-
sh history (pp. 325–27). Boswell's quoted parallel from "lib. vii.
p. xx. 'De Strategemate Regis Hachonis per Frondes'" of Olaus
[agnus's "Northern History" finds no place among the others
I. 257.7).

A few other omissions in the New Variorum volumes should be
oticed. Antony's mounting an "arm-gaunt steed" gave the com-
entators much trouble and still continues a crux. Boswell's full
te reads

> If Sir Thomas Hanmer's emendation "arm-girt" should not be
> adopted, I know not what to make of this difficult passage. Till some
> instance shall be produced of the epithet *termagant* being applied to
> a steed, I apprehend Mr. Steevens will have few followers in the
> sanction he has given to this wild alternation; which would at the
> same time destroy the measure of the verse. May I be permitted to
> throw out a conjecture, as to which I myself have no great confidence.
> *Gaunt* is certainly *thin*; but as it is generally used in speaking of
> animals made *savage by hunger*, such as a *gaunt* wolf, a *gaunt* mastiff,
> it is possible that it may derivatively have acquired the sense of
> *fierce*, and an *arm-gaunt* steed may signify a steed looking fierce in
> armour. The reader need scarcely be informed that formerly the horse
> was often protected by armour as well as his rider. But I prefer
> Hanmer's reading. (XII. 210.7)

e New Variorum editor hardly does him justice by quoting
ly the third and fourth sentences of the note, thereby, among
her things, depriving him of his last thought on the matter, i.e.,
at he still preferred Hanmer's emendation to his own con-
cture. Boswell's closely argued refusal to see satire on Shake-
eare's other works in lines 14–19 of the Prologue to *Henry VIII*
eserves a full airing, since the editor of the New Arden edition
that play only refers to it in a few words (p. 5), although I
lieve it germane to his discussion on p. xxviii. of his introduc-
n. Boswell wrote

> That Jonson was the author of the Prologue and Epilogue to this
> play, has been controverted by Mr. Gifford. That they were not the
> composition of Shakspeare himself, is, I think, clear from internal
> evidence. But whoever wrote them, if the conjecture which I am
> about to hazard should meet with the reader's acquiescence, there
> will appear to be no ground for Dr. Johnson's suspicion that a covert

censure of Shakspeare's other works was designed. It is, indeed, highly improbable, that even the most careless author should not have perceived and resented such an attack upon his literary character prefixed to his own play. According to my hypothesis, in the lines referred to neither Shakspeare nor the general practice of the stage in his time were the objects of satire; but the intention of the writer was to contrast the historical truth and taste displayed in our author's Henry VIII, with the performance of a contemporary dramatist, "When You See Me You Know Me, or the famous Chronicle Historie of King Henry the Eighth, &c. by Samuel Rowley." In the Prologue which we are speaking of, great stress is laid upon the truth of the representation

> "——Such as give
> "Their money out of hope they may believe
> "May here find *truth* too."

A few lines further he speaks of "our chosen *truth*." But in Rowley's play the incidents of Henry's reign are thrown together in the most confused manner. It commences with the death of Queen Jane Seymour in child-birth; and a few scenes afterward, the two following marriages of the King are thus for the first time succinctly stated:

> "Commend me to the Ladie Katharine Parry,
> Give her this ring, tell her on Sunday next
> She shall be queene, and crownd at Westminster:
> *And Anne of Cleave shall be sent home again.*"

The danger which Queen Catherine Parry incurred by meddling with polemical divinity, and her adroit escape, are narrated as we find them in history; and soon after, that is to say, when he had been dead about sixteen years, Cardinal Wolsey begins to be suspected by the king, whose opinions on this subject are principally influenced by Will Summers, his jester. This personage, whom I take to be the

> "——fellow
> "In a long motley coat guarded with yellow,"

is one of the most important characters in the play; and that th audience might have enough of that species of humour in this merr *bawdy play*, for the second of these epithets is still more applicabl to it than the first, Wolsey's fool Patch is also introduced to be a foil t the superior jocularity of the royal jester. *The noise of targets*, imagine, refers to an incident in this drama. The king goes out i disguise at night to ascertain whether the police of London is we conducted, and in the course of his adventures meets with a higl wayman called Black Will, with whom he thus enters into conversation. "*King.* Well overtaken, sir. *Black Will.* Sblood, come before me, sir: What a Divell art thou? *King.* A man at least. *Black.* And art thou valiant? *King. I carry a sword and buckler, you see!*" After a friendly dialogue they resolve to fight in order to try their manhood with sword and buckler, and, after a contest with the watchmen who interfere to part them, are both taken into custody. This play was first printed in 1605; but the second edition appeared in 1613, the very year in which Mr. Tyrwhitt supposes that Shakspeare's Henry VIII. was revived under the new title of All is True. (XIX. 500–502)

ie discussion of Rowley's play in the New Arden edition (p. xvii) owes much to, and is at the same time much less full than, oswell's note. Some notice of Boswell's pioneer efforts in this atter might also have been taken by the editor of Rowley's play the Malone Society Reprints (1952): "Who fished the murex o? / What porridge had John Keats?"

As so many of Boswell's notes are devoted to parallel passages words and phrases in Shakespeare's plays, it is understandable at most of this part of his commentary should not appear in odern editions. Yet no assessment of his total contribution to iakespeare studies can be made without taking these parallels to account. Most modern editions of Shakespeare are chary of printing parallels, both because of limitations of space and cause the meaning and currency of so much of Shakespeare's cabulary, established by these very parallels, are taken for anted. One or two notes are of more than sufficient interest as to erit quotation. The necessity for closer scrutiny of early editions of Shakespeare is further dramatized by quotation of oswell's long note on "the hundred merry tales" alluded to by eatrice in *Much Ado*. Steevens had conjectured that the book entioned might be a translation of an old French book, *Les nts Nouvelles Nouvelles*, and Reed found a reference to the indreth Merry Tales, a work he could not identify. Boswell ote

Such were the guesses with which those most conversant in old English literature were obliged to content themselves; but it is now clearly ascertained that the Hundred Merry Tales was, as I have stated, a jest book of the time. A fragment of an early edition of a compilation of that kind, under the title mentioned by Beatrice, was discovered a few years ago, by my friend Mr. Coneybeare, Professor of Poetry, in Oxford; which, by his permission, was published for the gratification of brother antiquaries. It must have appeared earlier than

1583, as it was from the press of John Rastell, who ceased to print in that year. Another work of the same nature, called "Tales and Quicke Answeres," perhaps of equal or nearly equal antiquity, has also been given to the publick. Scoggin's Jests, Tarleton's Jests, and Peele's Jests, show that this title was not always adhered to; but the Hundred Merry Tales continued for a long period to be the most popular name for collections of this sort. An hundred indeed seems to have been a favourite number with our ancestors even upon graver occasions, of which the celebrated Marquis of Worcester's Century of Inventions, may, out of a multitude, be mentioned as an instance. The quotation already given from the London Chaunticleres, will show that the Hundred Merry Tales was still hawked about among the common people as late as the middle of the seventeenth century; and I can close this account, as Dr. Farmer has done the disquisition on stewed prunes, by stating the price. In "The true State, of the Case, of John Butler, B.C. &c. treating of a Marriage dissolved and made null by Desertion, 1697," the author maintains, and avows that he has carried into practice, a doctrine not unlike to that of Milton, in his Tractate of Divorce; although he does not appear to have been aware of his having had so illustrious a precursor. His notions on the subject having been controverted, he makes this angry reply to one of his antagonists, "I have collected thereout (i.e. from the work he answers) a centiloquy of lies, &c.: Had they been collected together as a little book I have seen when I was a school-boy, called An Hundred Merry Tales, perhaps it might have fetched a penny a book. (VII. 165–66)

Furness, without naming them, cited Steevens's and Reed's theories and Professor Coneybeare's edition of a fragment of the jest book (p. 72). No word about Boswell, who first called attention to Coneybeare's work.

Dr. Johnson remarked in his General Observation on Troilus and Cressida that "Shakespeare has in his story followed, for the greater part, the old book of Caxton, which was then very popular; but the character of Thersites, of which it makes no mention, is proof that this play was written after Chapman had published his version of Homer." Steevens stated that "an anonymous interlude, called Thersytes his Humours and Conceits, had been published in 1598," and Malone stated that the interlude was "published long before 1598," but Boswell was able to put the matter beyond doubt, as

A copy of the interlude of Thersytes was discovered a few years ago, and an account of it is given in the British Bibliographer, vol. i, 172, from which it appears to have been acted as early as 1537.

does not seem likely to have furnished any hints to Shakspeare. The classical reader may be surprised that our author, having had the means of being acquainted with the great Father of Poetry through the medium of Chapman's translation, should not have availed himself of such an original instead of Lydgate's Troye Booke; but it should be recollected that it was his object as a writer for the stage, to coincide with the feelings and prejudices of his audience, who, believing themselves to have drawn their descent from Troy, would by no means have been pleased to be told that Achilles was a braver man than Hector. They were ready to think well of the Trojans as their ancestors, but not very anxious about knowing their history with much correctness, and Shakspeare might have applied to worse sources of information than even Lydgate. Of this Hardyng's Chronicle will supply a ludicrous instance:

> "Lamedone gat the kyng Priamus,
> Who made agayne his palais Ilion,
> And Troyes citie also more glorious
> Then thei were before their subvercion,
> And royall without pervercion,
> In joye and myrth thei stode many a yere,
> And Achilles with him his brother dere."
>
> (VIII. 449–50)

Others of Boswell's notes might be quoted in demonstration of the utter inaccuracy of the statement in the *DNB* that he contributed "various readings and notes of no great importance," but enough has been said here to insure him a solid place in the company of editors of Shakespeare.

Volume XX of the 1821 edition contains Shakespeare's poems, with commentary largely by Malone and Steevens, most of it from Malone's 1780 *Supplement* and his 1790 edition of the works, but with some remarks by a few other critics. Boswell's contributions to this volume have received no little attention from Hyder E. Rollins, editor of the New Variorum *Poems* and *Sonnets*, but I wish to accord them somewhat more prominence than the nature and scope of the New Variorum volumes would allow. Boswell introduced the volume with the following Preliminary Remarks:

> It would, I apprehend, be unnecessary to assign any other reason for reprinting the following poems than that the editor who undertakes to publish Shakspeare, is bound to present the reader with all his works. Mr. Steevens has, indeed, spoken of them with the utmost bitterness of contempt; but in the course of about forty years, the

period which has elapsed since they were first described by the critick as entirely worthless, I will venture to assert that he has not made a convert of a single reader who had any pretensions to poetical taste. That these youthful performances might have been written without those splendid powers which were required for Othello and Macbeth may be readily admitted, but I question if they would suffer much in a comparison with his early dramatick essays, The Two Gentlemen of Verona, The Comedy of Errors, or Love's Labour's Lost. If they had no other claims to our applause, than that which belongs to their exquisite versification, they would, on that ground alone, be entitled to a high rank among the lighter productions of our poetry. The opinions of Mr. Malone and Mr. Steevens, on this subject, will be found as they originally appeared in various parts of the volume; and I have no doubt as to the decision of the public, who, I am satisfied, will gladly welcome an accurate republication of poems glowing with the "orient hues" of our great poet's youthful imagination.

As an early and vocal admirer of The Rape of Lucrece, differing in this preference from Malone, Boswell expressed his views in an end-note to the poem.

> I cannot by any means coincide with Mr. Malone in giving the preference to Venus and Adonis, which appears to me decidedly inferior to the Rape of Lucrece, in which we find not only that liquid lapse of numbers which Mr. Malone has pointed out, but upon some occasions an energy both of expression and sentiment which we shall not easily find surpassed by any poet of any age. It may be added, that he has in this poem been much happier in the choice of his subject, not only as affording greater variety, but in a moral point of view. We have here nothing that the "wiser sort" whom Gabriel Harvey speaks of, had any cause to reprehend; but even in early time it was thought that there was some hazard when the "younger too delight" in the other. In the Latin comedy, Cornelianum Dolium 1638, supposed to be written by Thomas Randolph, Cornelius displeased at finding it in the possession of his daughter:
>
>> Venerem etiam et Adonidem petulantem
>> satis librum
>> In sinu portat, eoque multo peritior evasit
>> Quam probae necesse est. (p. 214)

Possibly as a result of this preference, Boswell contributed several notes to the commentary on that poem, most of them of some value.[14]

Boswell was the first to gloss "sawne" of line 91 of A Lovers Complaint as "sown, i.e. all the flowers sown in Paradise. Th word is still pronounced *sawn* in Scotland." While this is Boswell's only note on that poem, he had much to say about that collection of poems known as *The Passionate Pilgrim*. Malone had pointed out that William Jaggard, who first published the collection, with Shakespeare's name as author, had included two pieces that had appeared in an earlier collection. Boswell's addition to these Preliminary Remarks of Malone is a long one. I quote only part.

So many instances have been given of Jaggard's want of fidelity in this publication, that I am afraid all confidence must be withdrawn from the whole. In addition to these poems which have been withdrawn by Mr. Malone as being the property of other writers, that which stands fourth in this edition may, upon equally good grounds, be added to the list, as it is found in a collection of Sonnets, by B. Griffin, entitled Fidessa more Chaste than Kinde, 1596, with some variations which I have pointed out in the notes. Fidessa was reprinted in the year 1815 by my friend Mr. Bliss. It will throw some additional doubt upon Mr. Malone's conjecture, that the little pieces which he has thrown together at the beginning were "essays of the author, when he first conceived the notion of writing a poem upon the subject of Venus and Adonis." Mr. Malone, indeed, has himself, at the end of that poem, produced several instances of the same topick being treated by preceding writers.

In Jaggard's edition of 1612 a distinction seems to be drawn between some of these poems and others, which are separated from them by a fresh title-page:

SONNETS
To sundry notes of Musick.

This second class contains the following

1   It was a lordings daughter
2   Oh a day alack the day
3   My flocks feed not
4   When as thine eye hath chose the dame
5   Live with me and be my love
6   As it fell upon a day

Here (we may observe) two of the poems not written by Shakspeare are found, namely, No. 5 and 6; and from thence we might at first infer that the first class belonged to him, and that the second, like Heywood's translations, was added, to fill up the volume, from other sources; for I cannot but consider No. 1, as totally unworthy of our poet, and Nos. 3 and 4 appear to me to be of an older cast than his writings, or those of his immediate contemporaries, and bear a nearer resemblance to the style of those uncertain authors, whose poems are

attached to Surreys, in Tottell's edition. But unfortunately this second part contains No. 2, which is perhaps the only unquestionable
production of Shakspeare in the volume, and in the first we find the
poem in praise of musick and poetry, which is claimed for Barne-
field. If we are not to consider the Passionate Pilgrim altogether as a
bookseller's trick, I know not why this last-mentioned composition is
to be surrendered without a question. If William Jaggard was a rogue,
John Jaggard may not have been much better, and may have stolen
Shakspeare's verses, which were afterwards restored to their rightful
owner. I should be glad if I could claim them with more confidence
for our great poet, not on account of their merit, which is small, but as
showing his admiration of Spenser, and the warm terms in which he
expressed it. (pp. 396–97)

Malone thought that the poem with the first line, "Take, oh,
take those lips away," partly introduced in *Measure for Measure*
and quoted in its entirety in John Fletcher's *Bloody Brother*, bore
marks of Shakespeare's hand and hence added it to *The Passionate Pilgrim*. Boswell disagreed:

I regret that I cannot agree with Mr. Malone in assigning this
exquisite little poem to Shakespeare. The argument, founded upon
one expression which is found in it, will prove nothing; for, if it were
not sufficient to say that it is an obvious metaphor, it would be easy to
produce a variety of instances in which it has been used exactly in
the same way by contemporary writers. The first stanza of this poem,
it is true, appears in Measure for Measure; but, as it is there supposed
to be sung by a boy, in reference to the misfortune of a deserted
female, the second stanza could not have been written for that occasion, as being evidently addressed by a male lover to his mistress. Mr.
Weber, in his edition of Beaumont and Fletcher, in a note on the
Bloody Brother, seems willing, according to the colloquial phrase, to
split the difference; and is of opinion that "the first stanza was
Shakspeare's, and that Fletcher added the second to suit his own
purposes." But the truth is, that this poem would not suit the purposes of either. In the one case, it is sung apparently to soothe the
melancholy of Marina; in the other, to amuse Rollo. If I were to
ascribe it either to Shakspeare or Fletcher, I should be compelled to
say, that the latter has a better claim. However inferior in all those
higher qualities which have constituted Shakspeare, "the sovereign
of the drama," his accomplished contemporary has, I think, been
more happy in the short lyrical compositions which are interspersed
in the plays by him and Beaumont. But, as we often find, in our old
dramas, the stage direction [Here a song], I have great doubts whether
this delicate little poem may not, from its popularity at the time, have
been introduced by the printer, to fill the gap, and gratify his readers,

from some now forgotten author. Many writers of that day, whose general merits have not been sufficient to rescue them from oblivion, have been remarkably happy in short poetical flights; and in what Warton harshly terms the *futile* novels of Lodge and Greene, we occasionally meet with lyrical compositions of exquisite beauty. (pp. 419–20)

The poem is not included in the New Variorum *Poems*; Boswell's was the keener sensibility here.

Boswell's interest in *The Passionate Pilgrim* also manifested itself in seven footnotes. Of the poem beginning "Sweet rose, fair flower, untimely pluck'd, soon faded" Malone had written, "This seems to have been intended for a dirge to be sung by Venus on the death of Adonis." Boswell was forced to demur, albeit with great deference:

> This note shows how the clearest head may be led away by a favourite hypothesis. Unless the poet had completely altered the whole subject of his poem on Venus and Adonis, which is principally occupied by the entreaties of the goddess to the insensible swain, how could she be represented as saying, "I craved nothing of thee still" [1. 12]. The greater part of it is employed in describing her craving. (403.5)

The phrase "merry jigs" occurs in a line in the poem, "My flocks feed not." Malone defined it as a "metrical composition," and Boswell, who thought very little of the whole poem wrote, "Jigs, as the word is commonly used, would do as well in this passage. I cannot help wishing that such jigs or metrical compositions had been quite forgot, rather than that they should have been attributed to Shakspeare" (412.3). At the conclusion of this same poem Boswell could restrain himself no longer, demanding to know if "it is possible that Shakspeare could have written this strange farrago; or what is, if possible, still worse—'It was a lording's daughter?'" alluding to another poem in the collection (415.5). A number of later editors and students of Shakespeare's poems share Boswell's views on these two pieces.[15]

As pertinent and astute as some of Boswell's comments and notes on Shakespeare's poems already discussed are, he has made a more lasting impression on later scholarship with his observations on Shakespeare's sonnets, beginning with four and half closely printed pages of Preliminary Remarks. Although these remarks should be read in their entirety, analysis of their content with some quotation will suffice to show how much in

advance of most of his contemporaries Boswell was in his criticism of the sonnets. He did not believe that Shakespeare had any
individual in mind in writing the sonnets, arguing convincingly
against Malone's hypothesis of a Will Hughes and Nathan Drake's
of the Earl of Southampton, i.e., Henry Wriothesley, "W.H." re-
versed. He put no stock in biographical interpretations of the
sonnets, citing as one example Malone's belief that in Sonnet III
Shakespeare "seems to lament his being reduced to the necessity
of appearing on the stage, or writing for the theatre." Boswell
asked, "But is there any thing in these words which, read without a preconceived hypothesis, would particularly apply to the
publick profession of a player or writer for the stage?," and
added, "The troubles and dangers which attend upon publick
life in general, and the happiness and virtue of retirement, are
among the tritest common places of poetry. Nor was such
querulous language likely to have proceeded from Shakspeare"
(p. 219). Nor could Boswell see any merit in the theory that the
sonnets were written by an old man looking back upon a life of
which he was not especially proud, especially in certain of the
sonnets in which he writes of "harmful deeds," of a branded
name, and of "vulgar scandal." "Upon the whole," he stated, "I
am satisfied that these compositions had neither the poet himself
nor any individual in view; but were merely the effusions of his
fancy, written upon various topicks for the amusement of a private circle, as indeed the words of Meres points out: 'Witness—
his sugred Sonnets among his private friends.' " He emphasized
the great popularity of the sonnet form as a "favourite mode of
expressing either the writer's own sentiments, or embellishing a
work of fiction" (p. 220). And he agreed with Malone that there
was no homosexuality in the sonnets, proposing as a classical
model for the kind of language addressed by male to male Virgil's
second eclogue, which was much admired, translated, and imi-
tated (p. 221). He concluded by suggesting that "the poetical
merits" of the sonnets were "almost universally acknowledged
notwithstanding the contemptuous manner in which they have
been mentioned by Steevens" (p. 222).

Boswell's note on "Mr. W.H." the "only begetter of these ensuing sonnets" states that "the *begetter* is merely the person who
gets or *procures* a thing, with the common prefix *be* added to it."
A parallel from Dekker's *Satiromastix* is adduced, and the note
concludes, "W.H. was probably one of the friends to whom
Shakspeare's sugred sonnets, as they are termed by Meres, had
been communicated, and who furnished the printers with his

copy" (p. 223). Although the identity of W.H. is a still unsolved mystery, Boswell's explanation found most favor with the editor of the New Variorum Sonnets.[16] And although the New Variorum does not include it, Boswell's next note, on the first line of the first sonnet, "From fairest creatures we desire increase," is more apposite than the two which are reprinted. Boswell quoted the twenty-ninth stanza of *Venus and Adonis* as a parallel.

> Upon the earth's increase why should'st thou feed,
> Unless the earth with thy increase be fed,
> By law of nature thou art bound to breed,
> That thine may live when thou thyself art dead;
> And so in spite of death thou dost survive
> In that thy likeness still is left alive.

Curiously enough, Hyder Rollins, editor of both the *Poems* and the *Sonnets* in the New Variorum, at this juncture in *Venus and Adonis*, cites a critic, writing in 1884, who compares this stanza to Shakespeare's first sonnet, Boswell having preceded him by more than sixty years.

Hyder Rollins considered others of Boswell's notes of importance. His parallel from Tibullus, "Tu manes ne laede meos: sed parce solutis / Crinibus, et teneris, Delia, parce genis," for "If thinking on me should then make you woe" of Sonnet 71 is the only note on that line in the New Variorum. Malone wrote a long note on sonnet 93, and although he did not think Shakespeare was writing as a deceived husband there, he believed that Shakespeare had written "more immediately *from the heart* on the subject of jealousy, than on any other; and it is therefore not improbable that he felt it. The whole is mere conjecture." Steevens wrote a longer note to disprove Malone's conjecture, and Boswell capped both notes, siding with Steevens and declaring that "if Shakspeare had been led to the description of jealousy from having felt it himself; and had to the last thought it well founded in his own case, which he must have done, if such was his motive for neglecting his wife in his will [one of Malone's arguments], he would scarcely have described it as he has uniformly done in his plays, as being causeless and unjust" (p. 309). Hyder Rollins gives the merest snippet from Malone's note, but not his last sentence, cites Steevens, but totally neglects Boswell. Boswell reprinted the long exchange between Malone and Steevens on the merit of the sonnets, Steevens being the detractor and Malone the rather half-hearted defender. His remarks began with the statement, "I do not feel any great propensity to stand forth as the champion of these compositions." Boswell closed the discussion with his own considered opinion.

> I cannot but admit that Mr. Malone, in his answers to Mr. Steevens, though, I think, to use Dr. Johnson's expression, they are conclusive *ad hominem*, has done but scanty justice to these beautiful compositions: nor can I agree with him in what he says of the author of the Allegro and Penseroso, even in the guarded phrase, that he *generally* failed when he attempted rhyme: but I must defend my late friend from the censure he has incurred for saying no more of Petrarch than "that he is slow to believe he is without merit." That he has not spoken more strongly proceeded from one of the most valuable parts of his character; his utter dislike to every thing like affectation or false pretences. He had but a limited acquaintance with Italian literature; and of Petrarch, as he himself tells us, he knew nothing. He need not indeed have disclosed this, for a multitude of books would have furnished us with encomiums upon that poet, which he might ostentatiously have delivered as his own. But it was much more consistent with his love of truth and sincerity to confess that he had never read him, and to abstain from expressions of admiration which could not be genuine. He has rather chosen to refer the reader to the concurring testimony of those best qualified to form an opinion, his own countrymen, for centuries past. I shall not presume to undertake the defence of the Sonnets; a mode of composition which has been cultivated by every poetical nation in Europe; but, as the authority of Lope de Vega seems to be produced against it by Mr. Steevens, I may as well remark that there are now lying before me more Sonnets written seriously by that poet, than are to be found in Shakspeare. (p. 363)

Here is a nice blend of loyalty to a dead friend and independent literary criticism.

In keeping with the best eighteenth- and early-nineteenth-century practice, I add an addendum on Boswell's "Addenda" in the last volume of the edition. There, with additional matter contributed by others, Boswell comments on five more passages. He finds a parallel in "the old play of King John" for "exempt" with the meaning of "taken away" as used in The Comedy of Errors (p. 450) and one in Middleton's *Anything for a Quiet Life* for "table" meaning "palm of the hand" in The Merchant of Venice.[17] In what the editor of the New Variorum 1 Henry IV calls "the most discussed passage in the play," i.e., Vernon' description of Hal and his comrades, "All plum'd like estridge that with the wind," Boswell defended the old reading, "wind,

against Johnson's emendation, "wing," remarking at the juncture
at which it appears in volume XVI that "it is not uncommon in
elliptical language to leave the verb to be understood" (p. 363).
This statement is quoted in the New Variorum edition, but
Boswell's later comment in the last volume is not. There he wrote
"when I attempted to defend the original text, I could not re-
collect at that time a passage in which the conjunction *with* was
used without a verb in the sense of *to go with*. I have since found
one in Massinger: 'Be not so short, sweet lady, I must *with* you.' *A
Very Woman. Gifford's edit.* vol. iv. p. 275" (pp. 466–67). In 1859
Halliwell glossed "with" as "go with," and this the editor of the
New Variorum edition, doubtless having overlooked Boswell's
"Addenda," does quote (p. 255). Boswell's next note is on
"Samingo" in *2 Henry IV*, and he there shows his acquaintance
with the poetry of "Gonzalo Berceo, an old Castilian poet, who
flourished in 1211. He was a monk, much of the same cast with
our facetious Arch-deacon Walter de Mapes. In writing the life of
the saint [St. Domingo], he seeks inspiration in a glass of good
wine." Five lines of the Spanish poem are quoted (p. 467).
Boswell's last note contains a quotation from Cotgrave's French
dictionary for the meaning of "doubted," in explication of "dout"
in *Henry V* (pp. 468–69).

   Had Boswell lived longer, I suspect that he would have continued to involve himself in Shakespeare scholarship, either
directly as editor or indirectly as contributor. Whether he would
have or not, one must be grateful to him for completing Malone's
edition and for his own independent contributions to that edition. Anybody with any pretensions to knowledge of English
literature has at least heard of James Boswell, the elder, Johnson's
Boswell; more scholars should know of the existence and work of
James Boswell, the younger, Malone's Boswell.

Epilogue

Without the notes of James Boswell, who was, after all, the editor of the 1821 *Shakespeare*, the other six men discussed contributed a total of some thirteen hundred notes to the commentary. The totals for each range from Blackstone's ninety to Tollet's four hundred and fifteen. There are notes on all the plays of the accepted canon as well as on the poems and on the apocryphal plays. The greatest number of notes was given over to parallels, followed by explications and glosses. Attempts at emendation were relatively few, although Tyrwhitt, a classicist, was tempted and succumbed. The extent of the combined erudition of these men, if such a hypothetical combination be allowed, as exhibited by the number and nature of the books and manuscripts they quoted or cited, can only be termed remarkable, at least by modern standards. A library composed of those books and manuscripts would be the envy of any bibliophile. And it must be remembered that Tyrwhitt, Blackstone, and Douce were busy with their own editorial projects, while Holt White was contributing a spate of learned articles to the GM. Henley is remembered, when he is remembered, for the translation of *Vathek* and his notes thereto, although he did other, less memorable, editorial chores. Only George Tollet published nothing, his only claim to limited fame residing in the notes to Shakespeare and the help with the *History and Antiquities of Staffordshire*.

Each of the six men brought not only general information to the explication of Shakespeare's text but also areas of knowledge in which they were especially interested. One would expect that Sir William Blackstone would be steeped in the laws of England. Indeed, who more? Thomas Tyrwhitt, the nearest of them all to the Renaissance *uomo di virtu*, the editor of Chaucer and of classical texts, the exposer of the Rowley hoax, brought his keen eye for textual anomalies to the task. That he was not always successful in his attempts to emend Shakespeare's text is true. If as I noted, however, Tyrwhitt had done nothing but resurrect Francis Meres's *Palladis Tamia*, with all that that has meant for Shakespeare studies, he should still be accorded a place among

Shakespeareans. Francis Douce, whose notes have been cruelly and inaccurately characterized as dry as dust, brought his knowledge of everyday life in the Elizabethan period to bear upon the commentary on the plays and left his mark thereon. The Reverend Mr. Samuel Henley, although overzealous in this respect, illuminated the commentary by bringing forth parallels from scriptural writings. George Tollet, whom I have described rather arbitrarily as a gentleman-farmer, brought his knowledge of country matters and customs. Tollet spent most of his life in Betley, Staffordshire; Shakespeare's youth was spent in Stratford-on-Avon, Warwickshire. If I have read maps correctly, the distance between the two places is some thirty-five to forty miles as the crow flies. There is, then, the possibility that Tollet's observations on country matters would also hold true for not-too-distant Stratford-on-Avon. And finally, always excepting Boswell, there is Thomas Holt White, whose first public appearance as a commentator came in 1768 in the pages of the *GM*, making him, with Tyrwhitt, one of the two earliest commentators among the six. Holt White's notes defy characterization, as they display many and varied areas of knowledge. Should the *DNB* ever be revised Thomas Holt White must be given a separate account, for he richly deserves to emerge from the shadow of his brother Gilbert.

There is no secondary literature on Boswell listed in the *NCBEL*. The *DNB* account, by Francis Espinasse, dismisses Boswell's part in that 1821 *Shakespeare*, as I have noted, in one sentence: "Boswell contributed a long preliminary 'advertisement,' various readings and notes of no great importance, with the completion of Malone's 'Essay on the Phraseology and Metre of Shakespeare' and the Glossarial Index." Sir James Prior could find nothing to record of the younger Boswell, if the index to the life of Malone can be trusted. And although the writer of an obituary wishes to put the subject of his obituary in the best possible light, it was probably the anonymous writer in the *GM* who did Boswell justice, insofar as the 1821 *Shakespeare* was concerned. I quote the pertinent parts from the March 1822 number, pp. 277–78.

> Mr. Boswell possessed talents of a superior order, sound classical scholarship, and a most extensive and intimate knowledge of our early literature. In the investigation of every subject that he pursued, his industry, judgment, and discrimination were equally remarkable; his memory was unusually tenacious and accurate; and he was always as ready, as he was competent, to communicate his stores of

information for the benefit of others. These qualifications, added to the friendship which he entertained for Mr. Boswell, influenced the late Mr. Malone in selecting him as his literary executor, and to his care Mr. Malone entrusted the publication of an enlarged and amended edition of Shakespeare, which he had long been meditating. Few months have elapsed since this laborious task was accomplished:—laborious it certainy was, as Mr. Malone's papers were left in a state scarcely intelligible; and no individual probably, excepting Mr. Boswell, could have rendered them available. To this edition, Mr. Boswell contributed many notes, and collated the text with the earlier copies. In the first volume, he has stepped forward to defend the literary reputation of Mr. Malone, against the severe attacks made by a writer of distinguished eminence, upon many of his critical opinions and statements; a task of great delicacy, and which Mr. Boswell has performed in so spirited and gentlemanly a manner, that his preface may be fairly quoted as a model of controversial writing. In the same volume, are inserted the memoirs of Mr. Malone, originally printed by Mr. Boswell for private distribution; and a valuable essay on the metre and phraseology of Shakspeare, the materials for which were partly collected by Mr. Malone; but the arrangement and completion of them were the work of Mr. Boswell; and upon these he is known to have bestowed considerable labour and attention.

The writer could state that "Mr. Malone's papers were left in a state scarcely intelligible; and no individual probably, excepting Mr. Boswell, could have rendered them available" (p. 277), because Boswell himself was authority for such a statement. In the Advertisement to the 1821 *Shakespeare* he had written, "it is not every one who could have deciphered his [Malone's] notes," adding that Malone "was in the habit of using the first scrap of paper which presented itself, and marking down his memoranda in a species of short hand, of which no one, who was not accustomed to his manner, could readily comprehend the meaning" (I. vi–vii). He apologized that "in some of the most important parts of his [Malone's] investigations, a chasm must be left which I am unable to supply; yet still I can, with confidence, assert, that enough will remain to justify the publick expectation, and gratify the admirers of our greatest poet" (p. vii). And he confessed, too modestly, "that in the course of the long labours which I have had to undergo, I have not been able entirely to refrain from occasionally appearing in my own person; but I trust that in this respect I shall not be found to have been unreasonably or ostentatiously obtrusive" (p. viii). The truth is that Boswell's "occasionally" translates into hundreds of notes. While the other six men discussed here helped, some more than others, in the advancement of Shakespeare studies, James Boswell, the younger, probably contributed as much as all the six together. He deserves to be remembered as James Boswell, the younger, *editor of Shakespeare.*

Notes

Introduction

1. See my *Samuel Johnson, Editor of Shakespeare* (Urbana: University of Illinois Press, 1956), pp. 102–15.

2. James Sutherland, *Preface to Eighteenth Century Poetry* (London: Oxford University Press), pp. 50–51.

Chapter 1. Thomas Tyrwhitt, Editor of Chaucer

1. Malone's *Supplement* (1780), II. 158n.

2. Reprinted in *Huntington Library Quarterly* 3 (1939–40): 23–36; see p. 24.

3. Claude Jones, editor of Reed's *Diaries*, indexes the "Mr. Tyrwhit" (see his p. 156) of Jesus College, Cambridge as "Thomas Tyrwhitt" without any warrant therefor.

4. *Alumni Oxonienses* has him a F.S.A., as does the *GM* obituary, 1786, ii. 717.

5. See *Letters*, I. 28–29; the mistaken attribution is Bertrand Bronson's in his biography of Ritson, pp. 89–90.

6. Respectively, pp. 4, 21, 27, 33, and 36.

7. See L. F. Powell, "Thomas Tywhitt and the Rowley Poems," *RES* 7 (1931): 316.

8. 1778, III. 135.4; IV. 201.5; IX 428.1. The last is quoted below.

9. 1773 Appendix I., IV. 340. See also 1773, II. 359.6; 1778, IV. 225.6, and IV. 354.1, all emendations anticipated by Theobald.

10. 1778, III. 506.7. See also V. 205.6.

11. 1778, IX. 341.2. Tyrwhitt is incorrectly said to have called "interrogatory" "a word of five syllables" by the editor of the New Variorum *Cymbeline*, p. 431.

12. Respectively, in 1778, III. 29.1, 67.7; IV. 62.6; V. 142.5 and 523.6.

13. II. 22.4, 43.9, and 71.4 in Malone; I. ii. 26; II. i. 12; and III. Chorus 1. 7 in New Arden.

14. C. F. Tucker Brooke, *The Shakespeare Apocrypha* (Oxford: Oxford University Press, 1908), p. xxx. Brooke makes no comment on the reference to Sunday, 13 July.

15. The other emendations are at VI. 320.8 and VII. 159.9.

Chapter 2. George Tollet, Gentleman-Farmer

1. James Boaden, ed., *Private Correspondence of David Garrick*, 2 vols. (London: H. Colburn and R. Bartley, 1831–32), I: 645.

2. In the 1778 edition here and in what follows, unless otherwise indicated.

3. The manuscript was of Sampson Erdeswicke's *Survey of Staffordshire*

(London: E. Carll, n.d.). I was alerted to Tollet's presence in Shaw's work by Mrs. Mavis E. Smith of Betley, Staffordshire.

4. The notes are in the Appendix in vol. X of the 1773 edition. They are, respectively, on VI. 28 and IX. 350.

5. Mistakenly listed under *The Winter's Tale* in Malone, I. 147.

Chapter 3. Sir William Blackstone, Solicitor-General to the Queen

1. In order of quotation: Y. c. 163 (1); W. b. 51 (2); and ART Vol. 2. 10. p. 242.

2. "The Manuscripts and Correspondence of James, First Earl of Charlemont," *HMC, Twelfth Report, Appendix, Part X,* i. 343. Printed for H. M. Stationery Office by Eyre and Spottiswood.

3. *Sir William Blackstone* (Chapel Hill: North Carolina University Press, 1938), p. 10; *The Life of Blackstone* (Charlottesville: University of Virginia Press, 1938).

4. *The Life of Blackstone,* Michie Co. p. 144.

5. Quoted in [D. Douglas], *The Biographical History of Sir William Blackstone* (London: The Author, 1782), p. xxix n.

6. The note is not in Johnson's *Shakespeare* (1765) and not in his *Miscellaneous Observations on the Tragedy of Macbeth* (1745), but appears for the first time in the 1773 Johnson-Steevens variorum, and thus refers to a time before 1745.

7. He emends also at III. 376; IV. 120 (both uninteresting); and at IV. 471, the long note on *Macbeth* quoted above, pp. 77–78.

8. *Some Account of the Life etc. of Mr. William Shakespeare,* paragraph 3.

9. G. Blakemore Evans assigns the play to 1594 or 1595, *The Riverside Shakespeare* (Boston: Houghton Mifflin Co. 1974), p. 50.

10. Evans (see note 9), p. 56 has it followed solely by *The Tempest, Henry VIII,* and *The Two Noble Kinsmen.*

Chapter 4. Thomas Holt White, Retired Ironmonger

1. Sir Geoffrey Keynes, *John Evelyn, A Study and a Bibliography* (Cambridge: England, 1973), p. 89, mistakenly accepts attribution of the edition to Samuel Pegge. See my note in *Notes and Queries,* "Thomas Holt White and the 1772 Reprint of John Evelyn's *Fumifugium,*" N.S. 27 (February 1980), 57–59.

2. William Cushing, in his *Initials and Pseudonyms* (New York: T. Y. Crowell and Co., 1885) identified "T.H.W." as "White, Thomas, An English writer"—nothing more.

3. These are largely a series of abstracts "of a register of the barometer, thermometer, and rain, at Lyndon, in Rutland" for the years 1780–98.

4. *Life and Letters,* I. 19–20; GM, LVIII, part 1 (1788), 32.

5. I. 64 in the 1778 *Shakespeare;* I. 82 in Malone's *Supplement.*

6. *Life and Letters* I. 156.

7. See *Life and Letters,* I. 288.

8. Reprinted in 1793: IV. 529.8; VI. 132.3 (Tyrwhitt); IV. 18.9.

9. Reprinted in 1785: IV. 376.5; V. 361.2; VIII. 217.4; X. 665.5.

10. V. 334.8 and 376.8.

11. The analogue is mentioned, although Holt White is not, in Geoffrey Bullough, *Narrative and Dramatic Sources of Shakespeare* (London and New York: Columbia University Press), I (1957), 59. Steevens thought well enough of the note to reprint it in 1793 (VI. 564.5).

12. References throughout are to this edition unless otherwise identified.

13. The New Arden editor's note on the charge that Wolsey caused his "holy hat to be stampt on the king's coin" in *Henry VIII* (p. 118) was anticipated by Holt White and by Francis Douce. See above, pp. 114–15.

14. See note 11 above.

15. See also pp. 217–18 of the New Variorum edition for his note on "A watchcase, or a common 'larum bell" in *2 Henry IV*, another crux in the play.

16. *Life and Letters* I. 19 and 20.

17. He described Coke as "the great oracle of the law" in the *GM* for February, 1789 (p. 146).

18. See p. 93 of the New Variorum *Cymbeline*.

19. See also VIII. 599.* for another use of Gilbert's *Natural History of Selborne*.

20. See my article, "A Forgotten Miltonist," *Milton Quarterly* 10 (1976): 31–39.

Chapter 5. Samuel Henley, Translator of *Vathek*

1. For information up to this point, see Fraser Neiman, "The Letters of William Gilpin to Samuel Henley," *HLQ*, XXX (1972), 159–69.

2. Almost surely Archibald Hamilton, the elder, printer. This letter and those of Steevens and Malone to Henley (above, pp. 126–27) form part of a collection of letters to Henley in the Boston Public Library.

3. II. 681–82; subsequent references in the text are to page numbers in this volume.

4. Page 700 for both notes; both are quoted in the New Variorum edition.

5. See George Tollet's note on this in the Appendix to vol. X of the 1773 *Shakespeare*. The note is keyed to VI. 28.

6. See Paul Bertram, *Shakespeare and "The Two Noble Kinsmen"* (New Brunswick, N.J.: Rutgers University Press, 1965).

7. See *The Two Noble Kinsmen*, ed. G. R. Proudfoot (Lincoln: University of Nebraska Press, 1970), pp. xvi–xvii.

8. See also pages 687, 701, and 709 for Devonshire definitions of *to drumble*, *peascods*, and *to pill* in *Merry Wives*, *As You Like It*, and *Richard III*.

9. Steevens's name is signed to this note in subsequent editions.

10. *The Royal Play of Macbeth* (New York: MacMillan, 1950).

11. *OED* corroborates.

12. V. 477.8; p. 43 in the New Variorum.

13. See also 1785, V. 550.3 and p. 230 of the New Variorum *2 Henry IV* for another note by Henley.

14. He was to quote the same source in 1793 in explanation of Ophelia's "herb of grace o'sundays" (XV. 277.6).

15. See also III. 175.5; VI. 532.5; V. 67.2, 418.5; VI. 216.7; VII. 175.2; VIII. 40.4; XI. 349.7: XII. 286.7; XV. 436.6; 589.5 for the other Scriptural notes.

16. III. 338.8, on *Merry Wives*, and VIII. 385.7 on *1 Henry IV*.

17. See also VI. 217.8, for a Warwickshire phrase.

18. See, also in this category, IX. 155.3; XI. 376.9, 518.8.

19. His notes on 1 and 2 Henry IV and on Troilus and Cressida can be found by recourse to the indexes in those volumes under his name and hence are not included in the following analysis.

20. XV. 489.4; the New Variorum Othello (p. 139) gives a much shortened resumé of the note.

21. The list is in a "Sketch of the Life of Rev. Samuel Henley" read to the Massachusetts Historical Society by Judge Mellen Chamberland and printed in that Society's record of meetings for February 1877, vol. XV, pp. 230–41.

22. Boyd Alexander, England's Wealthiest Son, A Study of William Beckford (London: Centaur Press, 1962), p. 14.

Chapter 6. Francis Douce, Keeper of MSS in the British Museum

1. But see Arundell Esdaile, The British Museum Library, a Short History and Survey (London: G. Allen & Unwin, Ltd., 1946), p. 59, who writes that, "except to his intimates," Douce was "of a rough and strange manner, and the episode [with the Trustee] may perhaps not be discreditable to the Museum."

2. Folger MSS. C. b. 10, items 60–67.

3. See below, p. 141.

4. This information is recorded in the 1803 Shakespeare (II. 152.3).

5. Quoted, in the New Variorum Much Ado, p. 252 and 1 Henry IV, p. 255, respectively.

6. (I. 238–39 and II. 129–31). Compare also 1793; III. 318.4 and 1807, I. 53–54; III. 375.5 and I. 66–67; IV. 162.2 and I. 117; IV. 335.2 and I. 140–41; IV. 336.3 and I. 140–41; IV. 399.2 and I. 164; IV. 452.6 and I. 172; V. 43.5 and I. 184–85; V. 89.7 and I. 193; V. 316.5 and I. 238–39; V. 345.4 and I. 240–43; V. 509.6 and I. 266–67; VI. 217.8 and I. 313; VI. 249.6 and I. 315–19; VI. 450.3 and I. 331; VIII. 546.9 and I. 438–43; IX. 424.9 and I. 502–3; IV. 442.3 and I. 505–6; XI. 128.3 and II. 48–49; XI. 137.9 and II. 50–51; XI. 593.5 and II. 70–71; XIII. 72.7 and II. 99–101; XIII. 498.2 and II. 129–31; XIV. 368–63 and II. 179–80; XIV. 528.2 and II. 196; and XV. 162.8 and II. 239–40.

7. See the 1803 Shakespeare, VI. 152.9.

8. See also the New Variorum As You Like It, p. 89, on "peascod" and compare Douce, VI. 50.7; the long third sentence of the 1793 note is omitted.

9. These are Marinus Mersennus, Harmonicorum libri duodecim in quibus agitor de sonorum natura, causis et effectibus and Michael Creutzberg Praetorius, Syntagmata musicum. The two other notes are V. 191.7 and XIV. 365.5.

10. See also, in the New Variroum volumes, Winter's Tale, pp. 246 and 276; King John, p. 376; I Henry IV, p. 279; Coriolanus, pp. 101 and 257; Cymbeline, p. 217; and Romeo and Juliet, p. 140, for notice of others of Douce's 1793 notes.

11. The New Variorum 1 Henry IV is squarely with Douce et al.

12. Douce's Illustrations is cited in the New Variorum Hamlet for this passage.

13. Douce gave his copy of Petrus de Crescentiis, Opus ruralium commodorum, "fol. Lovanni per J. De Westfalia, 1474" to the Bodleian Library. See Catalogue of the Printed Books and Manuscripts Bequeathed by Francis Douce, Esq. to the Bodleian Library (Oxford: Oxford University Press, 1840), p. 76.

14. As listed in his will, reprinted in the obituary in the *GM*, August 1834, p. 216. See also for a more detailed account W.D. Macray, *Annals of the Bodleian Library* (Oxford: Oxford University Press, 1890), pp. 326–28 and note 13 above.

15. V. 43.5; the same book is cited at VI. 18.2.

16. Douce bequeathed to the Bodleian Library a *Catalogue de l'oeuvre de Jacques Jordaens a la fin du cat. des estampes d'apres Rubens par R. Hecquet.* See p. 146 of the Catalogue of his bequests.

17. He mentions a print by F. Valeggio and a "very elegant cut in *Loniceri Venatus et Aucupium.* Francofurti, 1582, 4to." (IV. 452.6) and one "after Wouvermans" (VI. 198). He had a 1641 edition of the works of Ambroise Paré. See the Catalogue, p. 208.

18. See V. 136.4; VI. 46.4; VII. 153.2; and XV. 162.8 for other biblical quotations or citations.

19. Macray, *Annals of the Bodleian,* p. 327 noted that "early French literature" was a "conspicuous feature" of Douce's collection.

20. IV. 234.5; expanded in his *Illustrations,* I. 492–97, where he casts doubt upon the authenticity of the story he cited in 1793.

21. IV. 335.2, 336.3, and 402.9; VI. 518.6; XI. 137.8.

22. Platt is Sir Hugh Platt, two of whose works Douce bequeathed to the Bodleian Library (*Catalogue,* p. 219); the two named in the note were not among the bequests.

Chapter 7. James Boswell, the Younger

1. See Stephen Parks, "Shakespeare and his Editors, 1594–1970 . . .," *Yale University Library Gazette,* Oct. 1975, item 58.

2. *Shakespeare's Lives* (Oxford: Oxford University Press, 1970), pp. 246–47.

3. IV. 197.2; see also IV. 122.*; VI. 161.9; VIII. 313.5; X. 212.3; XII. 165.2, 287.8; XVIII. 43.5; XIX. 351.9 and 435.6. There are not very many more.

4. XI. 71.9 and 182.1; see also XI. 106.8; XIV. 179.6 and 253.4.

5. See also IV. 189.5, 372.8, 373.2; V. 71.3, 177.7, 199.3, 232.2, 470.9; VI. 137.3, VII. 111.1, 157.1; X. 148.3, 382.4; XI. 67.7, 192.9; XII. 37.7, 371.8; XIV. 317.9; XV. 105.6, 142.8, 173.8; XVI. 187.6; XVIII. 122.8, 191.3, 211.5, 503.7; XIV. 15.4, 308.5 (esp. interesting); XXI. 12.6 and 17.2 (on alexandrines in Shakespeare's plays).

6. Gifford's criticism of Malone (and Steevens) is in volume VI of his edition of Jonson's works (p. 364). For others of Gifford's differences with Malone see XI. 196.4; XII. 328.9; XIII. 273.5; XVII. 293.5; XIX. 499.3.

7. VII. 157.1; see also V. 393.1 for Steevens and alexandrines.

8. XIV. 275.6; see XXI. 9.* for a blanket condemnation of Steevens's silent emendations.

9. VII. 348.6. See also IV. 132.1; VII. 354.4 and 5; VIII. 160.3 (defends Malone); XV. 101.6; XXI. 127.4 (corrects Steevens's Latin quotation).

10. See under February 1766 in the *Life* for Johnson's remarks on the line from Goldsmith's *The Traveller.*

11. X. 301.*. See also VI.238.5 and, especially, XVII. 117.7, for the differences with Ritson.

12. See IV. 111.1; XI. 249.7; and XVI. 325.1 for the latter.

13. VII. 205.4; see also VII. 229.4, on "the noble substance of a doubt" which is also severely cut.

14. Pages 126, 134, 138, 143, 154, 172, 194; pp. 153, 165, 185, 210, 239 in the New Variorum, with pp. 134 and 143 of 1821 quite understandably ignored.

15. His other notes are on pp. 401, 402, 403, and 418; of the seven notes the New Variorum edition includes the three quoted above and that on p. 401.

16. See Appendix VII. pp. 166–76, esp. 167 and 176 in vol. II.

17. Pages 450–51; no parallel is adduced in the New Variorum edition, pp. 75–76.

Index

The abbreviations for S's plays and poems are those given in the *Shakespeare Quarterly* Bibliography, volume 6, number 6 (1985), pp. 691–92. A number of entries for the plays are for pages where the titles are not named but easily recognizable characters are. Articles in the titles of works indexed are omitted; many titles are abbreviated without benefit of ellipses, but are still identifiable by author and/or first words of those titles. Names of works abbreviated in the text are expanded in the index, i.e. Boyer's *Dict.* is expanded to Boyer, Abel, *Royal Dict. Abridged.* Long titles in the text will be abbreviated in the index, i.e. Stebbing Shaw's *History and Antiquities of Staffordshire* appears simply as *Hist.* The entry for Shakespeare is for his works only. Some names are abbreviated: Chas., Geo., Robt., Thos., Wm. Easily understandable abbreviations are used in titles and in some other entries: *Hist., Wks., Eng.* (England or English). Place names are not indexed, nor are the notes.